PENGUIN BOOKS
Pure Evil

Geoffrey Wansell has observed criminals with whole-life sentences, often up close and very personal, for over twenty years. In this chilling yet fascinating book, he looks for answers, and in the process reveals shocking insights into the foulest crimes known to mankind.

Pure Evil

Inside the Minds and Crimes of Britain's Worst Criminals

GEOFFREY WANSELL

PENGUIN BOOKS

PENGUIN BOOKS

UK | USA | Canada | Ireland | Australia
India | New Zealand | South Africa

Penguin Books is part of the Penguin Random House group of companies
whose addresses can be found at global.penguinrandomhouse.com.

First published as *Lifers: Inside the Minds of Britain's
Most Notorious Criminals* by Michael Joseph 2016
This edition published in Penguin Books 2018

001

Copyright © Geoffrey Wansell, 2016

The moral right of the author has been asserted

Set in Garamond MT Std
Typeset by Palimpsest Book Production Ltd, Falkirk, Stirlingshire
Printed and bound in Great Britain by Clays Ltd, St Ives plc

A CIP catalogue record for this book is available from the British Library

ISBN: 978-0-718-18983-9

For my son Dan Wansell and
my editor Dan Bunyard

Contents

Preface: Death's Shadow

This is a book about murder, and the men and women who commit the foulest crime known to mankind. But it is also a book about the ultimate penalty those killers face under English law – a whole life sentence of imprisonment, which means they must spend the rest of their natural lives behind bars with only the remotest possibility of release.

It also asks a question – does locking the worst of the worst offenders up forever and throwing away the key represent the right response from society? Indeed, do we as a society truly understand the consequences of a whole life sentence?

Are we comfortable, for example, in sending a young man in his early twenties to jail for the next sixty, or even seventy years of what remains of his life? Are we so determined on revenge for the victims and punishment for the offender that we can sentence a young woman in her early thirties to spend the rest of her life behind bars?

One lifer himself once memorably said, 'What keeps me going is knowing I'll be dead soon enough anyway of natural causes. The average male only lives until he's sixty to sixty-five. The way I see it, I'm closer to death than birth.'

As an author who has written two books about individuals sentenced to spend the rest of their lives in a cell – the Gloucester serial killer Rosemary West and the bus stop killer Levi Bellfield – I wanted to try and find an answer to that question, and others. Did I think, for example, that either of those killers should ever qualify for release?

That is an important question as we no longer have the death penalty in this country. It disappeared in 1965 – fifty years ago last year – and I have no quarrel with that. The possibility that any man or woman should have their life taken away by the state when there is even the remotest possibility that there could have been a miscarriage of justice has always seemed to me an unanswerable argument against the death penalty. No civilised society should ever allow for the possibility that it can send an innocent man or woman to the gallows.

The most severe penalty that any murderer in this country can now receive, therefore, is a whole life sentence, and there are more than fifty people currently serving that sentence today, two of whom are women, the rest men. Indeed there are now more prisoners serving whole life sentences than at any time in our history, and the number has more than doubled in the past fifteen years.

How did that come about? In 1965, in place of the death penalty came a mandatory life sentence for all murder convictions, on the understanding that every convicted killer theoretically forfeited his liberty to the state forever. In practice, however, nearly all lifers in the twenty years after 1965 were released on licence at some point, when they were deemed to no longer present 'a risk to society'. The average life sentence at that time was around ten years, which aroused increasing public concern as the years passed, in part encouraged by the controversy over the Yorkshire Ripper's sentence in 1981.

That concern eventually provoked a political reaction, and in 1983 the then Conservative Home Secretary, the late Leon Brittan, began to set minimum terms that certain convicted killers were compelled to serve behind bars before they could be considered for release on licence. He also gave any future

Home Secretary the power to keep a killer imprisoned beyond the recommended term, as was the case for the Moors Murderer Myra Hindley. In 1985 Brittan imposed a thirty year minimum upon her that meant she should remain in prison until at least 1995 – thirty years after her original arrest.

In 1989, however, the Conservative Home Secretary David Waddington imposed a whole life tariff on Hindley, after she confessed to having been more involved in the murders than she had previously admitted. Hindley was then persistently denied release by succeeding Home Secretaries and was kept in prison far beyond the thirty-year term she had been allocated. In fact Hindley remained a prisoner until her death on 15 November 2002 at the age of sixty – having spent thirty-seven years of her life behind bars.

In May 2002 the European Court of Human Rights ruled that the decisions about sentencing made by the Home Secretary were an abuse of power, and that the responsibility for deciding the length of sentence should be transferred from politicians to the judiciary. The then Labour Home Secretary David Blunkett accepted the ruling, but insisted on providing a new set of mandatory guidelines to judges about how long offenders who committed the most heinous crimes should serve under his new Criminal Justice Act, passed in 2003.

In particular, Blunkett's guidelines suggested, where an offender was twenty-one or over at the time of the offence and the Court took the view that the murder committed was so grave that it demanded the most severe penalty – he or she should spend the rest of their life in prison on a 'whole life order' – that was the 'appropriate starting point'.

Those grave cases were defined as including: the murder of two or more persons where each murder involved a substantial degree of premeditation, the abduction of the victim, or sexual or sadistic conduct; the murder of a child if it involved the abduction of the child or sexual or sadistic motivation; a murder done for the purpose of advancing a political, religious or ideological cause; and the murder by an offender previously convicted of murder.

Over the past twelve years those guidelines have been subtly amended to allow judges increasing leeway to pass a whole life sentence if they feel the murder is particularly heinous, even if it does not exactly satisfy those definitions.

Gradually, however, this has led to ambiguity about what exactly constitutes a sufficiently heinous crime to demand a whole life sentence. In the case of the brutal massacre of Fusilier Lee Rigby in Woolwich, London in May 2013, for example, one of his very public attackers was given a whole life sentence while the other was not, even though both were convicted by the jury of the same murder.

Yet after a dozen years of leaving sentencing powers in the hands of the judiciary, there are still underlying moral questions that remain unanswered. Do we take the draconian action of denying a killer freedom forever just to satisfy the demand for punishment and revenge on the offender from the families of the victims? Or does the general public demand it? Intriguingly, England and Holland are the only countries in Europe that still have a whole life sentence for the most heinous murders – the judiciary in Scotland decided on a fixed term when a life sentence was imposed in 2001, after which the offender had at least to be considered for release.

I wanted to look at the killers and the murders they committed, as well as at the reactions of the victims' families, the police who investigated the crimes and the judges who sentenced the offenders, to see if I could discern a pattern.

Most of all, I was anxious to put the murders in context – focusing not just on the details of the crimes themselves but also on the human reactions to them. Have our views about the severity of sentencing hardened over the past two decades, so that we as a society increasingly demand the most severe penalty? What do the lifers themselves feel about their sentences?

I was also determined to look at the less high-profile murderers who nevertheless warranted a whole life sentence. I did not want to revisit the best-known cases where there were fixed public attitudes to the killer, rendering a debate about a whole life sentence all but irrelevant. So this book does not contain a lengthy re-examination of the cases of the Moors Murderer Ian Brady, the serial killer Dennis Nilsen or the Yorkshire Ripper Peter Sutcliffe. There are excellent examinations of those crimes already – Brady himself has written at length about his own case, my friend Brian Masters wrote brilliantly about Nilsen, while Michael Bilton's extraordinary book on Sutcliffe left no stone unturned.

We know that Brady died in May 2017, at the age of seventy-nine, while he was still imprisoned at Ashworth Hospital, the secure psychiatric unit on Merseyside; that Nilsen, who is now sixty-nine, seems content to remain in custody; and that Sutcliffe, who is sixty-eight, is campaigning for a transfer from Broadmoor (also a secure psychiatric hospital) to a lower-security unit.

Instead of these three notorious cases, I wanted to look at some of the slightly less publicised ones that nevertheless offer insight into the minds of the murderers themselves and the judges who sentence them. I have included Michael Adebolajo and Michael Adebowale, the killers of Fusilier Lee Rigby, whose appeals against their sentences I watched in the Court of Appeal in London in the autumn of 2014. I have also included Anwar Rosser and Jamie Reynolds, whose appeals against their sentences I also attended just a month later. But I could not neglect Rosemary West, every day of whose trial and appeal I witnessed, nor Levi Bellfield, at whose trial I was also present throughout.

This is my third book about killers and it is fair to say that writing about the most foul of murders is a profoundly difficult thing to do, and to survive. The details that you are forced to consider lodge in your brain. They have stained my consciousness forever, but they also mean that I feel strongly that the families of the victims have every right to express the strongest views about what should happen to the man or woman who robbed them of a loved one.

Many of the cases in this book brought tears to my eyes, as the suffering inflicted on so many of the victims almost defies human understanding. The mutilation of innocent men, women and children to satisfy the urges of an evil killer who seems to have no grasp whatever of human decency or compassion can bring one to doubt one's own humanity.

And yet, I still find it difficult to sympathise entirely with the argument that the only acceptable response to their actions is to lock them up forever and throw away the key – denying them all hope of redemption.

It is a genuine moral dilemma, and one which is little discussed. It nevertheless provided me with the inspiration to write about it. On the one hand there is society, the law and the victims, demanding punishment; on the other the lives of the prisoners themselves. I would never say the 'rights' of the killers, for they surely abandoned those rights once they committed the dreadful crime of murder.

Perhaps there can never be a resolution to this powerful dichotomy, but – after working on this project for more than two years – I am increasingly convinced that there can. I believe it is time to put an end to the whole life sentence, not because the European Court of Human Rights decided in 2013 that we should, but because the failure to do so is, in my view, morally indefensible.

In its place we should establish a maximum fixed term for life imprisonment at fifty years, half a century behind bars, after which point the offender must at least be offered the possibility of freedom.

I hope this book illuminates how I reached that conclusion, and why I believe it is correct. But I am not turning my head away for one moment from the contradiction that I can argue for a fixed term for a life sentence, after which there should be the possibility of release, while at the same time I have included in this book case after case of men released on licence after serving a life sentence who then go on to kill again.

How can I also argue that society would ever be truly prepared to accept a notorious serial killer back into its midst – even if they were given a fresh identity? Would not the outcry overwhelm the good intention of trying to accept a whole life prisoner's redemption?

Perhaps it would, but this book argues that a higher moral standard should apply – the possibility that the passage of time may allow even the worst of the worst offenders to change for the better – and that to deny them any hope whatever is too high a moral price to pay.

I am still an old-fashioned liberal at heart who believes society should set itself the highest moral standards, and I have not changed in that view throughout the seventy years of my life.

In my first book, *Caught in the Act* – about the treatment of young offenders – written in 1973 with my friend and former colleague Marcel Berlins, we argued for the need for a system of carefully supervised institutions to allow young offenders the appropriate therapeutic help that they needed, but under strictly secure conditions.

That was more than forty years ago, but I believe it holds true today, and it is even more true for men and women in this book. It is the reason I suggest a 'supermax' prison offering both an extremely secure and a specifically therapeutic environment for whole life prisoners.

Most of all, however, I hope this book sparks a debate about how we treat the worst of the worst offenders, no matter how unpopular or little discussed that subject may be. In doing so, we are confronting one of the central questions in any civilised society – how it copes with the greatest evil and wickedness.

For that can lie in the most unlikely places, as this book shows.

No Mercy, No Remorse

Jamie Reynolds

The scene is a neat semi-detached house in a polite, well-kept road in the small town of Wellington in Shropshire, not far from the border between England and Wales. It is approaching dusk on the evening of a quiet Sunday, 26 May 2013.

Everything looks as normal as it possibly could in this provincial street of well-kept hedges and tidy gardens. But behind the lace curtains of this unostentatious little house, something utterly unimaginable is happening – the most depraved, despicable murder is being committed.

A sparkling-eyed, redheaded girl of just seventeen years and nine months in age – Georgia Williams, with her whole life ahead of her, and who hoped to become a model – has fallen into the clutches of a baby-faced young man just five years her senior, who looks as harmless and innocent as the day is long, and has been her 'friend' for five years. His name is Jamie Reynolds.

But Reynolds is certainly not behaving like an innocent 'friend' on this particular Sunday evening. Telling her it will further her modelling career, he has persuaded Georgia to take part in a bizarre private 'photo shoot'. It involves her changing into a set of clothes he has specially selected for her. He has brought her a black leather jacket and shorts, and shortly before eight she poses for him in the kitchen and hall of that neat little house in Avondale Road.

A few minutes later, Reynolds takes another set of photographs of Georgia, only this time she is standing on a box in the upstairs hallway with a red rope around her neck attached to an oar placed across the trapdoor entrance to the attic above, in a makeshift gallows. She is still wearing the leather jacket and shorts, while her hands are free, hanging by her side.

When she agreed to take part in this extraordinary 'photo shoot' Georgia was probably smiling, giggling even, as she cheerfully acquiesced to Reynolds' weird demands. She almost certainly believed that she had nothing whatever to worry about. After all, she had told her father, Steve, a detective constable with West Mercia Police, and her mother, Lynette, that she was going to see Reynolds, so what harm could she possibly come to?

That thought must have been in Georgia's mind as Reynolds quietly suggested in his wheedling voice that she should climb on to the box and allow him to slip the red rope around her neck. Once she had climbed on to it, Reynolds stepped back once again and started taking photographs with his stepfather's camera. The shutter clicked time after time, as he took frame after frame, and cajoled Georgia to smile for the camera.

Just a minute or so later, Reynolds photographed her with her hands tied behind her back. Georgia was still smiling, but tragically she did not know what was in store for her.

Far from being Georgia's friend, Reynolds was about to become her executioner, for as soon as he briefly stopped shooting, he reached up and pulled the noose tight, tying it to the banister. That forced Georgia on to her tip toes and started cutting off the blood supply to her brain.

Now plainly terrified, Georgia, who had been head girl at her secondary school and was a corporal in the Royal Air Force cadets, started to struggle, but Reynolds showed the helpless girl not a shred of mercy. Instead, he applied further pressure to tighten the rope by putting his knee in her back and pulling downwards, shortly before kicking the box Georgia had been standing on away from beneath her so that she was left swinging helpless in the void, the noose tightening around her neck, her legs kicking in wild panic.

Then, as Georgia's life ebbed away, he calmly stepped back and started taking pictures again – delighting in his power over her, relishing the horrific fantasy that he had created of killing a young woman by hanging, and doing nothing whatever to prevent her death. As the breath finally began to leave her body, he simply grinned in triumph and took yet another photograph. He gloried in his betrayal of the teenager and her horrifying, grotesque death.

Within a few minutes of Reynolds kicking the box away from beneath her feet, the pretty young woman, who was still legally a child no matter how mature she may have looked, was dead at the end of Reynolds' rope. Yet, tragically, her ordeal did not even end there.

The twenty-two-year-old Reynolds carefully took Georgia's body down from his makeshift gallows and laid it on one of the three beds upstairs in his family home. His parents were away in Italy for a week, and so there was no chance whatever that the lonely – but undeniably persuasive – Reynolds would be disturbed.

That was precisely how Reynolds had planned it, for Georgia's murder was the culmination of a fantasy that had been playing out in his mind for months. He had even foretold it in one of the forty violent, sexual 'stories' he had written depicting what he intended to do to various young women he knew of in the local area.

Reynolds took pleasure in one story in particular, started on 27 January 2013 on his iPhone, five months before the murder. It was entitled 'Georgia Williams in Surprise', and it described in graphic detail exactly how he intended to abuse and kill the teenager after he had persuaded her to come to his parents' house while he was alone there. He had revised the story repeatedly over the months, the last time in early May, three weeks before the murder.

In his story Reynolds went into pornographic detail about what he intended to do to the innocent seventeen-year-old, including a description of her hanging. 'Her feet start kicking wildly as she hangs,' he wrote. 'She dances wildly at the end of her rope.'

Soon after he had written his story for the first time, he started texting Georgia, telling her how much he liked her and how interested he was in her. She displayed no interest in him whatsoever, but that did nothing to deter Reynolds as he went on to describe how he was interested in 'artistic' photography, and told her that he wanted to use a 'simulated hanging' as a scenario.

Just before that fateful Sunday evening, he sent Georgia a text saying, 'Fake hanging. Just want to double check to make sure you are cool with it because it is "totally safe".'

Along with his depraved written fantasies, which were also directed at other young women, this pasty-faced young man with a stubbly excuse for a beard also assembled a vast electronic library of violent pornography, including no fewer than 16,800 images and seventy-two videos of extreme pornography, including 'snuff' movies that depicted the death and sexual mutilation of young women.

Acting out these fantasies on the helpless body of Georgia

Williams, Reynolds ruthlessly set out to destroy the dignity and grace of the young woman who had brought 'light and joy' into the lives of her family and friends, and had been a school counsellor to victims of bullying in her school, as well as a fine sportswoman.

In the last hours of that Sunday evening, Reynolds systematically sexually abused the lifeless body of Georgia Williams. He posed her body on all three beds in the house, including his parents', and gradually stripped her until she was naked. He took photographs of her, and then of himself – by now also naked – as he violently assaulted her in every conceivable perverted way.

Then he transported her naked corpse downstairs to the kitchen, only to resume the attacks and continued to do so for hours – after taking care to close the living room curtains. Reynolds was only too aware that suburban streets have many watching eyes. He was later to be described as both 'narcissistic' and 'necrophiliac', and there can be no denying that it is all but impossible for an ordinary human being to conceive of the depravity that Georgia Williams was subjected to during that evening.

Reynolds' actions defied all human conscience. They were the work of a young man who can only be described as truly evil, and who glorified in being in charge of the body of a lifeless teenage girl and relished the humiliation he was subjecting her to. But just as Reynolds had taken care to ensure that no prying eyes would catch a glimpse of his depravity, so he had sculpted a plan that, he thought, would ensure that he got away with Georgia's murder and monstrous violation.

Reynolds' escape plan was every bit as careful and calculated as the fantasy that led to Georgia's death. For, as the evening wore on, he used the dead teenager's mobile phone to pretend to be her and sent a text message to her mother saying, 'Ended up going out. Don't know when I'll be back.' He then added a second message: 'Phone about to die too,' clearly intent on covering his tracks.

When Mrs Lynette Williams picked up that message the following morning she immediately texted her daughter to find out exactly where she was and what she was doing. Reynolds used Georgia's phone to reply, texting, 'Stayed with friends. I'll see you tonight.'

The subterfuge did not end there. On the Monday morning Reynolds texted Georgia's older sister Scarlett – using his own mobile phone this time – to suggest that he was worried about where Georgia might be and offering to help Scarlett to look for her. Reynolds then texted Georgia's own phone from his own mobile, repeating his concern. It was a callous attempt to both conceal his own tracks and manipulate every member of the Williams family, while all the time privately gloating over his crime.

It had the additional benefit of ensuring that Georgia's family did not contact the police at once, even though her father Steve was a detective.

But all the time Reynolds was sustaining the pretence that Georgia had left him the evening before, he was also executing his plan to escape the consequences of his actions. He used his stepfather's white Toyota van, which was parked in the driveway outside the Avondale Road house – with its rear doors facing the front door – and secretly loaded Georgia's naked body, wrapped in a cloth, into the back. He also loaded her underwear, some jewellery, as well as the clothes he had dressed her in, and the rope and the handcuffs he had used to subdue her.

Meanwhile, Reynolds deleted the incriminating pictures from his stepfather's camera and loaded them instead on to an external hard drive for his computer, which already contained other examples of his obsession with extreme and violent pornography. He was clearly intending to relive the previous evening's dreadful events at his leisure in the future.

Then, shortly before lunch on Monday 27 May 2013, after waiting for a visit from his sister – during which he pretended to Georgia's sister Scarlett that everything was completely normal and explained that he was going off on a 'camping trip' for a few days – Reynolds set off in his stepfather's van to dispose of Georgia's body.

He even knew exactly where he was taking her. Reynolds crossed the border and drove into North Wales, and then through the picturesque Nant-y-Garth pass to the upright little market town of Wrexham. He parked the van – with Georgia's body in the back – had something to eat, and went to the Odeon cinema while waiting for dusk to fall, so that he could play out the final act in the tragedy of Georgia's young life.

That evening, as the light began to fade, Reynolds drove back to the remote woodland valley of Nant-y-Garth and up a track into an isolated wooded area. But he did not get very far as the van got stuck in the mud. So he hauled Georgia's body out of the back of the van and dragged it deeper and deeper into the trees before depositing it in a remote stream – clearly hoping that it would never be discovered, and not caring what animals or insects might do to her naked body in the wilderness.

But then came the first hitch in Reynolds' careful plan. His stepfather's van was stuck in the mud and he needed help to get it out. A passing motorist finally stopped, but then happened to take a photograph of the van. Realising that the picture placed the van in North Wales, Reynolds slipped into a panic – so much so that he immediately drove north to Glasgow in Scotland, where he bought a new watch, once again went to the cinema, and then checked into the Premier Inn in the city centre for the night.

As a result of Reynolds' delaying tactics, Georgia's parents did not inform the police of her disappearance until Tuesday 28 May – by which time Reynolds had disappeared with her body – but an alert was put out for him that day and he was quickly located on the morning of Wednesday 29 May, three days after the murder, at the Premier Inn he had chosen in Scotland's second city.

The following evening, West Mercia Police launched an appeal on BBC Television's *Crimewatch* programme in an effort to track down the white van's whereabouts. Their appeal was an immediate success, and by Friday 31 May, Georgia's body had been located – though sadly not before it had suffered dreadfully during the three days and nights it had lain naked in dense woodland. At a nearby layby police found the rope used to kill her; the leather jacket and shorts and the handcuffs were also discovered, although her jewellery and mobile phone were never found.

When Georgia's parents went to identify the body formally they were traumatised by the damage she had suffered, so traumatised, indeed, that they would never be able to eradicate the vivid images of her dreadful fate from their minds in the months to come.

In the days that followed his arrest, Reynolds repeatedly insisted during his police interviews that it was all a mistake, and that Georgia had gone to see a friend and he did not know where she was. But when the officers revealed that they had found the external hard drive with the pictures of Georgia both alive and dead, Reynolds claimed total memory loss – until, as a result of the *Crimewatch* appeal – they also told him that they had photographs of his van stuck in the mud in Wales and of Georgia's body.

Asked if he accepted responsibility for her death, Reynolds only replied, 'Even though I don't remember it, it does certainly look that way. I hate myself for it . . . I never wanted to hurt her.' It was the only remorse he was ever to admit to in the months that followed.

Then, and only then, did Reynolds, the former shop worker and petrol pump attendant, finally admit that he had 'little flashes' of memory in which he thought he might have dragged her naked body into the woods.

For almost seven months Reynolds firmly denied his responsibility for the murder and mutilation of Georgia Williams. It was not until five days before his trial at Stafford Crown Court was due to begin in December 2013 that he accepted his own guilt and admitted that he had indeed killed her. But he did not claim that he had done so in an act of 'madness' that might diminish his culpability for the crime.

Reynolds simply stood in the dock of Stafford Crown Court, before Mr Justice Wilkie, and replied, 'Guilty,' when he was asked how he responded to the charges put to him. There was no emotion on his face, no weeping or cries of remorse, not even a plea for mercy from the Court. It was as if Georgia was merely a memory that he had wiped from the hard drive of his brain.

After Reynolds' plea of guilty it was revealed that he had attempted to commit similar crimes in the past, luring girls he knew from the local area to his house and subjecting them to brutal sexual attacks.

In January 2008, when Reynolds was still only seventeen, he had persuaded a red-haired young woman to come to his home to pose for photographs which had an eerie similarity to those he finally took of Georgia. When she refused to go upstairs with him, he attacked her and attempted to strangle her. She only escaped by fighting Reynolds off, which left her with red marks and swelling on her neck. When the police were called, they discovered that he also had photographs of other unknown, naked young woman being strangled, as well as two pictures to which he had digitally added a noose around their neck. One of those photographs depicted the young woman he had just attacked.

Astonishingly, in the light of what was to happen five years later, and regardless of the apparent seriousness of the attack, West Mercia Police did not insist that he stand trial for the attack. Instead they issued the seventeen-year-old teenager with what they called 'a final warning'. He was also referred to the Youth Offender Service and monitored by the Child and Adolescent Mental Health Service. It did nothing whatever to stop him.

In 2010 he began contacting a second red-haired young woman. She turned him down flat, but he continued to pester her. Finally in August 2011, she confronted him in a car park and told him to his face to stop. Reynolds responded by reversing his car straight into hers at considerable speed. She went on to feature in one of his forty 'stories', as well as appearing in a digitally created image with a noose around her neck.

In February 2013 Reynolds invited a third red-haired young woman into his parents' house, having modified a Facebook photograph of her to show a rope around her neck, her arms and legs tied, and yet more sexual violation. After she arrived he locked all the doors and pretended not to know where the keys were.

As a result, the young woman was trapped in the house for almost an hour, screaming, shouting and threatening to climb out of the window, while Reynolds attempted to persuade her to stay the night. In the end he pretended to 'find' the keys and she left. She was extremely fortunate, because Reynolds had left himself a note to remind him to remove the oar from the loft's hatch. She was clearly intended for the same fate as Georgia Williams.

Four more digitally altered images created by Reynolds of local young women with nooses were found in his bedroom, and in the week leading up to Georgia's death he sent messages to some sixteen young women, trying to persuade them to come to his house on Sunday 26 May. Astonishingly, two or three of them showed an interest, but could not make that evening. On the morning after Georgia's murder he contacted them to say that he had a mechanical problem with his camera, and that they should postpone their visit for twenty-four hours.

In the weeks before Reynolds pleaded guilty in December 2013, he was examined by the distinguished forensic psychiatrist, Professor Bob Peckitt, in a series of interviews. In his report the professor explained that although Reynolds had experienced some physical and emotional abuse as a child – his mother had escaped from the relationship with her first husband and married again. But the professor also noted that his stepfather and mother had given him a 'comfortable and supportive' home.

Professor Peckitt concluded that Reynolds did not have 'a sufficiently disturbed upbringing' to account for his adult behaviour, and he also discounted the possibility that he had a 'recognised mental disorder' or an 'abnormality of mental functioning'. In other words, he was clinically sane.

But the professor also stated firmly that Reynolds suffered from a 'long-standing necrophiliac fantasy' which involved hanging a young woman and having sex with her corpse. He concluded that he was an 'intelligent and plausible' young man who had the potential 'to progress to being a serial killer' who posed a 'grave risk to women' and would continue to do so for the rest of his life.

It was one of the bleakest statements ever made about a convicted killer of a single human being in a British criminal court, and it was about a young man who was not even twenty-four years of age. It sealed Reynolds' fate.

When Jamie Reynolds was summoned back to the dock of Stafford Crown Court on 19 December 2013 to hear Mr Justice Wilkie pass sentence, he knew that he faced a life sentence for the murder of Georgia Williams seven months earlier. The only question in his mind was how long the minimum term that the judge would recommend would be.

He thought that the fact that he had pleaded guilty (although only after waiting six months before deciding to do so) and thereby not putting Georgia's family through the ordeal of a trial, and that he was still only twenty-three years of age, would weigh in his favour.

But Reynolds' legal team would have warned him that in the past fifteen years the minimum terms of imprisonment for a life sentence had been growing steadily longer. In 1997, for example, the average length of time a prisoner served under a life sentence before being released on licence was only some nine years, now it was almost double that – at seventeen years or so.

The atmosphere in the well of Stafford Crown Court on the chilly morning of Friday 19 December 2013 could hardly have been more charged, and the tension grew even more dramatically when fifty-four-year-old Detective Constable Stephen Williams stood in the well of the court to read his 'impact statement' to the judge before sentencing. Unable to hold back the tears, his whole body appeared to be trembling as he stood up to read the brief statement that he held in his hand.

The grey-haired police officer was in such obvious distress that Mr Justice Wilkie offered to read the statement for him, but Stephen Williams bravely replied, 'Thank you for your consideration but I'd like to do it myself.' Struggling to control himself, he said in a voice on the verge of breaking: 'I cry endlessly from morning to night . . . we have been damned by evil to endure this misery to the end of our lives.' The loss of the young woman who had been his 'truly wonderful daughter' was clearly almost too much to bear.

Mr Justice Wilkie began his sentencing remarks by addressing Reynolds directly, and telling him, 'You have, for at least five years, been obsessed with sexual violence against women, particularly in the form of hanging, or strangulation, and by sexual violation of them in death. Repeatedly you have sought to engineer situations where you were not simply the viewer of fictional fantasies but were the real life assailant.'

Jamie Reynolds must have realised at that precise moment that his fate was likely to be far worse than a simple life sentence with a fixed minimum term.

A Scots-educated, thoughtful man of almost sixty-six, with a careworn face and the manner of an academic, Wilkie had dealt with serious murderers before. He had presided over the conviction and sentencing of the predatory wheel clamper and drug dealer Levi Bellfield for the murder of Surrey schoolgirl Milly Dowler just eighteen months earlier. He was no stranger to evil.

Not long after he began his sentencing remarks, Mr Justice Wilkie made it clear to everyone in court that the life of the prisoner in the dock was about to change forever when he told him firmly, 'The only sentence I am empowered to pass is one of life imprisonment and I do so.' But then he paused and added, 'My next task is to consider whether this is a case which calls for a whole life term and, if not, to fix a minimum term before the expiration of which you, Jamie Reynolds, will not be considered for release on licence.'

The words would have chilled Reynolds' bones to the

marrow, for Wilkie had suggested that – even at his age – he might join the group of fifty or more men (and two women) condemned to end their lives in prison, with barely any hope of release beyond the onset of a terminal illness.

Reynolds was facing the ultimate punishment that the English law could pronounce on a prisoner – after the replacement of the death penalty by a life sentence which gave nothing but the slimmest chance of release. Only two men in recent memory had walked out of jail after receiving such a sentence – when their innocence was proven many years after they were sent to jail. There was no chance of that for Reynolds – he had pleaded guilty.

As the sentencing went on it became clearer and clearer that the judge had been strongly influenced by Reynolds' meticulous planning of Georgia's murder and his desire to keep a record of it. The pictures taken while Georgia was suspended with a noose around her neck, while she was still alive, clearly profoundly shocked and moved Mr Justice Wilkie, who said, 'Seeing those photographs of her, totally trusting and helpless, unknowing of what you were about to do to her, has been almost unbearable . . . You then, as you had envisaged, enjoyed the spectacle of her final ghastly minutes as she struggled for life, knowing that she had been betrayed and that she was facing death. At no stage have you expressed any genuine remorse for your horrific actions.' Mr Justice Wilkie added, 'It follows that, whilst your plea of guilty has in fact saved Georgia's family from having to endure a trial, in the context of this case, where the evidence against you is so overwhelming, that, as a mitigating factor, is of little significance.'

In his quiet, studious voice the judge then began to explain to Reynolds that basis under which the Court could sentence him to spend the rest of his life behind bars. It came under

Section 269 of the Criminal Justice Act 2003, and allowed a judge to make this ruling where: '... the Court is of the opinion that the offence is so serious that no order should be made providing for the possibility of release'. In those circumstances 'the Court must make a whole life order.'

But under the provisions of Section 269, the judge explained, the Court also had to consider factors that had to be taken into account when looking at the 'seriousness of the offence', using the guidelines laid out in Schedule 21. In particular, these pointed out that when the seriousness of the offence was 'exceptionally high' and the offender was over twenty-one, the starting point for the Court was a whole life order, especially if there was either the murder of two or more people, which included premeditation or planning, as well as sexual or sadistic content – or the 'murder of a child involving abduction or sexual or sadistic motivation . . .'

After looking at the legal precedents in other cases involving a whole life order – and reminding Reynolds that whole life was a 'draconian penalty' reserved for cases of 'exceptionally serious criminality', he then touched on the debate going on between the European Court of Human Rights and the Courts of the United Kingdom about the legality of a whole life term of imprisonment – which had been brought to a head by a European judgement in the summer of 2013. After that Mr Justice Wilkie reached his conclusion. It did not make comfortable hearing for Jamie Reynolds, standing in the dock.

The judge reminded Reynolds that he had 'long anticipated' the murder of Georgia Williams, had planned it and decided what steps he would take to avoid being caught. It was also designed to give him 'sadistic and sexual' pleasure, that he had the opportunity to save her but instead allowed her to suffer 'horribly'.

'After the killing you took sexual pleasure by repeatedly violating her body,' he added in the hushed courtroom. 'You then treated her body with contempt, dumping it in a remote spot, far from home, naked, without burial, intending that it should not be found for a long time, during which it would be vulnerable to the ravages of nature.'

The catalogue of depravity did not even end there.

'This was not a one off, directed at one person,' Wilkie continued, proved by the fact that Reynolds had invited two other young women to come to his parents' house the following day. Finally the judge reminded the twenty-three year old that his killing of Georgia was the result of his long-standing preoccupation with violent sadistic pornography, as was made clear by his collection of doctored digital images of young women, and the fact that he had attacked two of them, in January 2008 and February 2013.

The conclusion was inevitable, but it still must have chilled the heartless Reynolds to the core of his being. Mr Justice Wilkie said simply, 'The sentence I pass is one of whole life imprisonment. The early release provisions are not to apply to you. I make a whole life order.'

At that moment Jamie Reynolds became the youngest person in British legal history to be sentenced to spend the rest of his natural life in prison. There was every prospect that he might end up staying there for more than sixty years, in a small cell, and with the opportunity for exercise a maximum of an hour a day.

As he was led back to the cells beneath the court, Reynolds's pasty, white face was emotionless. Perhaps he was stunned, perhaps he did not care what he had done, but one thing is certain: he displayed not one ounce of remorse for his crime.

Outside the court, however, emotions were high. West

Mercia Police's investigating officer, Detective Chief Inspector Neil Jamieson, branded Reynolds 'a sadistic, very dangerous and manipulative individual'.

But it was DC Steve Williams who somehow captured the sense of despair that had swirled around the courtroom.

'There is no sentence that we can ever say that we're satisfied with because it'll never bring Georgia back,' he told the assembled crowd of reporters and television crews, his voice still wavering. 'She's dead, she's gone physically and lives in our hearts.' Clearly still deeply hurt by his daughter's murder, he went on: 'The one thing that will always get to us and cause us grief is the fact that even though Jamie Reynolds is serving a full life sentence, he still has life to hang on to.'

Sadly, the suffering inflicted upon Steve Williams and his family was not to end there. Even though, in January 2014, Jamie Reynolds' solicitors announced that he would not launch an appeal against his sentence, just three months later he changed his mind. On 14 April 2014, he announced that he would indeed be launching an appeal on the grounds that the 'sentencing judge did not give enough weight to his age and plea of guilty,' and that he intended to take the European Court of Human Rights' view that full life sentences were 'incompatible with the human rights convention'.

The Williamses were devastated. 'We thought that was the end,' Steve Williams announced. 'But now it's almost like there's a new trial coming up. It makes you feel sick. It makes you feel angry and it devalues Georgia's life.'

Every bit as distraught, his wife Lynette added: 'It's made us really upset and angry. You do worry how people can contemplate how he should serve anything less than full life.'

Moments later, her husband brutally summed up the feelings of all his family, and, quite probably, the millions more who had taken an interest in the case in the press, on radio and on television. 'But to me, the pure evil of it all was how he orchestrated Georgia's death to fulfil his own sexual fantasy – like I've said before, if you are going to kill somebody in cold blood for a few moments of perverted sexual pleasure you should accept the consequences. He's saying his age hasn't been taken into account, but you look at life expectancy now and he's probably taken about seventy years of Georgia's life and that's what we should have taken – the whole of his life. He has never shown an ounce of remorse. He has never apologised. He could have stood up in court and said I'm really sorry. He knew us. We had contact with him. But he couldn't face us in court. He didn't even look at us.'

The ordeal of Georgia Williams' parents would not end for another eight months – until Reynolds' appeal was heard in the Court of Appeal in London. But their case would highlight for the world the importance, and significance, of a whole life term of imprisonment.

2

Should Life Mean Life?

The words of fifty-four year-old Detective Constable Steve Williams should haunt us all.

It was April 2014, with his wife Lynette beside him, when he told reporters bitterly that Reynolds' claim that his age had not been taken sufficiently into account when he was sentenced, and neither was the fact that he had pleaded guilty, made a mockery of everything he and his wife felt about their daughter's brutal murder.

'He's probably taken about seventy years of Georgia's life,' Williams said, 'and that's what we should have taken – the whole of his life.'

In that one sentence Williams precisely encapsulated how millions of people in Britain feel about how the worst of the worst murderers should be dealt with. 'Lock them up and throw away the key,' is the cry time and time again from the families of victims of murder.

The political cries ring out meanwhile: 'Tough on crime, and tough on the causes of crime,' – and so the demand for longer and longer sentences for murder grows ever louder. 'There are no votes for being soft on crime,' politician after politician tells the world, and so the prison population expands and expands exponentially.

But is that the correct response? Should a just and humane society be sentencing a twenty-three year-old young man to spend what could be the next seventy years behind bars?

That is what this book is about. Are we right to answer the demands of the families of victims and allow men and women to spend half a century or more locked away?

Is anyone who commits multiple murder necessarily sane – or should their mental health be taken into account in their prison sentence? Will the prison system be able to deal with an ever-ageing population of killers? Are prison officers correctly trained to deal with the worst of the worst? Should we create a 'supermax' prison to house the worst offenders? What do other countries do about prisoners who commit the worst of offences? Does every other country lock them up and throw away the key?

Those are some of the questions this book will seek to examine and answer. Because the reality is that ever since the suspension of the death penalty for capital murder in 1965, British society has never been quite sure how it feels about 'whole lifers', a phrase coined by the distinguished legal commentator Joshua Rozenberg to mean those men and women who are given 'whole life terms of imprisonment'.

The Ministry of Justice declines to give a precise figure for the number of prisoners serving that tariff, but this book can reveal that there are more than fifty, if not sixty 'whole lifers' – including two women. Each and every one of those prisoners is effectively destined to end their lives in jail, even though some of them were never formally sentenced to serve a 'whole life' term in the first place.

They range from the eighty-seven-year-old paedophile Sidney Cooke (also known as 'Hissing Sid'), who is now largely bed-ridden in Wakefield Prison, to Robert Maudsley (whose nickname remains 'Hannibal the Cannibal', even though it is highly unlikely that he actually did eat the brains of the prisoner he killed in jail), who also lives in Wakefield Prison in a specially constructed 'glass cage' in the basement with his own staff of six prison officers and no contact with any other prisoners.

They include the tattooed Peterborough killer Joanna Dennehy, who stabbed and murdered three men in 2013 and claimed afterwards, 'I killed to see how I would feel, to see if I was as cold as I thought I was. Then it got moreish'; Steven Wright (the Suffolk Strangler), who killed five prostitutes in 2006; and former abattoir worker Mark Bridger, convicted of killing five-year-old April Jones in 2013, even though her body was never discovered.

They also include Rosemary West, convicted of the killing of ten young women, including her daughter Heather; and Ian Brady (the Moors Murderer) who has been on hunger strike and demanding the right to die for more than a decade, while firmly refusing to tell the authorities the whereabouts of the last of his five victims, fourteen-year-old Keith Bennett.

Each and every one of them has their own depraved story to tell, but they each confront society with the same perplexing dilemma – should they spend the rest of their lives imprisoned with little or no hope of release?

Some argue that it would be better to reintroduce the death penalty – as their crimes are so odious that imprisonment, at the state's considerable expense (about £90,000 a year), is 'too good' for them. It is not an argument I agree with – the concept of one innocent man or woman being sent to the gallows, or given a lethal injection, is simply too repugnant to consider. You can set an innocent prisoner free, but you can never bring them back to life.

Yet, for half a century, Britain has puzzled over what

the supreme penalty for taking a human life in a heinous crime should be. The truth is that there is no truth. There is no correct answer. There will only ever be a debate – but it is a debate that must be had, for it is not enough to ignore it and allow the present muddle to continue for another fifty years.

For my part, I believe that rehabilitation can, sometimes, be possible – but, equally, that many of the very worst offenders will never be redeemed. The very worst have no conscience or regret about their crimes and would commit them again tomorrow – given the chance. That may not be what they tell the Parole Board when they are being considered for release on licence, but, as this book will show repeatedly, more often than not they cannot resist the urge to kill again.

To my mind, the concept of an eye for an eye – that a murderer should pay for his or her crime with their own life – was rightly suspended in Britain in 1965. For the previous eight years there had been two degrees of murder, 'capital murder' which carried the death penalty and 'murder' which did not, although it carried a mandatory sentence of 'life imprisonment'.

That was abandoned in the wake of Labour MP Sydney Silverman's Private Members' Bill in 1965 that saw the death penalty suspended for five years. It remained theoretically in place for offences including espionage, treason and piracy, but was never used. The suspension became permanent on 16 December 1969, when the then Home Secretary, James Callaghan, proposed it to the House of Commons. It was not finally abolished in Northern Ireland until 25 July 1973.

The firm understanding in the House of Commons when the death penalty was suspended was that murder of any kind should always attract a life sentence, providing the killer was over twenty-one years of age. Yet in the years that followed, a life sentence for murder seldom meant life. Indeed by the late 1970s, the average term of imprisonment served by a murderer was around nine years. Many of those sentenced to life for murder emerged from prison to resume normal lives, but a substantial minority did not, and often went on to commit further crimes, including murder. That infuriated many members of the public, as did the fact that the sentence did not seem to deter murderers who might fairly be called 'the worst of the worst'.

There emerged a strange confusion about what a life sentence meant, not least because it no longer seemed a sufficient penalty for the most depraved and ruthless killers, many of whom killed more than one victim, or were responsible for the deaths of children. As a result, trial judges started to add a 'minimum term' to a life sentence in the worst cases of murder – by specifying, for example, that a convicted killer sentenced to life should serve a minimum period (say twenty-five years) in prison before he or she could be considered for parole.

Then, gradually, the politicians of the day started to override the judges' decisions about a minimum term and insist that particularly heinous offenders should receive a 'whole life tariff', regardless of the judicial view. That reflected an ever-increasing clamour from the general public, often incited by the media, for harsher and harsher sentences for those who had committed the worst crimes.

That fervour came into full flood a few weeks after the death penalty had been legally suspended. Just one month later, Greater Manchester Police arrested two of the most notorious killers in British criminal history, Ian Brady and his female accomplice Myra Hindley, who would become known as the Moors Murderers for their killing of five children between the ages of ten and seventeen, four of whom they also sexually assaulted.

The crime shocked the nation, a shock that deepened still further when Brady and Hindley came to trial in April 1966. The prosecution played the jury a fifteen-minute tape recording of one of their female victims, ten-year-old Lesley Anne Downey, being tortured by the pair and pleading for her life. It left even the most hard-nosed reporters in the press gallery traumatised and in tears.

At the end of the trial, after the jury had convicted them both, the judge, Mr Justice Fenton Atkinson, described them as 'two sadistic killers of the utmost depravity' and Brady as 'wicked beyond belief'. He recommended that they should both spend 'a very long time in jail' but, significantly, he did not recommend a 'tariff' – or minimum term – for Brady. He did, however, recommend that Hindley serve a minimum of twenty-five years.

In fact, due to a series of decisions by successive Home Secretaries, Hindley was never released and died, still a prisoner, in 2002 at the age of sixty – from bronchial pneumonia. Brady too was destined never to be released, again through the intervention of the Home Secretary, being declared criminally insane in 1985 and transferred to the Ashworth high security hospital near Liverpool. Brady died in May 2017, at the age of seventy-nine, after spending the last seventeen years of his life on hunger strike, although one that allowed him to make toast and drink packet soup – 'to help him to survive'.

It was the Moors Murders that first brought into clear focus the difficulties of just having a simple 'life' sentence for murder. Surely, some argued, there had to be a distinction between a domestic argument that led to a single death and a determined effort to kill a police officer, for example, or several people, especially children?

That question came into sharp focus again just a few months after Brady and Hindley were convicted when a small-time armed robber named Harry Roberts was caught after the killing of three Metropolitan Police men in East Acton, London, in what became known as the 'Massacre in Braybrook Street'. On the afternoon of 12 August 1966, just a few days after England had won the World Cup at Wembley, Roberts and two associates were on their way to commit a robbery carrying two handguns, when they were stopped by an unmarked police car carrying two detectives and a young constable.

Convinced that the officers would discover the guns, Roberts, then aged thirty, shot first one and then a second officer dead, while one of his accomplices shot and killed the third. Desperate to escape justice, Roberts went on the run, hiding out in east London's Epping Forest using the military training he had been given as a soldier during the Malayan Emergency between 1948 and 1960. He was finally captured after ninety-six days on the run, sleeping in a barn on the edge of the forest.

At his trial in 1967 Roberts was sentenced to life imprisonment for killing the officers, and the trial judge recommended that he serve a minimum of thirty years. In fact, once again, after the repeated interventions of a succession of Home Secretaries, each fully aware of how strongly the police service felt about the killing of policemen, Roberts remained in prison until November 2014.

By then aged seventy-nine, Roberts had been refused parole on a number of occasions after repeated attempts to escape and a five-year campaign of brutal intimidation, ending in 2006, against the female owner of an animal sanctuary, where he was on 'day release' in preparation for his potential freedom. Eight years later the Parole Board allowed his release on licence.

Both the Moors Murderers and Roberts concentrated the

public mind on what a life sentence truly meant – especially when it came to multiple murders – but there was no political appetite to revisit the whole issue so quickly after the formal suspension of the death penalty under Harold Wilson's Labour Government. For the most part, both politicians and the public were prepared to allow the uncertainty of whether 'life should mean life' to continue.

This typically British compromise was sustained because the public were prepared to accept that politicians – and particularly the Home Secretaries of the day – could and should decide whether a murderer should remain in prison, regardless of what the trial judge may have said. This left the issue to be decided on a case-by-case basis, usually depending on the political assessment of how far the public would be appalled if a particular prisoner were to be released.

The contradiction is that by allowing the compromise, British society – so determined to suspend and then abolish the death penalty – covertly accepted a system that allowed some killers to spend their entire lives behind bars, while others were deemed sufficiently rehabilitated to be freed 'on licence'.

There is no finer example of that covert acceptance of the confusion than the case of Britain's longest-ever serving prisoner, John Straffen, who spent more than half a century in jail. The Hampshire-born Straffen, son of an army officer, killed two young girls, aged five and nine, with no apparent motive in 1951. At his trial that October he was found 'unfit to plead' because of his mental health, and sent to Broadmoor Special Hospital in Berkshire.

Just a few months later, in April 1952, he escaped and, during his four hours of freedom, killed another five-year-old girl. At his subsequent trial he was convicted of murder – as the jury were apparently convinced that he was sane.

Straffen was sentenced to death, but was reprieved due to his mental deficiencies. He was to spend the rest of his life in prison, before his eventual death in November 2007. He had served a total of fifty-six years, and had become the oldest prisoner serving a whole life term. Yet at no point had he ever received that sentence from a judge.

Straffen was an exception. For the majority of other prisoners convicted of murder during the 1970s and 1980s, a life sentence meant serving an average of nine years or so in jail. Yet, as they did so, the public clamour of being 'tough on crime' and especially murderers steadily gathered in pace. As the years passed and the twentieth century drew to a close, so the public, and therefore political, demand for longer and longer sentences for murder grew and grew. Slowly but surely, a form of 'sentence creep' began to take hold, so that murderers, and especially multiple ones, received ever longer terms of imprisonment.

One reason for that lay in a group of high-profile cases that increased public revulsion at what a murderer could be capable of – thereby increasing the call for 'life to mean life'.

The first major crime to accelerate the growing call for 'whole life' terms involved the balaclava-clad 'Black Panther', Donald Neilson, who shot dead three sub-postmasters during robberies in various parts of England between 1971 and 1974. Then, early in 1975, he abducted seventeen-year-old heiress Lesley Whittle from her home in Shropshire.

Neilson attempted to ransom the terrified daughter of the owner of a successful coach hire business for £50,000, while keeping her hostage in a water drainage shaft in Staffordshire. The ransom attempt failed and her body was finally recovered almost seven weeks later. She had fallen, and the tether that Neilson had placed round her neck to restrain her from trying to escape had strangled her to death. In July 1976

Neilson was given four life sentences, and the judge recommended he be given a 'whole life' term, which the Home Secretary accepted.

Thirty-two years later, in 2008, Neilson attempted to have his sentence reduced to a minimum of thirty years, but his appeal was refused. That same year he was diagnosed with motor neurone disease and he died, still a prisoner, in December 2011, at the age of seventy-five. He had spent more than thirty-five years behind bars. For millions of people throughout Britain Neilson epitomised a man who would have been a candidate for the death sentence, had one still existed.

Perhaps more than any other, Neilson's was the case that began the escalation in the length of imprisonment meant when a life sentence was imposed. He ushered in an era in which a life sentence increasingly came to mean exactly that – and his case was followed just five years later by another which would confirm public opinion about the treatment of serial killers. It was the conviction of the thirty-five-year-old lorry driver, Peter Sutcliffe, 'The Yorkshire Ripper', who was charged with the murder of thirteen women and the attempted murder of a further seven, after a killing spree that had lasted for five years and terrified the female residents of Leeds and Bradford in Yorkshire.

At Sutcliffe's trial in May 1981, he pleaded guilty to the murders, but claimed diminished responsibility on the grounds of his paranoid schizophrenia. Sutcliffe claimed that he had killed as a result of a 'divine mission' and as the result of hearing the 'voice of God'. The jury heard some horrifying details of his killings – many of his victims were prostitutes who were beaten about the head and their bodies mutilated after their deaths – and declined his argument of diminished responsibility. They unanimously found him guilty of murder and attempted murder and the trial judge at the Central Criminal

Court in the Old Bailey, Mr Justice Boreham, imposed a sentence of thirty years, calling Sutcliffe 'an unusually dangerous man' and recommending that he serve the full term before even being considered for release.

In fact, Sutcliffe only spent the first three years of his sentence in prison. He was transferred to Broadmoor Hospital, a top-security psychiatric unit, in 1984 as a result of his paranoid schizophrenia and he has remained there ever since. As the end of his thirty-year minimum term approached in July 2010, he appealed against his sentence, but was told by Mr Justice Mitting at the Court of Appeal that, in his case, life would indeed mean life. The families of some of his victims were appalled that there should ever be a chance that he be released, not least because of his mutilation of his victims with a hammer, a sharpened screwdriver and a knife.

In March 2011, Sutcliffe returned to the Court of Appeal once more, on the grounds that his incarceration without a fixed period raised major issues of law, but the Court, this time led by the then Lord Chief Justice, Lord Judge, rejected his bid for the case to go to the new Supreme Court because of the serious issues of law that it raised. Sutcliffe also claimed that he was now 'much better' and no longer 'uniquely dangerous'.

Lord Judge accepted Sutcliffe was 'disturbed' when he went out to commit the murders, but then added, 'There is no reason to conclude that the appellant's claims that he genuinely believed he was acting under the divine instruction to fulfil God's will carries any greater conviction now than it did when it was rejected by the jury,' before suggesting that Sutcliffe's crimes were 'criminal conduct at the extreme end of horror'.

As a result Lord Judge confirmed that the Court's view

was that 'the interests of justice require nothing less than a whole life order. That is the only available punishment proportionate to these crimes.'

During Sutcliffe's years of incarceration, the atmosphere and culture that surrounded the worst offenders changed significantly. Sutcliffe may have gone to prison originally in a less ferocious climate of public opinion, but over time that had been transformed beyond recognition by a string of high profile cases, of which his was one of the earliest and most significant.

Sutcliffe too had changed during his years in Broadmoor, where he has spent the last thirty years. Still diagnosed as suffering from mental health problems, he adopted his mother's maiden name of Coonan, became a Jehovah's Witness and struck up a long-lasting friendship with the late – and now disgraced – radio disc jockey Jimmy Savile.

Only a matter of months after Sutcliffe's conviction, however, the British public were presented with another infamous serial killer, the Scottish-born ex-policeman Dennis Nilsen. In his own way, Nilsen became every bit as notorious as Sutcliffe had in 1982, when it was discovered that he had murdered and dismembered no fewer than twelve young men – most of whom were homeless, homosexual or prostitutes – in two north London flats over a period of five years between 1978 and 1983. He then stored their body parts in the flats – by doing so, he was, in his own words, 'killing for company'.

Nilsen later told the police, 'I wished I could have stopped, but I couldn't. I had no other thrill or happiness.' But he did not deny that he washed, clothed and retained his victims' bodies within his two flats for weeks or even months at a time, before burning some of them on bonfires and hiding others under the floorboards, or flushing their bones down the lavatory. He did deny that he was a necrophiliac, though accepted that he had engaged in sexual acts with the bodies of six of his victims. The revelations shocked the British public to the core.

After his conviction on 3 November 1983 at the Central Criminal Court at the Old Bailey, the judge, Mr Justice Croom-Johnson, recommended that he should serve a minimum of twenty-five years as part of his life sentence. But successive Home Secretaries – again reacting to public and media opinion – decided that the extreme seriousness of his crimes and the public revulsion that accompanied his trial meant that he should never be freed. He remains in prison today more than thirty years after his conviction, and complains that he has been denied the right to publish his autobiography, *History of a Drowning Man*, as well as some music and poetry that he has written.

Just three years later came another equally controversial case that again underlined the public desire for killers to be locked up forever. It involved a twenty-five-year-old former waiter in a Little Chef restaurant called Jeremy Bamber, who was charged with shooting dead his adoptive parents, his sister and her twin six-year-old sons at the family home, 'White House Farm' in Essex, so that he could claim a large inheritance. He shot the boys twenty-six times.

The killings became one of the most dramatic multiple murder cases in Britain, but Bamber insisted that his sister, Sheila, who was a diagnosed schizophrenic, had actually committed all four of the other murders before turning the gun on herself. At his trial in October 1986 the jury decided that Bamber's story about his sister was concocted to save himself, and found him guilty of the five murders.

In sentencing Bamber to life imprisonment, with a minimum term of twenty-five years, the judge suggested that he found it 'difficult to foresee' that he would ever be released, and in 1994 the Home Secretary let it be known that he would indeed never be released.

Now, almost thirty years later, Bamber remains in prison. But he is exceptional in that he is the only 'whole life' prisoner who has never accepted his guilt. Indeed he has vigorously protested his innocence from the day of his conviction, and is continuing to appeal against his sentence – and his continued imprisonment – to this day.

In 2003 Bamber won a case in the European Court of Human Rights in Strasbourg, stating that his whole life term was a breach of his human rights, and he is still pursuing that argument with the British Courts from his prison cell. Indeed, it was Bamber's appeal which led indirectly to the ECHR deciding that whole life terms were 'inhuman' in 2013.

Two cases in the 1990s further underlined the ever-increasing demand from the public – and the families of the victims – that 'life should mean life', especially for the most heinous crimes. The first major case to escalate the steadily increasing appetite for whole life terms of imprisonment, handed out by successive Home Secretaries, was that of the paedophile Robert Black.

Finally tracked down in 1990, Black abducted, raped and murdered four schoolgirls aged from five to eleven between 1981 and 1986. He was also convicted of the kidnapping of a fifth schoolgirl and the attempted kidnapping of a sixth in the years before his eventual capture.

Black was finally caught by the police after he was seen snatching a six-year-old girl off the street in Stow, in his native Scotland, and throwing her into the back of his van. The police chased the van and finally caught up with it, but not before Black had sexually assaulted the girl. The police officer who saved her turned out to be her father. The case made headlines around the country. He was in jail for the abduction when he was finally charged with murder.

Black finally went for trial in April 1994 and denied all the charges against him, but the jury disagreed and in May 1994 he was convicted. The judge recommended that he serve a minimum of thirty-five years before he could even be considered for release, which meant that he would not have been considered for parole until 2029, by which time he would be eighty-two years of age. But in October 2011 Black was found guilty of the murder of another schoolgirl, this time in Northern Ireland in 1981, and given a further life sentence. Robert Black died in January 2016, shortly before he would have been charged with the murder in 1978 of Genette Tate.

The other case in the 1990s that confirmed the public desire for whole life sentences concerned the only woman, apart from Myra Hindley, to be given a whole life term at that time. She was, of course, Rosemary West, wife of the Gloucester-based serial killer Frederick West, who killed himself on 1 January 1995, before he could stand trial. She was charged with the murder of her daughter Heather, aged sixteen, eight other young women who had visited her husband's house at 25 Cromwell Street in Gloucester, and West's daughter by his first marriage, eight-year-old Charmaine.

When Rosemary West was convicted at Winchester Crown Court of the murder of ten young woman and children, in November 1995, the trial judge Mr Justice Mantell memorably concluded: 'If attention is paid to what I think, you will never be released.' In fact, West was officially given a life sentence with a minimum term of twenty-five years before she could be considered for release. It was the Labour Home Secretary Jack Straw who decided two years later that she should serve a 'whole life tariff' and die in prison.

West has since decided that she has no wish to appeal against her sentence. Now aged sixty-two, she is reportedly content to spend the rest of her life in prison, although, of course, she would be entitled to change her mind as the years continue to pass. She has, after all, spent two decades already behind bars and there is every possibility, given reasonable health, that she may spend a further three decades in the same predicament. The difficulty, of course, is that her very notoriety will make any decision to release her a matter of great controversy – just as it was for Myra Hindley.

But it was the European Court of Human Rights that ended the twentieth-century discussion between judges and the Home Secretary over who should decide how long the worst murderers should serve in prison. In November 2000, in the wake of an appeal to the ECHR on behalf of Robert Thompson and Jon Venables, the ten-year-old child killers of two-year-old toddler James Bulger, the European Court ruled that the Home Secretary should lose the right to set a tariff for defendants under the age of eighteen as it did not consider it was appropriate for a politician to interfere in the judicial process. At their trial in 1993 the judge had sentenced Thompson and Venables to eight years each, but the then Home Secretary, the Tory Party's Michael Howard, set a tariff of fifteen years – partly as a result of the public outcry over the case. The House of Lords overturned that increase, criticising Howard for putting too much weight on public opinion.

Two years later a similar decision in respect of adult offenders followed an appeal on behalf of the convicted double-killer Arthur Anderson, who had been sentenced to life imprisonment in 1988 with a recommended minimum term of fifteen years – only to be told by the Home Secretary of the day, Labour's David Blunkett, that he would have to serve twenty years. Anderson appealed to the House of

Lords who decided that the decision breached his human rights. Their decision was upheld in the European Court of Human Rights.

These two cases effectively cost the Home Secretary any discretion over the length of life and other sentences. In response to the change in the powers of the Home Secretary over sentencing, David Blunkett, as Home Secretary of the Labour Government, introduced the Criminal Justice Act of 2003 which responded to the loss of the Home Secretary's sentencing power, and gave the judiciary detailed guidance about what factors they had to take into account in their sentencing decisions. Many commentators saw it as David Blunkett's revenge for the decision to strip the Home Secretary of his powers. Judges are not formally obliged to stick to the guidelines, but must explain the reasons if they depart from them.

Now the only occasion when a politician may intervene in the judicial sentencing process comes when the Government's Attorney General exercises his right to petition the Court of Appeal if he thinks that the sentence passed by a judge has been 'unduly lenient'. Only judges can now set a minimum term for life imprisonment, and only the Court of Appeal or the Supreme Court can amend their decision.

The sentencing guidelines laid down in the Criminal Justice Act 2003 are still the subject of debate between judges and politicians, and have given rise to further appeals to the European Court of Human Rights, but they nevertheless lay the foundations for sentencing the worst offenders in Britain.

Under the 2003 Act a minimum term (which was formerly called a 'tariff') became the minimum number of years a prisoner serves before he can even be considered for parole – it does not mean that the prisoner will be released after the minimum period has passed. That will only take place when the prisoner 'is judged no longer a risk of harm to the public', by the Parole Board.

The starting point for a 'whole life' order is that the offender must be aged over twenty-one – Jamie Reynolds, for example, only just came within its terms at the age of twenty-three, and Schedule 21 of the Act lays down the types of murder that might attract a 'whole life' term. They include multiple murders, where each murder involves premeditation, abduction, or sexual or sadistic conduct; the murder of a child involving abduction or sexual or sadistic conduct; any assassination committed to further a religious, political, racial or ideological cause; and any murder by a person previously convicted of murder.

The trial judge can also pass a whole life order if he considers the offence so serious – or the combination of offences that make it so serious – to be exceptionally high.

In 2011 three prisoners sentenced to whole life orders, all of them murderers, Jeremy Bamber, Peter Moore and Douglas Vinter, disputed the rights of the British Courts to pass a 'whole life' term, and appealed to the European Court of Human Rights that whole life orders breached their human rights. They argued that to sentence them to spend the rest of their life in jail was 'inhuman'. The three killers lost their case in 2012 when the ECHR found that the whole life prisoners could apply to the Home Secretary for compassionate release, and therefore their human rights were not breached.

But on 9 July 2013, after a further appeal by the same three men, the ECHR found that there had to be the 'prospect of review' for prisoners subjected to whole life orders, and that any impossibility of parole would violate their human rights under Article Three of the European Convention.

Just seven months later, on 18 February 2014, the Court

of Appeal in England and Wales fundamentally disagreed with the European Court in their ruling on appeals by three different whole life prisoners, Mark Bridger (killer of five-year-old April Jones in 2013), Lee Newell (guilty of murdering a fellow prisoner, while in jail for murder) and Matthew Thomas, whom it was later discovered had not been sentenced to a whole life term and whose case was, therefore, not considered.

Led by the Lord Chief Justice, Lord Thomas, the five-strong Court, which included Lady Justice Hallett, found that the ECHR in Strasbourg was not correct when it concluded that English and Welsh law never allowed whole life orders to be reduced. Lord Thomas specifically pointed out that the Home Secretary could review them in 'exceptional circumstances'.

On behalf of the Court, the Lord Chief Justice explained that they believed there are some crimes which were so heinous that Parliament was entitled to allow 'a sentence which includes a whole life order'. He concluded: 'In our judgement the law of England and Wales therefore does provide to an offender "hope" or the "possibility" of release in exceptional circumstances . . . Judges should therefore continue as they have done to impose whole life orders in those rare and exceptional cases.'

In effect, the Court of Appeal denied the European Court's assertion that there was no possibility of parole or release under a whole life order, no matter how exceptional the circumstances might be. This did not, therefore, breach an offender's human rights under the European Convention.

Interestingly, only four prisoners serving 'whole life' terms have ever been released on compassionate grounds by a Home Secretary. Three of them were Irish Republican Army sympathisers released as part of the 'Good Friday' agreement for peace in Northern Ireland, including the infamous Paul 'Dingus' Magee, who originally escaped during his trial for the murder of an SAS soldier in 1981, and was sentenced to a term of thirty years in his absence. Magee was finally imprisoned for killing a policeman in England in 1992, but was repatriated to Northern Ireland in 1999 as part of the 'peace process' and eventually released in December 2000, when he was given a pardon under the Royal Prerogative of Mercy.

The only other theoretical 'whole life' prisoner, whose existence in that category was never officially confirmed, was the London gangster Reggie Kray, who had been diagnosed with terminal cancer when he was released by the Home Secretary on 1 October 2000. He died within a matter of weeks. The reality is that the possibility of release on compassionate grounds is, to put it politely, remote – unless the prisoner is facing a terminal illness.

It was against this background that Jamie Reynolds's legal team came to the Court of Appeal in London on Thursday morning 16 October 2014 to argue that his whole life order should be amended because the trial judge had not taken into account his young age and the fact that he had pleaded guilty to the charges. His legal team knew the Court's ruling that whole life orders were legal, in spite of the European Court's decision, but they also knew that the weight of the argument would once again revolve around whether life should indeed mean life for the twenty-three-year-old convicted murderer.

In the low-key atmosphere of the wood-panelled Court Five on the first floor of the Royal Courts of Justice, Reynolds' case was placed before the Lord Chief Justice, Lord Thomas, sitting with two other Appeal Court judges, by Reynolds' defence team. The Court's attention was drawn to his eventual plea of guilty – though it had not taken place until a psychiatrist had warned that he could not claim any 'diminished responsibility' for his crime as a result of the meticulous planning he had demonstrated.

The Court also heard that the closeness of age between Reynolds and his victim should play its part in weighing the length of his term of imprisonment as it was not the murder of a young child, but rather one of a mature teenager. The Court was then told by the Crown, on behalf of the prosecution, that the closeness of age between Reynolds and Georgia Williams had effectively helped him commit murder and in no way mitigated against the sentence.

Sitting in Wakefield Prison, watching proceedings by video link from the Court of Appeal, Reynolds looked pale and uncertain. No longer sporting the partial beard he had worn during his trial, he looked for all the world like a terrified schoolboy, rather than the depraved killer that he had appeared at trial. Only speaking when asked to confirm his name, his voice was high-pitched, almost strangled, and he sat there watching the proceedings, staring blankly at the screen in front of him showing the London hearing, while nervously biting his nails.

No judgement was reached on that Thursday morning, however. The Lord Chief Justice and his two colleagues promised to hand down a written judgement on Reynolds as soon as they could – although they did ask if they could see the photographs of Georgia Williams' ordeal that the trial judge had seen when he sentenced Reynolds to spend the rest of his life in jail.

It was an ominous harbinger of what their decision would be. If the Court of Appeal was as appalled by Reynolds' detailed record of his crime as the trial judge clearly had been, then the chance of his receiving a shorter sentence seemed less and less likely. Two weeks were to pass before the Court of Appeal handed down their judgement on James Reynolds' appeal against his whole life term. Their decision would confirm whether or not there was any judicial sympathy for sentencing a young man barely in his twenties to spend six decades in prison.

Rot in Hell

Barely two months after Mr Justice Wilkie sentenced Jamie Reynolds to a whole life term of imprisonment at Stafford Crown Court in December 2013, another judge passed exactly the same sentence on a thirty-three-year-old former soldier and alcoholic drifter named Anwar Rosser.

At Bradford Crown Court on the morning of Thursday 13 February 2014 – ironically, the day before the Court of Appeal was to make its historic judgement that whole life orders in England and Wales did not contravene the European Convention on Human Rights – Mr Justice Coulson ruled that Rosser too should spend the rest of his life behind bars.

In some ways Rosser's crime was even more heinous than Jamie Reynolds' sexual and sadistic killing of teenager Georgia Williams – because it involved the death of an innocent, cheerful, loving four-year-old boy called Riley Turner. The facts alone chill the bones.

Shortly after 4.00 on the snowy morning of Sunday 20 January 2013, Rosser, for no clear reason other than sexual perversion, savagely murdered this little boy in his own bedroom in the house he lived in with his mother, Sharon Smith, and stepfather, Guy Earwaker, in Keighley, Yorkshire. His twin brother and eighteen-month-old baby brother were also asleep in the house when he was killed.

At the time, Rosser was living in a flat just across the road from Riley's parents in Harewood Road, Keighley. The couple had befriended the ex-soldier – even to the extent of helping him to furnish his flat – but on that bleak Saturday night which turned into an even bleaker Sunday morning their friendship fractured forever.

On Saturday evening, 19 January 2013, Rosser had gone to his local pub, the Bracken Arms, and got drunk, though not incoherent or incapable. Filled with alcoholic bonhomie – and lust – he met two local women there and invited them to 'make a party of it', but instead of going back to Rosser's flat he suggested they all went to visit Riley's parents instead.

Things did not go to plan for Rosser, however. As the evening turned into the first hour of Sunday morning the two women left, and Rosser asked Riley's parents if he could sleep on their sofa in the living room instead of walking back to his flat across the road. His excuse was that he was afraid that some people to whom he owed money might be waiting outside his flat intent on beating him up.

Out of compassion, Riley's parents agreed that their neighbour could stay on the sofa and went upstairs to bed themselves at about 1.00 on that Sunday morning. What Riley's parents did not know was that Rosser had another, far darker, reason for wanting to stay in their house that night – he almost certainly wanted to seriously injure one or more members of the family. To do so, he had even brought with him a four-inch knife with a brown handle, which he had stolen from the pub where he worked as a part-time chef.

Rosser may have been carrying the knife partly out of a sense of paranoia about the men who he claimed could be waiting for him outside his flat, but that was certainly not the principal reason, as he was soon to reveal. Shortly after 4 am, Rosser got up from the sofa and crept upstairs armed with no fewer than four knives, including the one that he had brought with him. The other three he had taken from the family's downstairs kitchen.

Rosser looked into Sharon Smith and Guy Earwaker's bedroom, but he did not wake them – nor did he attack them. For reasons known only to himself, he had decided to attack their son Riley. So he crossed the landing and entered the bedroom of the four-year-old, who was sound asleep.

Quite without warning, Rosser attacked the little boy in the most depraved and brutal way, repeatedly stabbing him in a frenzy as the boy lay in his bed. In total Riley suffered no fewer than thirty stab wounds, all inflicted by the brown-handled knife Rosser had brought with him that evening.

But Riley's ordeal did not end there. Rosser also attacked the boy sexually, stabbing him in the scrotum and then inserting objects into his rectum when – according to the report of the coroner – he was still alive. He finally removed Riley's pyjama bottoms when they were soaked with urine, and one of the objects found nearby contained traces of the child's faeces and blood.

Riley endured fourteen stab wounds to his neck – one of which severed his windpipe – while another almost severed his spine. There were five stab wounds to his back, and five to the chest, which had punctured the toddler's lungs. There were also six wounds in the abdomen, one of which had penetrated his stomach wall. Yet even that grotesque violence was not enough for Rosser. There was also a deep bite mark on Riley's upper left thigh, a mark that matched the former soldier's teeth.

Finally thirty-two year-old Rosser placed his hands around the little boy's neck and strangled him. Yet Rosser did not flee into the night after committing such a dreadful crime: quite the opposite. After destroying the tiny, innocent toddler's body and covering his bed with his blood, Rosser went into Riley's parents' bedroom and curled up on the floor on Sharon Smith's side of the bed.

At about four thirty that Sunday morning, Sharon Smith woke up suddenly to discover Rosser lying beside her on the floor. She quickly woke up Guy Earwaker, who told Rosser to get out, which he did, but only after apologising and asking for some tobacco. But he did not leave the house. Rosser simply went downstairs and waited. He wanted to hear the devastated reaction of Riley's parents when they found his body.

That only took a few moments. Guy Earwaker looked out into the hallway after Rosser had gone downstairs and saw that the light was on in Riley's bedroom. He went to investigate and discovered Riley's blood-soaked corpse lying on his bed.

Unable to speak, Earwaker went back to find Sharon Smith, who followed him into Riley's bedroom. She screamed, and it was only then that the couple heard the front door slam downstairs as Rosser finally left. Earwaker chased him outside into the street, but lost sight of him in the darkness and returned to the house to comfort his wife and call for an ambulance and the police.

Later that morning Earwaker joined in the police hunt for Rosser, and within just a few hours he found him hiding in a caravan that he had broken into on a smallholding not far away from Harewood Road. There was blood on the snow outside the caravan, and smears of blood inside the caravan itself.

'I have ruined my life,' Rosser told Earwaker. Then, after the police arrived and he had been arrested he said, 'I know

I have done summat but I don't know what. After what I have done I am a piece of shit.'

Nevertheless, in spite of the blood smears in the caravan and the fact that he had clearly been in the house when Riley Turner died, Rosser continued to deny any knowledge of the boy's death. It was to be a year before Rosser finally pleaded guilty to killing Riley Turner.

Throughout those months, Rosser took legal refuge behind his defence team's call for expert reports. Time and again the deadlines for delivery were missed and those delays saw his trial postponed from July 2013 to October 2013 and finally until February 2014. It was only after the experts concluded that his 'antisocial personality disorder' and psychopathic personality did not mean that he had not known exactly what he was doing when he killed the four-year-old, that Rosser accepted that he could not hide behind his mental condition to diminish his responsibility for the killing.

Sentencing Rosser on Thursday 13 February 2014, Mr Justice Coulson referred to two 'victim statements' about the effect the slaughter of this 'bright, lively, happy, innocent four-year-old' had had on his family. They were made by Riley's mother Sharon Smith and her own mother. They make heart-rending reading.

'I wish I had told that monster "no" that night when he asked if he could sleep,' Sharon Smith wrote to the Court. 'He said people were outside his house and were going to beat him up and I believed him. I didn't want him to get beaten up, but all along he had a knife in his pocket, plotting to hurt one of us, or all of us. I feel so much guilt that my poor son had to go through such horrific things because my kind heart didn't want to let that monster get beaten up. Now my kind heart cost me my son's life.'

But Sharon Smith did not end there. 'The guilt eats away at me every day,' she went on. 'What he's done is unforgiveable, he's ruined our lives. I don't look forward to life any more. I wake up now and just want to be with my son Riley so that he's not alone. I can't bear to think he's sad and alone.'

She ended by explaining the impact of his death on his twin brother. 'It's very upsetting,' she wrote, 'to hear my boy cry for his brother all the time and wonder where he's gone and why he isn't coming back. Some questions I can't answer to my boy. I try my best but I don't understand myself and I never will.'

Mr Justice Coulson was clearly deeply moved by Riley's mother's testimony, but it was the horrors of the crime itself that made the strongest impression. In particular, he drew attention to the sexual and sadistic elements of the killing. He pointed out that both the prosecution's and defence's psychiatrists had expressly identified the 'sexual element' in Rosser's motivation and conduct.

'On any view, this murder involved a strong sexual component,' Mr Justice Coulson said. 'That can be seen from the removal of Riley's pyjama bottoms, the slicing open of his scrotum, the biting, and, in particular the repeated insertion of items into his rectum.' He went on to point out that the sadistic element included Rosser's determination to stay in the house until he had heard Riley's parents' reaction to the killing.

Mr Justice Coulson also suggested that the killing was 'a gross breach of trust' because Riley's parents had specifically invited Rosser to stay that night. He added that the murder was clearly premeditated because he had brought one knife with him, and remarked that Rosser had a history of violence, including a December 1996 assault that resulted in actual bodily harm – although he had only received a police caution for the offence.

The reality was that from the age of eight, Rosser had been a 'poorly controlled' boy with a penchant for starting fires. At the age of sixteen he had attacked a boy when he was sleeping, smashing a sporting trophy into his head, a wound that demanded four stitches. Shortly after that attack, for which he received a police caution, Rosser joined the Fifth Regiment, Royal Artillery, but he never saw active service, ending up spending time in an Army jail for his violent behaviour when drunk. He was discharged from the Army as a result.

'Thereafter, your life was punctuated by drink-fuelled outbursts and anger and violence,' Mr Justice Coulson told Rosser, 'something of which you were aware but seemed incapable of doing anything about.'

For his part, Rosser remained motionless in the dock, his thin, pale face expressionless.

When it came to the details of the sentence, Mr Justice Coulson – taking a lead from Mr Justice Wilkie's decision in the case of Jamie Reynolds just two months earlier – saw no reason why the European Court of Human Rights' decision should prevent him passing a whole life order.

Mr Justice Coulson bluntly told the prisoner before him: 'The evidence demonstrates beyond doubt that you are an exceptionally dangerous man, and there is nothing to say that such a condition could ever be modified or improved.'

He pointed to the evidence from the forensic psychiatrist appointed by the prosecution, who considered that he posed 'a real risk of further acts of sadistic homicide which could involve further child victims'. Rosser did not blink. He simply remained impassive as Mr Justice Coulson told him, 'You must go to prison for life. I therefore impose a whole life order. That means you will remain in prison for the rest of your natural life.'

At that moment Riley Turner's parents, who had been in Court throughout the brief trial and the sentencing, leapt to their feet, clapping and shouting, 'Yes, rot in hell.'

As he was led down to the cells by the five guards who surrounded him in the dock, Rosser showed no trace of emotion, he simply looked blank, almost as though he could barely understand the significance of what had just happened to him.

Outside the court, the senior investigating officer in the case, Detective Superintendent Mark Ridley, told a group of reporters that Rosser had never offered any explanation whatever 'for his savage and gratuitous actions'. The superintendent added: 'He has shown no remorse or compassion for the pain suffered by Riley's family . . . Today brings to an end what has been a very sad and disturbing case.'

It was not to be the end, however. On Thursday 16 October 2014 Rosser sought leave to appeal against his whole life sentence at the Court of Appeal in London.

It was here that Rosser's case and that of Jamie Reynolds came together as they were both considered by the Lord Chief Justice, Lord Thomas, sitting with Mr Justice Wyn Williams and Mr Justice Sweeney in the book-lined and wood-panelled Court Five in the Royal Courts of Justice. Both Rosser and Reynolds appeared in Court by video link from the prison in which they were serving their sentences – Wakefield in Yorkshire.

But it was Anwar Rosser's appeal that was heard first.

Looking drawn and still a little numb on the video link, he sat there in silence as his legal team raised their concerns about the sentence that he had received from Mr Justice Coulson. Rosser said nothing – beyond confirming his name.

His barrister explained to the Court that they felt his whole life sentence was 'manifestly excessive', and that Mr Justice Coulson should have sentenced him to a 'very long but finite' period instead.

In particular, they questioned whether there was indeed a 'sexual element' to the murder of Riley Turner and whether there had been any 'premeditation' to the crime. They also pointed out that he had pleaded guilty 'at the earliest possible opportunity', and that he suffered from a 'severe personality disorder', which led him to suffer from fits of paranoia. The conclusion, Rosser's defence suggested, was that his case was only 'borderline' for a 'whole life term'.

For their part, the prosecution, on behalf of the Crown, firmly told the Court that there clearly had been a 'strong sexual component' to the death of Riley Turner, not least because his pyjama bottoms had been removed, and that there had been premeditation because Rosser had carried a knife to the crime.

'The judge took the view that he decided to stay the night because of what he intended to do,' the prosecution insisted, before adding that there was clearly also a 'sadistic' element to Riley's killing because of Rosser's decision to stay and listen to the reaction of his parents when they discovered the body – which clearly showed his desire to derive a sadistic pleasure from their suffering.

Briefly rebutting the Crown's arguments, Rosser's barrister told the Court that it was clear that he was in an 'immensely disordered state' and that there had been earlier examples in the last days of 2012 and the first days of 2013 of his suffering from bouts of paranoia, and a fear that 'money lenders' were going to attack him.

Lord Thomas, the Lord Chief Justice, then announced that they would not pass judgement that day, but would hand down their written conclusions at some point in the future. When Jamie Reynolds' appeal was heard immediately after Anwar Rosser's, the Court also explained it would pass down a written judgement of both cases at some point in the future.

That came just two weeks later. On 31 October 2014, the Lord Chief Justice and his fellow judges in the Court of Appeal found, in the case of Rosser, that: 'There is no basis on which it can properly be argued that a whole life order was wrongly imposed.'

In particular, the Court insisted, 'It was not and could not be disputed that the murder involved sadistic motivation,' and then added, 'We cannot accept the argument that the judge was wrong in finding it also had a sexual component.' The three judges pointed to the attacks on Riley's rectum 'before he died' and the deep cut into his scrotum.

They also declined to accept that there had not been pre-meditation in Rosser's actions: 'Rosser went upstairs with four knives and the plain intention to kill,' just as they turned down the significance of his plea of guilty, especially because 'the evidence against him was irrefutable', and finally the Court of Appeal dismissed the suggestion that Mr Justice Coulson had failed to take fully into account Rosser's mental condition, saying firmly, 'None of the experts suggested that the disorders significantly reduced culpability.'

Anwar Rosser was thereby condemned to spend the rest of his natural life in prison – or until the Secretary of State found enough 'compassionate grounds' on which to release him on licence towards the very end of his life.

The Court's written judgement, dismissing Rosser's right of appeal, then proceeded to detail their opinion on the fate of Jamie Reynolds.

The Court were no more sympathetic to Reynolds' claim

than they had been to Rosser's. They found that Mr Justice Wilkie had indeed taken into account the reasons for the lateness of Reynolds' plea of guilty, and that he had also given enough significance to his young age in his original sentence of a whole life term.

'Reynolds did not admit he committed the killing until a few days before the trial,' the Lord Chief Justice and his two colleagues concluded, even though 'the evidence was overwhelming and we can find nothing in the psychiatric evidence that in any way justifies the failure to admit the killing.' The Court then added the telling remark: 'He showed no remorse'.

But that was not the only reason the Court dismissed the arguments put forward by Reynolds' legal team in their appeal against his sentence. Turning to his young age, the three judges concluded firmly that his intention to commit 'the kind of grotesque murder that he carried out was of long standing'.

'The planning of the murder was very careful,' they went on, 'the suffering inflicted was indescribable and motivation both sadistic and sexual,' while there was no psychiatric evidence that excused him from his sentence. 'Reynolds was a clever, resourceful and manipulative man who was determined to carry out a murder for sadistic and sexual pleasure,' and furthermore, Georgia was still a child in the eyes of law.

The Court did not feel it was necessary for them to elaborate on all the 'aggravating factors' that made Reynolds' crime so particularly heinous – but they did point to 'the long-standing desire to commit such a crime, the detailed planning, the females he had in reserve, the way in which he watched Georgia slowly die, his degradation of her body by his sexual violation of it, the taking of trophies and the dumping of the body.'

Given all that they had said in their summing up, the Court's conclusion was inevitable.

'Quite apart from the future danger Reynolds poses,' they argued, 'the judge was plainly entitled to conclude . . . that the only just punishment for the murder of Georgia was a whole life order. There is no basis on which it can properly be argued that a whole life order was not required.'

The fates of the twenty-three-year-old shop worker and occasional petrol pump attendant were confirmed. Jamie Reynolds was to spend the rest of his natural life behind the bars of an English prison, a period that could very well exceed sixty years, given the life expectancy of the average man in Britain. Arguably, it was the most draconian sentence ever handed down by an English Court.

Yet the Lord Chief Justice Lord Thomas and his fellow judges were nonetheless careful to explain the background to their decisions in the cases of both Reynolds and Rosser. In particular, they sought to lay out the responsibilities of the Courts in whole life cases and the case law that lay behind their decision.

The three judges started by referring back to the decision taken on 18 February 2014 stating that the Court of Appeal in England and Wales had concluded that the Courts had every right to continue to impose whole life terms of imprisonment, no matter what the European Court of Human Rights may have concluded in July 2013. The ECHR had ruled then that whole life terms were incompatible with Article Three of the European Convention of Human Rights, as they offered an offender no 'hope' of release and should therefore be abandoned.

In their judgement on 18 February 2014, Lord Thomas, Sir Brian Leveson, Lady Justice Hallett, Lord Justice Treacy and Mr Justice Burnett had disagreed. Lord Thomas concluded firmly: 'In our judgement the law of England and Wales . . . does provide to an offender "hope" or the "possibility" of release in exceptional circumstances which render the just punishment originally imposed no longer justifiable.'

The five judges pointed out that 'circumstances do change in exceptional cases', and that each case had to be treated quite separately 'given that the heinous nature of the original crime justly required punishment by imprisonment for life'.

Now, just a few months later, in the 31 October judgement in the cases of Rosser and Reynolds, Lord Thomas pointed out that the Court of Appeal's February decision had concluded: 'A Court must only impose a whole life order if the seriousness is exceptionally high and the requirements of just punishment and retribution make such an order the just penalty.' That was exactly why the Court of Appeal could now confirm the whole life sentences on Rosser and Reynolds.

But the Court was also aware that a detailed consideration of the brutal, ugly details in both cases was required in order to make their judgement, and explained: 'It is therefore regrettably necessary to set out the horrific circumstances of each of the murders, because only by an objective analysis of the circumstances can a judgement be made as to whether the requirements of just punishment necessitated a whole life order in each case.'

Indeed, so aware were they of the horrors of the Rosser and Reynolds murders that the Court of Appeal took the exceptional step of suggesting that the details should not be made widely available. 'The media, in reporting the decision of the Court,' it suggested, 'will, the Court knows, report the matter in such a way that the families of the two murdered children are not subjected to even greater anguish.'

The deaths of four-year-old Riley Turner and seventeen-year-old Georgia Williams had taken enough toll on the two families without making their suffering even more acute by replaying the horrific details all over again, and yet the Court knew that it could not render its judgement without describing the grotesque treatment that they had both been subjected to.

Sitting in Court Five of the Royal Courts of Justice that morning in October 2014, I felt once again that the legal system found itself caught in the paradox of insisting that the draconian term of a whole life in prison with little hope of release should be imposed while, at the same time, trying to protect the families – and, by implication, the general public – from the repeating the worst details that made that whole life order inevitable.

The worst murderers may justify the harshest treatment, but the general public should be protected from knowing too many details out of respect for the victims' families. That was not to prove possible in the next case to provoke a whole life term of imprisonment – for that was to be played out in full view of the television cameras and the onlookers' mobile phones – and involve the massacre of an innocent soldier in broad daylight.

3

'An eye for an eye, a tooth for a tooth'

Michael Adebolajo and Michael Adebowale

Few people in Britain will ever forget the sunny Wednesday afternoon of 22 May 2013 when, just after 2.20 pm, two young Muslin extremists, Michael Adebolajo and Michael Adebowale, then aged just twenty-eight and twenty-one, hacked to death twenty-five-year-old Manchester-born drummer Lee Rigby from the Royal Regiment of Fusiliers in a quiet side street just yards from his base at Woolwich Barracks in south-east London.

There were puffy clouds in the sky and a gentle breeze, but the barbarity of the killing in broad daylight – that left the young soldier almost beheaded – and his attackers proclaiming for every passer-by to see that they had killed in protest at the death of Muslims at the hands of British soldiers, left the nation stunned.

A separated father of a two-year-old son, Rigby, who had served in Afghanistan, was making his way back to his barracks after spending the morning working as a recruiting soldier for the British Army at the Regimental Headquarters in the Tower of London. He had got off the train at the nearby Woolwich Arsenal station shortly after 2.10 pm and was walking down Wellington Street on his way back to the Royal Artillery Barracks.

Lee Rigby was not in uniform, he was simply wearing a hooded T-shirt inscribed 'Help for Heroes', the charity for wounded soldiers.

Unbeknown to Rigby his killers had decided, to advance their extremist cause, to murder a British soldier in broad daylight and to do so in such a brutal way as to attract the maximum of publicity to their cause. They hoped it would culminate in their being shot dead by armed police officers who would be bound to be called to the scene of such a public execution. Adebolajo and Adebowale expected to become martyrs and gain their place in paradise.

In the days before their attack the two young men, both British born, though of Nigerian descent, had acquired an old handgun – a revolver – which did not work, but nevertheless looked sufficiently realistic to ensure that members of the public would not threaten them until the armed police they expected had arrived. The day before the attack they had also bought five knives and a knife sharpener, which they used to sharpen some of the knives before the attack.

They met up in the morning of Lee Rigby's murder, and eventually drove to Wellington Street, close to Woolwich Barracks, an area Adebolajo knew well, having lived there and handed out leaflets supporting the cause of Islamic jihad outside the Poundland store in the High Street. Adebolajo drove them to Wellington Street in a Vauxhall Tigra car, where the two young men waited for their utterly innocent victim. They were carrying the handgun and no fewer than eight knives.

Adebolajo and Adebovale were both tall and slim, both London-born to Christian parents, both having converted to Islam some years before, and both were equally convinced of the justification for their murder, their own private jihad against a British soldier.

Lee Rigby was to become their innocent victim. There was little doubt he was a soldier. He was wearing a 'Help for Heroes' hooded top and carrying his Army day sack. He was fresh-faced, outgoing, cheerful and energetic, the epitome of an excellent young British soldier. He had done nothing whatever to deserve what Adebolajo and Adebowale had in mind for him.

The two young extremists watched Rigby as he walked down Wellington Street, crossed John Wilson Street, which formed part of London's South Circular Road, and entered Artillery Place on the way to the barracks. Once he had passed the blue Vauxhall Tigra, Adebolajo, who was driving, started to follow him, and then – when he had his back to them – accelerated to between thirty and forty miles an hour and ran him down from behind.

The impact threw Rigby on to the bonnet of the Vauxhall, breaking five vertebrae in his back and five ribs, and leaving him unconscious. With his body on the bonnet the car then careered across Artillery Place before mounting the pavement and crashing into the support of a road sign. The sudden stop meant that Rigby's inert body was dumped in front of the car. There was no way that the unconscious soldier could defend himself against the barbaric attack that was to follow.

Rigby's two tall attackers jumped out of their car, Adebolajo carrying a knife and a meat cleaver, Adebowale carrying a knife and the handgun. In the next three minutes the two men butchered Rigby – there is no other word to describe it. Adebolajo concentrated on trying to decapitate him, hacking at his neck with the cleaver before switching to another knife, while Adebowale concentrated instead on his chest and torso, stabbing him in a frenzy with the most severe force.

In broad daylight, with the sun filtering through the clouds, the two men rained blow after blow on the helpless Rigby until he was unrecognisable. It was a bloodbath, the most relentless, barbaric attack on an innocent young man that could ever be imagined. So bad were the young soldier's injuries that he could only be formally identified later by using his dental records.

Still not content, Adebolajo and Adebowale then dragged the now dead body of Rigby into the centre of Artillery Place and dumped it there – bringing the traffic to a halt and attracting – as they had planned – an ever-increasing group of passers-by. Some tried to see if there was anything at all they could do to help Rigby, while others engaged the two attackers in conversation.

Adebolajo – bloody meat cleaver still clasped firmly in his hand – explained to one female passer-by: 'The only reason we have killed this man today is because Muslims are dying daily by British soldiers . . . By Allah, we swear by almighty Allah we will never stop fighting until you leave us alone.'

Aware that he was being filmed on a mobile phone, Adebolajo launched into a political diatribe in defence of his and Adebowale's actions that afternoon – as retaliation for the deaths in Muslim countries, and hoped that his statement would be broadcast around the world.

'This British soldier is an eye for an eye, a tooth for a tooth,' he then added, before handing another passer-by a two-page note trying to justify their actions.

As Mr Justice Sweeney was to comment at the trial of both men for murder six months later: 'Your sickening and pitiless conduct was in stark contrast to the compassion and bravery shown by the various women at the scene who tended to Lee Rigby's body and who challenged what you had done and said.'

At 2.34 on that May afternoon, thirteen minutes after the attack on Lee Rigby had begun in earnest, a group of armed police officers arrived at the site of the attack in Artillery Place. They immediately confronted the two Muslim extremists with their weapons drawn and shouted, 'Armed Police . . . Put down your weapons!' Both men refused to do so.

Michael Adebolajo's response was to run towards the police brandishing the meat cleaver above his head, having thrown away the knife, preparing to attack one or more of the armed officers. Michael Adebowale, meanwhile, crouched down and pointed the handgun at the officers, as if preparing to shoot. The police responded by firing eight times at close range, shooting them both. However, they immediately sought to offer first aid, even though Adebowale pointed the handgun at them again after he was shot the first time.

The incident ended with both attackers being taken to hospital with gunshot wounds, while the body of Fusilier Lee Rigby was eventually removed to the mortuary.

The killing provoked a political storm and a ferocious backlash among the British people. Within a few days, more than £600,000 had been donated to Help for Heroes and the emergency Cabinet committee, COBRA, had met twice in Downing Street, the first session chaired by the Home Secretary, the second by the Prime Minister. There were genuine, and persistent, fears that such a barbarous killing in broad daylight by two men with close connections to Islamic jihad would incite a fierce anti-Muslim reaction from the British public.

In the days after Rigby's killing an extra 200 uniformed police officers were put on patrol on the streets of London in an attempt to ensure there would be no backlash against Muslim communities in the capital; but right-wing groups, including the British National Party and the English Defence

League, organised demonstrations condemning Rigby's killing.

The fears about a backlash proved fully justified. In the ten days after Rigby's killing there was an eight-fold increase in anti-Muslim attacks across Britain. These ranged from ten attacks on mosques to physical abuse of Muslim women in the street and an attack on an Islamic Centre in Muswell Hill, north London, which was used by Muslim children after school. One charity estimated that there were more than 200 anti-Muslim attacks in London in the aftermath of Lee Rigby's brutal murder.

Once Adebolajo and Adebowale were released from their separate hospitals after treatment for their gunshot wounds, both attackers were formally charged with the murder of Rigby and the attempted murder of police officers, and then remanded in custody. That did not prove a pleasant experience. Adebolajo was reported to have lost two front teeth as a result of an attack at the high-security Belmarsh Prison in south-east London, barely a mile from the scene of the attack.

On 27 September 2013, Adebolajo and Adebowale appeared by video link at the Central Criminal Court in the Old Bailey in London and both pleaded not guilty to the murder of Lee Rigby – in spite of Adebolajo's confession at the scene of the crime, which had been captured by a bystander on a mobile phone, and in spite of the considerable closed circuit television evidence showing them taking part.

When their trial began just two months later, on 29 November 2013, Adebolajo asked to be referred to in Court as Mujaahid Abu Hamza, while Adebowale asked to be known as Ismail Ibn Abdullah. Throughout the next three weeks, both men persistently attempted to make jihadist speeches inciting violence against British soldiers from their places in the dock. At no point did either demonstrate the slightest remorse for their barbarous public attack in broad daylight on a quiet suburban street in south-east London.

Nor did their attitudes suggest that they might have been in any way deterred from their brutal actions by the threat that they might spend the rest of their lives in a British prison now that they had been denied their dreams of martyrdom and a place in paradise because the armed Metropolitan Police officers had not killed them. They were all too clearly so swept up in their own obsessive extremism that any rational thought was beyond them.

The same attitude applied throughout their trial at the Central Criminal Court in Old Bailey. Neither Adebolajo nor Adebowale appeared to pay the slightest attention to the proceedings in front of them in Court. Both ignored argument in favour of political statements and posturing. For his part, Adebolajo gave a rambling account of his views of Islam and the importance of jihad against the killers of Muslims, while Adebowale claimed that his actions had been a 'military strike' commanded by God and that he was a 'soldier of Allah'. In fact, both men appeared almost unconcerned as the evidence against them was emphatically revealed by the prosecution, led by Richard Whittam QC.

Nevertheless, during the trial something of the background of both men gradually began to emerge. It steadily became clear that Adebolajo had been a polite, well-mannered, church-going schoolboy from a loving home, and the fact that he had taken part in this vicious murder came as a profound shock to many of his friends who had known him at school. Although he had been born in Lambeth, south London, Adebolajo had been educated at Marshalls Park

School in Romford, Essex, where he was known as an 'ordinary boy' who liked football and came from a close family who dressed in traditional Nigerian clothes on Sundays. When he left school in 2001 he was described as 'always a good guy' who would 'do anything for anyone'. Although one near neighbour described Adebolajo as having a 'fierce' temper, that was not a widely held view. After school, he had gone on to study sociology at the University of Greenwich, though he never completed a degree. What seemed certain was that his character seemed to begin to change once he converted to Islam at that age of nineteen in 2003. At that point the young man born Michael in December 1984 insisted that from now on he wanted to be known as Mujaahid ('one who engages in jihad') and started to attend meetings of the militant Muslim group Al-Muhajiroun, which was later to be banned in the wake of the London bombings on the underground and bus network on Wednesday 7 July, 2005.

There was clear evidence that he was determined to support the jihadist cause. In particular, Adebolajo had been arrested outside the Old Bailey in 2006 during a protest against the trial of Mizanur Rahman, a British Islamic activist of Pakistani descent who was accused of inciting racial hatred, of which he was eventually convicted, although the jury could not reach a verdict on the further charge of inciting murder.

Within four years Adebolajo had journeyed to Kenya in an apparent attempt to join the militant Al-Shabaab group in Somalia linked to al-Qaeda, but was arrested by the Kenyan authorities without reaching his destination and deported back to Britain.

When Adebolajo returned from East Africa he was interrogated repeatedly by officers from the Secret Intelligence

Service about 'certain other individuals' he may have come into contact with. Adebolajo later claimed that he was repeatedly asked to work for British Intelligence in the wake of these conversations, but that he refused to do so.

What is not in doubt is that both he and Adebowale were both known to the SIS, and that Adebolajo was 'one of a small number of hard core fanatics who regularly protested alongside some of Britain's most notorious hate clerics', in the words of one newspaper report.

In the years before the killing of Lee Rigby, Adebolajo was often to be found standing outside the Poundland store in Woolwich High Street in south-east London wearing a skull cap and dark jacket while handing out pro-Islam leaflets and haranguing passers-by for hours at a time in what one person called 'a constant rambling monologue' about jihad.

Even though it also emerged that Adebolajo was married with four stepchildren and two children of his own, that did nothing to detract from the fact that he was a man trapped in the certainty of his own obsession – and, as such, a potential target of interest to Scotland Yard's counter-terrorism command.

Rather less emerged about Adebolajo's younger companion, Michael Adebowale. Some reports suggested that he had studied alongside Adebolajo at the University of Greenwich, but those claims were formally denied by the university. It was certain, however, that he too came from a strong Christian family, and had not attracted any particular interest at school. His mother was an active probation officer, while his father was a member of the staff at the Nigerian High Commission in London. The precise date of his conversion to Islam was not revealed, although it appeared likely to have been after that of Adebolajo.

The comparatively ordinary backgrounds of the two men in the dock did nothing to dissuade the jury from the firm conviction that they were both guilty of the barbaric murder of Fusilier Lee Rigby, and the attempted murder of the armed police officers who confronted them after that killing. Just a week before Christmas, on Thursday 19 December 2013, three weeks after the trial had begun, the jury found both Adebelajo and Adebowale guilty.

But Mr Justice Sweeney, the trial judge, adjourned sentencing until after the Court of Appeal had ruled on the arguments over whether a 'whole life' order was lawful in England and Wales in the light of the ruling by the European Court of Human Rights in July 2013 that it was 'inhumane' and incompatible with Article Three of the European Convention on Human Rights.

On that very day, at Stafford Crown Court, not far from Stoke-on-Trent, Mr Justice Wilkie had taken exactly the opposite view when he sentenced Jamie Reynolds to a whole life term of imprisonment for the depraved murder of seventeen-year-old Georgia Williams. In his sentencing remarks he explained: 'I am persuaded that the proper approach for this Court is to apply the domestic authorities which are binding on me' and leave the issue of 'compliance with Article Three' to the Court of Appeal or the Supreme Court.

At the Old Bailey, however, Mr Justice Sweeney took a quite different view, arguing that the issue of 'whole life' orders that had been stalking the Courts in England and Wales for almost six years had to be resolved before he would feel comfortable passing sentence on either Adebolajo or Adebowale.

The issue of whether a 'whole life' order could be passed, and, indeed, whether it should ever be passed, was thereby thrown into high relief. Yet again, there seemed to be uncertainty about the most draconian punishment that could be handed down in a Court in England and Wales.

That uncertainty was dispelled when, on 14 February 2014, the Court of Appeal in England and Wales, led by the Lord Chief Justice, Lord Thomas, and having among the panel of five senior judges Sir Brian Leveson, handed down their final decision on the issue of the European Court of Human Rights' judgement over whether a 'whole life' order contravened Article 3 of the European Convention on Human Rights.

The Lord Chief Justice and the Court emphatically confirmed the right of the Courts in England and Wales to pass 'whole life' orders for the most heinous crimes, and insisted that those orders were humane, not least because – contrary the European Court's view – they did allow for the possibility of release, at least on compassionate grounds.

Just eleven days later, on Tuesday 25 February 2014, Mr Justice Sweeney returned to the Old Bailey to pass sentence on Michael Adebolajo and Michael Adebowale. It was to provide some of the most dramatic moments ever seen in the long history of the Central Criminal Court in Old Bailey, and resulted in both men being taken physically from the dock, screaming abuse at the judge and the judicial system.

It quickly became apparent that neither Adebolajo nor Adebowale were prepared to accept the authority of Mr Justice Sweeney to sentence them at all. They were the first al-Qaeda-inspired terrorists to murder on British soil without killing themselves in the process – and therefore the first to come before a British Court. The London bombers of 7 July 2005 had all committed suicide as they detonated their explosives. In contrast, their passage to paradise had been blocked, and now they were confronted with the full force of the law, and neither young man was prepared to accept it.

Nevertheless, for a time, Adebolajo and Adebowale were prepared to let the judicial system take its course. They, albeit grudgingly, allowed their barristers to make pleas of mitigation on their behalf, and for the 'victim statements' on behalf of Lee Rigby's family to be heard in Court.

After hearing from Adebowale's defence that a 'whole life' term of imprisonment would be 'inhumane' for the twenty-two-year-old young man, and a similar plea from the defence – though not based on his age, more on its 'inhumanity' – on behalf of Michael Adebolajo, Mr Justice Sweeney started to pass sentence.

After outlining the fact that they had been convicted 'on overwhelming evidence' of the 'barbaric murder' of Fusilier Lee Rigby on 22 May 2013, and the fact that they were British citizens aged twenty-nine and twenty-two, Mr Justice Sweeney went on to say that he was 'sure of the following facts': 'You each converted to Islam some years ago, Thereafter you were radicalised and each became an extremist – espousing a cause and views which, as has been said elsewhere, are a betrayal of Islam and of the peaceful Muslim communities who give so much to our country.'

The judge's opening remarks provoked a furious reaction from the two young men in the dock. 'That's a lie!' Adebowale shouted at the top of his voice, jumping to his feet. 'You know nothing about Islam,' he yelled, before throwing the water in the plastic cup in front of him at one of the nine security guards surrounding him in the dock. He then hit him and spat at him.

'I swear by Allah that America will not be safe,' the younger of the two defendants added, again at the top of his voice.

That incited Adebolajo to turn and grapple with another

officer and a full-blown scuffle broke out in the dock, after which both defendants were forced to the ground – with only their legs in the air and showing above the wooden front of the dock.

Mr Justice Sweeney continued for a moment, and then paused before saying, 'Gentlemen, you have a choice . . .' But events in the dock had already gone from bad to worse.

With the fight still in full flow, Adebolajo shouted 'Allahu Akbar!' (God is the Greatest) before he and Adebowale were physically carried out of the dock and down the stairs to the cells head first.

As they departed, the sounds of their shouts of 'Lies, Lies!' and 'No betrayal!' continued to echo around the court-room reducing the family of Fusilier Rigby, sitting just a few feet away, to tears.

It was only when peace and quiet were restored that Mr Justice Sweeney resumed his summing-up, doing so with the specific agreement of the barristers for both men and the prosecution.

'It is no exaggeration to say,' Mr Justice Sweeney said, addressing the defendants as though they were still in the dock before him, 'that what the two of you did resulted in a bloodbath. Aspects of all this were seen, as they were intended to be, by members of the public.'

Drawing attention to the fact that the numbers of passers-by increased during the thirteen minutes it took the police to arrive, the judge continued: 'You both gloried in what you had done, Each of you had the gun at one point or another and it was used to warn off any male member of the public who looked as though he might intervene.'

Describing the killing as 'sickening and pitiless', Mr Justice Sweeney then drew attention to the 'severe and lasting impact on those close to Lee Rigby'.

Looking across at the now deserted dock, and accepting that Michael Adebolajo was now firmly in the cells in the bowels of the Old Bailey, Mr Justice Sweeney then spoke to the Court and to Lee Rigby's family and friends in his firm voice.

'You, Adebolajo, were the leader of this joint enterprise – albeit that Adebowale played his part enthusiastically. It was you who provided much, if not all, of the equipment and the car, and you were the mouthpiece of the day.'

'That said,' the judge went on, 'neither of you, I am sure, has any real insight into the enormity of what you did, nor any genuine remorse for it either – only regret that you did not succeed in your plan to be shot dead, which has resulted in you being brought to justice before the courts. Equally you, Adebolajo,' he added, 'who I have observed at length, have – I am sure – no real prospect of rehabilitation.'

There was a hush in the courtroom as Mr Justice Sweeney went on to explain that a life sentence is mandatory for murder, and that he must 'identify the minimum term that you must serve'. The prosecution had insisted that this murder was for the purpose of advancing a political, religious, racial or ideological cause, which meant that he fell within Schedule 21 of the Criminal Justice Act 2003 that called for a 'whole life' term.

The prosecution also alleged, he said, that the crime fell within the provisions of the Counter Terrorism Act 2008 and had a terrorist connection.

Adebolajo's pleas for mitigation on the grounds that the murder was motivated by 'simple religious hatred', which might suggest he should consider a lesser sentence than a 'whole life' term, and – equally – that there were signs that there was some hope that he was capable of rehabilitation, as well as that he had not acted as part of a wider group, were all rejected by Mr Justice Sweeney.

Insisting that in Adebolajo's case there was no mitigation whatever, although this was not a case of 'mass or repeated murder', the judge concluded that it was 'one of these rare cases where not only is the seriousness exceptionally high' but that the 'requirements of just punishment and retribution make a whole life term the just penalty. Accordingly in your case I propose to impose such a term.'

The defendant was not in Court to hear his fate, and neither was his young partner, who suffered only a little less severely at the hands of Mr Justice Sweeney.

Again sentencing without the defendant in the dock in front of him, Mr Justice Sweeney concluded that in his case a whole life term was not appropriate.

'In your case, Adebowale, I am persuaded that a combination of your lesser role, your age and your pre-existing and continuing mental condition mean that it is not appropriate in your case to impose a whole life term,' the judge said. 'Nevertheless, in your case there must be still a very substantial minimum term. The term I propose to impose is one of forty-five years, less the 272 days spent on remand.'

That meant that Adebowale, then still only twenty-two, would not be even considered for release until he was at least sixty-seven years old, and there was no guarantee of his freedom even then.

Outside the Court, Lee Rigby's family thanked the judge and told the assembled large crowd – including demonstrators carrying banners calling for the restoration of the death penalty, some of them holding replica gallows complete with a noose – 'We feel that no other sentence would have been acceptable . . . and we feel that justice has been served for Lee.'

Fusilier Rigby's wife, from whom he was separated, but who was the mother of his son, had said earlier that her husband would 'never be forgotten'.

Neither will his trial. Yet the dramatic events of that Wednesday morning of 26 February 2014 did nothing to deter Adebolajo from announcing just two months afterwards that he intended to appeal against the judge's decision to the Court of Appeal – citing what he alleged were 'mistakes' made by Mr Justice Sweeney during the three-week trial.

So it was that on Wednesday 3 December 2014, ten months after their sentencing, the cases of Michael Adebolajo and Michael Adebowale came before the Court of Appeal in London. The more aggressive Adebolajo declined to appear – even by video link from his prison, Full Sutton, near York – but his partner Adebowale agreed to do so from Broadmoor Hospital, where he had been transferred in the months after his sentence.

Matters did not go well for either defendant. Taking the absent Adebolajo's case first, his barrister argued that there were a number of technical legal issues that rendered Mr Justice Sweeney's sentence unreasonable – including the fact that the defendant believed he was acting as 'soldier' for the jihadist cause and should therefore be judged as someone who was active in combat and not therefore obliged to follow the criminal law. He also questioned whether the killing of Fusilier Rigby should be classified as terrorism or not.

For Adebowale, his barrister argued that his relative youth – he was just twenty-two – should mitigate against such a long sentence; that he was not the driving force within the decision to kill Lee Rigby; and that his medical condition was such that he was 'edging ever closer to an enduring and lasting illness', as was clear from the decision to remove him from prison and place him in Broadmoor, a special hospital for the criminally insane.

The Lord Chief Justice, Lord Thomas, and his two fellow

judges were not swayed by either argument and brushed aside both applications for leave to appeal in a brutally critical judgement that made it abundantly clear that the Court of Appeal fully supported Mr Justice Sweeney's decisions in February.

Reviewing the details of the crime, Lord Thomas pointed out that both men had become radicalised and had decided to murder a British soldier in broad daylight and in public as part of their personal jihad. They also, he continued, intended to get themselves killed in the process of the killing and had planned these actions over a period of time, taking with them eight knives and a old handgun that did not work, but could be used to frighten members of the public who might be tempted to interfere.

The idea, Lord Thomas went on, was to cause the most impact on the general public, which is why they had gone to such lengths to attempt to decapitate Fusilier Rigby at the scene of the attack, and that they both 'gloried' in what they had done.

Turning to Adebolajo's contention that he was some kind of 'soldier', Lord Thomas dismissed it as 'hopelessly misconceived' as an argument 'which should never have been advanced'. Indeed he described the entire appeal as 'having no merit at all'.

There was more than enough evidence, he concluded, to suggest that the murder had been committed to advance the two Nigerians' 'political cause', and that it had been a quite deliberate action which they had both 'wholly understood'. It was, he added, a 'barbaric murder' committed against 'our state' and 'our society' which had also had a devastating effect on the Rigby family.

As for Adebowale's appeal, the Lord Chief Justice was equally dismissive, insisting that he had been fit enough to stand trial and that his mental health at his appeal did not reduce his culpability for the crime. Lord Thomas concluded that 'the judge was entitled to pass the sentence that he did', adding that he did not feel a 'whole life' term was appropriate in the younger defendant's case.

The irony was that the twenty-two-year-old Adebowale will at least be eligible to be considered for release when he is sixty-seven years old – after committing one of the most brutal and public murders in modern times – whereas his co-conspirator Michael Adebolajo will never have that privilege. Neither will Jamie Reynolds, of almost exactly the same age, who is condemned to spend the rest of his days behind bars without the possibility of release – except in the most exceptional circumstances.

As I sat there watching the appeal, I could not avoid thinking that the confusion over exactly what represents the grounds for sending a killer to prison for the rest of his life remains. When does a 'heinous crime' become sufficiently 'heinous' to warrant a whole life term of imprisonment?

4

'I killed to see how I would feel'

Joanna Dennehy

Michael Adebolajo was not the only person to be given a whole life sentence for murder in the final days of February 2014.

Just two days after Mr Justice Sweeney imprisoned the Islamic extremist for the rest of his life for the barbarous killing of Fusilier Lee Rigby, Mr Justice Spencer, also sitting at the Central Criminal Court in Old Bailey, sentenced another vicious killer to spend the rest of their life in prison – the only difference was that this killer was a woman.

On 28 February 2014, thirty-one-year-old Joanna Dennehy, who was born to a respectable middle-class family in the affluent town of St Albans in Hertfordshire and had played netball for her school team before descending into severe drug and alcohol problems as a teenager in 1997, became the first woman ever to be sentenced to a whole life term by a judge.

Only two women before Dennehy had ever been condemned to end their days behind bars – the 'Moors Murderer' Myra Hindley, who died at the age of sixty in November 2002 without seeing freedom since her arrest in 1965, and Rosemary West, who is now sixty-two and has been in jail since April 1994, with no prospect whatever of release.

Both of those women, however, had originally been given fixed terms of imprisonment by the judges in their cases – only for those twenty-five-year terms to be extended to whole life by the Home Secretary of the day. In the case of Hindley, this was done by the Conservative David Waddington and confirmed by his successor Michael Howard, and in West's case by Labour's Jack Straw.

Indeed, no woman had been subject to a whole life sentence since the last days of 2003, when the Home Secretary lost the power to amend any term of imprisonment under the new Criminal Justice Act, which became law in November of that year. At no point during the ensuing decade had any woman committed a crime so heinous that she should be considered as warranting the most draconian penalty under English law. But in the case of Joanna Dennehy that was to change.

On the surface, Dennehy hardly looked as though she could deserve such a punishment. A thin, white-faced young woman with piercing eyes, she may have sported a green star tattoo beneath her right eye, but she appeared to be nothing more than a troubled teenager who had never quite managed to grow into maturity.

Her appearance could not have been more deceptive, however, for behind the mask of normality Dennehy was a psychopath who suffered from a severe antisocial personality disorder that revealed itself in ferocious bouts of 'anger, aggression, impulsiveness and irresponsibility' – in the words of one psychiatrist who interviewed her. No matter how harmless she may have looked, she killed for her own amusement and, to use her own words, 'to see how I feel'.

Indeed, so severe was her personality disorder that Dennehy was later diagnosed as suffering from a condition known as paraphilia sadomasochism, in which the sufferer derives sexual excitement from the infliction of pain, humiliation and bondage. A woman with severe drug and alcohol addiction, Dennehy liked to give – and receive – pain.

Yet her life had not started out like that. As a child, Dennehy had been very close to her sister Maria, who was two years younger; so close, indeed, that they slept in bunk beds and invented their own secret language. But as Dennehy made the transition into adolescence, her personality changed. She became involved with a group of older boys who introduced her to 'skunk', a strong form of cannabis, and she started drinking and skipping school.

Then, at the age of fifteen, she met and ran away with John Treanor, who was five years her senior. They left St Albans and eventually ended up living rough in East Anglia. Dennehy briefly returned home, but at sixteen left again to live with Treanor, first in Luton and then in Milton Keynes. Within the next four years, while still a teenager, she had two children with him, even though she insisted that she 'didn't like kids', and all the time her relationship with Treanor was disintegrating. Unsettled and uncertain, Dennehy would leave him for days or weeks at a time, cheat on him with both men and women, only to return and beg his forgiveness.

The couple tried moving to East Anglia again, but Dennehy's drinking got worse as she worked as a farm labourer – sometimes even taking her wages in alcohol. She also started to have violent tantrums, in which she would repeatedly hit Treanor for no apparent reason. She was equally violent towards herself, cutting her arms, body and neck with razor blades – she even tattooed the green star beneath her right eye herself. Eventually, in 2009, Treanor left her, taking their two children with him, and Dennehy started to drift around East Anglia, often working as a prostitute to sustain her drug and alcohol habits. In the following four years she spent short periods of time in prison for minor offences, and was also treated for mental health problems.

Then, in 2011, Dennehy met the man who was to become her 'slave', a seven-foot-three-inch-tall burglar called Gary Stretch, who was then in his early forties and had a long criminal record, including one term of five years' imprisonment and one of four years for offences including burglary and handling stolen property. In 2008 Stretch had also been sentenced to fifteen months for harassing his former partner, and threatening – through a mutual friend – to kill her.

By the beginning of 2013 Stretch had become utterly infatuated with Dennehy, so infatuated, indeed, that he devoted himself to satisfying her increasingly violent whims. At the end of March that year, for example, just before and during the Easter holidays, Stretch helped Dennehy fulfil her most violent fantasies, in a spree that lasted just ten days. She had finally lost control, and the tall, muscle-bound Stretch assisted her in every way he could.

And so it was that on Thursday, 21 March 2013, Dennehy killed her first victim at 11 Rolleston Garth, the rooming house that she had been living at in Peterborough, Cambridgeshire, though she had recently moved near by. As she had done so often before, she used her sexuality to ensnare a man – this time a thirty-one-year-old Pole named Lukasz Slaboszewski, whom she had met just a few days earlier.

Like many men before him, the Pole had rapidly fallen in love with the white-faced young woman with a green star tattoo beneath her right eye. He even texted a friend saying how beautiful the world was now that he had Dennehy as his girlfriend. Tragically, it was the last message he was to write. He had met his nemesis.

Alone that Thursday afternoon, without Stretch, Dennehy invited Slaboszewski to the rooming house she had recently left, and then – without any warning whatever – stabbed him through the heart with one of the many knives she had taken to keeping with her at all times. The single stab was delivered with such force that it killed him outright at once. But Dennehy showed not the slightest emotion.

She paused for a time and then, after a little thought, decided to leave the body in a wheelie bin outside the house, while she decided how she would dispose of it. Before she did that, however, Dennehy brought a fourteen-year-old girl called Georgina Page, whom she had recently befriended in the rooming house, to look at the dead Pole's body in the wheelie bin, taking a bizarre pride in the killing.

Slaboszewski's body remained in the wheelie bin for two days before Dennehy finally made an attempt to dispose of it. She had realised that she needed a car, and borrowed some money from Kevin Lee, the landlord of the rooming house that was now living in – 38 Bifield in Peterborough – to buy one. She settled on a blue Vauxhall Astra and took a taxi with Gary Stretch to collect it. Later that evening, under the cover of darkness, Dennehy and Stretch drove around the more remote outskirts of Peterborough looking for the right spot to dump the Pole's body.

The site they chose was the isolated area of Thorney Dike, where Stretch had lived some years earlier. After dumping the corpse in a stream at the side of a field far away from any houses, the two complimented each other that 'No one will ever find it,' even boasting about it to teenager Georgina Page when they got back to Peterborough.

But Dennehy's murderous spree was only just beginning.

No sooner had she dumped Slaboszewski's body than she started planning her next killing. Her next victim was to be

John Chapman, a kindly, inoffensive man of fifty-eight who lived in another of the rooms at 38 Bifield. An alcoholic who had served in the Royal Navy, he had been drinking with Dennehy in the days after she disposed of the Pole's body, but, for some reason, Dennehy had taken against him, telling him that she would get him out of the house 'by any means'. In return he had described her to another tenant in the rooming house as 'the mad woman'.

In the early hours of Good Friday, 29 March 2013, Dennehy did indeed get rid of Chapman by any means. She killed him in his own bed-sitting room on the top floor of the house. She stabbed him once in the neck, severing the carotid artery, and five times in the chest. Two of the stab wounds penetrated the heart, and one was delivered with such violence that it passed through the breast bone. Chapman's blood alcohol limit was four times over the limit for driving and it is quite possible that Dennehy stabbed him while he was asleep in bed.

Leslie Layton, another occupant of the rooming house at 38 Bifield, and another man who had fallen under Dennehy's spell, took a photograph of Chapman's blood-soaked body at 7.32 on that Good Friday morning – just a few hours after the murder.

By now consumed with an intense, unremitting desire to kill, Dennehy quickly identified her next victim, another man who had become infatuated with her over the previous months. Kevin Lee was forty-eight, a husband, father and her landlord. In the time since they had first met in the autumn of 2012 he had fallen under her spell completely. He had employed her in his property letting business and had provided her with rooms in the series of bedsits in the houses that his company owned. For her part, Dennehy had confided in him, hinting that she had been abused as a child, and then, following her first killing, confessing to him what she had done. The police later suspected that she may even have shown him the Pole's corpse.

What is not in doubt is that Dennehy lured the likeable, compassionate Lee to 11 Rolleston Garth – by telling him that when he arrived on that Good Friday afternoon she was going to 'dress him up and rape him'. It would not have been the first time that Dennehy and Lee had engaged in sado-masochistic sex games together, and Lee was clearly looking forward to a repeat.

No one knows exactly how far they went in their sexual charade; it is possible that she had already dressed him in a black sequinned dress that she owned – leaving his buttocks exposed. Whatever the truth, it is clear that Dennehy stabbed him five times in the chest, penetrating both his lungs and heart. Lee tried to defend himself, but the attack was so unexpected and so fierce that he had no chance.

Now Dennehy had two dead bodies – John Chapman and Kevin Lee – at two separate addresses in Peterborough, one at 38 Bifield and the other at 11 Rolleston Garth. The question was: how to dispose of them and where? Naturally enough, she recruited her ever-willing lover Gary Stretch, but this time she also recruited her other loyal follower Leslie Layton – the photographer of Chapman's bloodied body – to collect the body of Kevin Lee.

Layton, in turn, borrowed a tarpaulin from another follower of Dennehy's, Robert Moore, who lived near by and had also been shown her first victim in the wheelie bin. He, like Lee and Stretch, was infatuated with the extrovert young woman with the dancing eyes and no conscience whatever.

The plan was for Layton to drive Lee's Ford Mondeo, with Lee's body in the boot, and follow Dennehy and Stretch as they searched for a site to dispose of his body. In the end, once again taking advantage of Stretch's local knowledge, they chose Newborough, another remote rural location on the outskirts of Peterborough.

But Dennehy had not finished humiliating Kevin Lee. She and Stretch pulled his bloodstained corpse out of the boot of his own car, while Layton remained in the driver's seat, and Dennehy posed it in the black sequined dress, with his buttocks prominently exposed and pointing upwards. Followed by Dennehy and Stretch, Layton then took Lee's Mondeo to an area of waste ground at Yaxley – a long way away from where its owner's body had been dumped – and set fire to it.

The three of them then returned to 38 Bifield in the Vauxhall Astra to dispose of John Chapman's corpse. Layton helped Dennehy carry Chapman's blood-soaked body down from the top floor. Stretch put it in the boot of the Astra. This time Dennehy and Stretch knew where they were going – back to the stream in Thorney Dyke where the body of Lukasz Slaboszewski still lay undetected. When they arrived, all three of them got out of the car and placed Chapman's body beside the Pole's corpse – confident that no one would ever find either of them.

Intoxicated by her killing spree, Dennehy took refuge in Gary Stretch's flat in Peterborough, but nevertheless she sensed that John Chapman's disappearance would be noticed and that the police were likely to investigate it, with every possibility that they would link his disappearance with her in view of their very public arguments. She quickly decided that they were going to need somewhere to hide out in case the police came looking for them.

The couple settled on the home of Robert Moore, who had provided the tarpaulin to transport the bodies the day before. Dennehy knew only too well that he was as much in her thrall as Stretch and Layton, and would literally 'have done anything for her', even if that meant harbouring her as a murderer.

On Saturday 30 March, she and Stretch went to stay with Moore in his house in Peterborough – it turned out to be a wise decision because, by the following day, the police had indeed begun a search in earnest to locate the missing John Chapman. One person they visited was Leslie Layton, seeing him first on that Easter Sunday morning and again the following afternoon of Monday 1 April. Still determined to protect Dennehy, he denied knowing anything about Chapman, and told the police he had not seen Dennehy since the previous Wednesday. It was, of course, a pack of lies.

By that time, however, Dennehy and Stretch had decided to remove themselves entirely from Peterborough for a while – not least because the police were actively looking for them both. In the late afternoon of Easter Monday the couple took a trip to King's Lynn to see Georgina Page, the fourteen-year-old whom Dennehy had confided in before. By now the disappearance of John Chapman had been widely reported and a police search was under way for both Dennehy and Stretch, who were being sought to 'help the police with their enquiries'.

The notoriety positively delighted Dennehy, who could not resist comparing herself with Bonnie Parker, the American gangster of the Depression era, who along with her partner Clyde Barrow robbed more than a dozen banks in the first years of the 1930s, and who was alleged to have killed seven people. Not that Dennehy thought she was going to end her life in a hail of bullets as Parker had done. Instead, she confessed to the impressionable young Georgina Page that she thought she and Stretch would eventually be caught and go to prison for 'a long time'. For his part,

Gary Stretch told her, 'My kids are grown up, so I don't care.'

That night the couple returned to Robert Moore's house, but, by then, they had decided to leave for another place well known to Stretch – the county town of Hereford on the border of England and Wales, where he was born. The couple had burgled a house in Norfolk on their way back from seeing Georgina Page and, because of his background, Stretch knew a group of criminals in Hereford who would give them money for the electrical goods they had stolen. On the way to see them, Dennehy and Stretch also burgled a house in Herefordshire to increase the amount of money they might make.

In a flat in Kington, about twenty miles from Hereford on the Welsh border, Dennehy and Stretch met the criminals he knew, who did indeed agree to help them sell the stolen property. One of them, named Mark Lloyd, agreed to go with them into the town. The idea was to sell the goods, although Stretch had also thought of a plan to rob one of the local drug dealers.

By then, Dennehy's appetite for killing had begun to return – and she told Stretch, 'You've had your fun. Now it's my turn.' The implication was clear – she intended to kill again, but this time choosing her victims at random. Her fantasy of being Bonnie Parker had overwhelmed her.

Before Dennehy left Kington, however, Stretch took a photograph of her brandishing a huge, jagged knife almost a foot long, while sticking out her tongue as she laughed for the camera. It was not a photograph of a young woman consumed by guilt or remorse. Indeed, shortly after the couple arrived in Hereford in their Vauxhall Astra – with an uncomfortable Mark Lloyd now a passenger in the back – Dennehy took an even more revealing photograph of herself on her mobile phone which shows her grinning at the camera, once again with her mouth open, as if she were about to take part in an adolescent prank.

Her intentions were far worse. This thirty-one-year-old mother of two had decided to kill again – and was depending on her loyal partner, Stretch, to help her find a victim. On the way into Hereford she visited a small store, where the closed circuit television cameras captured her in high spirits, indeed almost a state of euphoria, about what she expected to happen next. Shortly afterwards, Stretch duly fulfilled his promise to her to help her find a victim by driving them to a secluded, wooded part of the county town where owners often walked their dogs.

In fact it was Stretch who spotted her next victim, a retired fireman called Robin Bereza, aged sixty-three, who on that Tuesday afternoon of 2 April 2013 had decided to take his dog for a walk instead of going jogging. Stretch may have asked Dennehy – 'Will he do?' – but what is not in doubt is that he pulled up the Astra some little way behind Bereza, no doubt so that Dennehy could attack him from behind.

No sooner had the car come to a stop than Dennehy jumped out of the passenger side, ran up behind the unsuspecting retired fireman and stabbed him in the back. She then stabbed him a second time in the upper right arm.

When he turned to face her Bereza asked, 'What on earth are you doing?'

'I want to hurt you, I am going to fucking kill you,' Dennehy told him.

The fireman responded by trying to fight her off, kicking out at her with his legs, and starting to run away. Dennehy pursued him, but not for long, as another car suddenly turned into this quiet road in Hereford.

Stretch had been driving the Astra slowly behind Dennehy as the attack took place, and he beckoned her to get back into it. She calmly did so – and smiled at the driver of the car that had just arrived.

Meanwhile Bereza was lying on the ground, in great pain from the serious injuries she had inflicted on him. The deep wound to his back penetrated the chest wall and had both bruised his lung and fractured a rib, while the other stab wound to his right arm shattered the shoulder blade and fractured his arm. He only survived the injuries because of the rapid response of the local paramedics and medical staff who treated him.

Dennehy's appetite for murder was not quenched by her attack on Bereza, however, and she encouraged Stretch to find her another victim near by, which he duly did, driving her to a cul-de-sac next to a path also used by dog-walkers and close to where his grandmother used to live. Once again Stretch spotted a potential victim walking away from their Astra down the path. He was John Rogers, a fifty-six-year-old man, not in the best of health, who was also walking his dog.

Once again Dennehy leapt out of the car and stabbed her victim from behind without any warning – or hesitation. Then, when he turned round, she stabbed him repeatedly in the chest, pushing him backwards as she did so. When Rogers finally fell over, she continued to stab him relentlessly in both the front and back in a frenzy of bloodlust, clearly determined to kill him. She stabbed him no fewer than thirty times, and when she finally stopped she left Rogers motionless on the path, picked up his dog and walked back to the car – clearly convinced that she had killed him.

Miraculously, Rogers survived, although once again principally due to the expert medical treatment he received rapidly after the attack. Dennehy's stab wounds to his chest, abdomen and back had left him with both lungs collapsed and his bowel perforated and exposed. The stab wounds had been delivered with such force that Dennehy had broken nine of his ribs, as well as wounding his hands and arms, which resulted in irreparable nerve damage.

Given that both these vicious, unwarranted attacks took place in broad daylight in an English county town on an ordinary Tuesday afternoon, it is hardly surprising that Dennehy and Stretch were caught by the police minutes after the second attack on the defenceless and unsuspecting guitarist and musician John Rogers, who was now so badly injured that he would never regain the dexterity he needed to be able to play his guitar again.

Yet the thin young woman with a penchant for wearing woolly hats, sticking her pierced tongue out and sniggering for the camera showed not a single trace of remorse for her killing spree as the truth about her murders was steadily revealed in the days after her arrest on 2 April 2013.

Instead, she gloried in her attempt to kill two innocent passers-by that afternoon. She even joked with the police officers that detained her, saying, 'It could be worse – I could be fat,' before telling one of the officers, 'You're a decent copper, I'm a crap criminal – you will read about it in the newspapers shortly. You will think, "That's the girl I arrested – I know her."'

Extrovert and unashamed to the last, and only too aware of her status as one of a tiny number of female serial killers, Dennehy performed what one officer later describe as a 'bizarre chicken walk' at the police station as she hunched her shoulders and clucked, before claiming, moments later, 'I'm The Incredible Hulk.'

When Mark Lloyd, the man she and Stretch had bullied into staying in the back of the Vauxhall Astra that day as they looked for potential victims, told the police about the couples' boast that they had left 'other bodies' where 'no one will ever find them', the police in Peterborough extended their search and discovered not only the two bodies in Thorney Dike, but also the body of Kevin Lee in Newborough.

Within a month, Joanna Christine Dennehy had been charged with three murders and two attempted murders, along with her seven-foot-three-inch accomplice Gary Stretch, and their associates Leslie Layton and Robert Moore, who had helped them dispose of the bodies and harboured them when they were known fugitives from the law.

During her time on remand in custody awaiting trial, it emerged that Dennehy had been in and out of prison, on short sentences, in the years running up to the Peterborough murders, mainly for offences that involved dishonesty, although she had been convicted early in 2012 of 'possessing a bladed article in a public place', namely razor blades, and later that year had been given a 'community order', that did not involve imprisonment, for an assault that caused actual bodily harm.

When Dennehy was examined by a psychiatrist during her remand, he diagnosed her as suffering from 'severe emotionally unstable personality disorder' and from 'antisocial personality disorder'. Significantly, however, he also suggested that she suffered from the rare condition of paraphilia sadomasochism, a disorder which led her to prefer sexual activity that involved the infliction of pain or humiliation or bondage.

In the psychiatrist's words, she suffered from 'psychopathic disorder, that is a personality disorder characterised by superficial charm, callous disregard for others, pathological lying and a diminished capacity for remorse.'

At one point Dennehy baldly confessed to him, 'I killed to see if I was as cold as I thought I was. Then it got moreish and I got a taste for it.'

But Dennehy did not rely on any psychiatric excuse for her actions when she appeared at an arraignment hearing at the Central Criminal Court in Old Bailey on 18 November 2013. She had travelled down from Cambridgeshire, where she was being held on remand before her trial.

Once in the dock, however, she suddenly, without warning, and to the astonishment of her own legal team, announced that she was pleading guilty to all the charges. When her startled barrister, Nigel Lickley QC, asked for more time to consult with his client, Dennehy interrupted him, saying, 'I'm not coming back down here again just to say the same stuff. It's a long way to come to say the same thing I have just said.'

But, on 28 February 2014, Dennehy did stand in the dock of the Central Criminal Court once again, this time alongside Gary Stretch, Leslie Layton and Robert Moore to hear Mr Justice Spencer pass sentence on them all. Her three accomplices, two of whom had pleaded not guilty at the trial, had been found guilty by a jury of the charges against them, and now all four would learn their fate. Typically, Dennehy was wearing a pink Adidas sweatshirt and grey tracksuit bottoms, much like the outfit she wore in the notorious mobile phone photograph of her brandishing a huge jagged knife with handcuffs at her belt which had been taken while she was on the run.

Mr Justice Spencer did not mince his words. 'You are a cruel, calculating, selfish and manipulative serial killer,' he told Dennehy as she sat in the dock opposite him. He then told the Court that she had written a letter to him 'claiming to feel remorse' for the stabbing of Robin Bereza and John Rogers in Hereford.

'I have no hesitation in rejecting that suggestion,' he told her firmly.

From the dock Dennehy shouted, 'Bollocks!'

Then she reverted to smirking and occasionally laughing out loud throughout the judge's remarks to the defendants.

That did nothing to deter the Mr Justice Spencer. Referring to the Court of Appeal's decision, just two weeks earlier, that a 'whole life' term was acceptable under English law, Mr Justice Spencer then pointed out to her that there was only one sentence for murder – life imprisonment. Therefore the only question for him was whether the seriousness of her offences was 'exceptionally high', which would warrant her spending the rest of her life in prison.

'You have shown no genuine remorse,' the judge pointed out. 'Quite the reverse. In the letter you have written to me you say in terms that you do not feel any remorse for the murders and to claim otherwise would be a lie.' He then went on: 'The only reason you can offer for the attempted murders is "drunken cruelty, plain and simple, compelled by my lack of respect for human life". As I have already made clear, I reject your protestations of remorse for these attempted murders.'

Then, in the most chilling moment of the trial, Mr Justice Spencer added: 'It is very significant, in my judgement, that from a single stab wound to the heart to kill your first victim you progressed by the end to the frenzied attack on John Rogers when you so nearly killed him, stabbing him more than thirty times. You told the psychiatrist you saw the killings as a kind of fetish and that you were sadistic.'

'I am quite satisfied,' he went on, 'that the seriousness of these murders is exceptionally high and that the element of just punishment and retribution requires the imposition of a whole life order.'

Mr Justice Spencer then sentenced Gary Stretch to life imprisonment, though with a minimum term of nineteen years.

'Thank you very much,' Stretch muttered from the dock.

Leslie Layton was sentenced to fourteen years' imprisonment for preventing the 'lawful and decent burial of bodies' and perverting the course of justice, while Robert Moore, who had pleaded guilty to the two charges he faced for harbouring Dennehy and Stretch while they were on the run, was given three years' imprisonment. 'It is clear to me from the pre-sentence report that you do not fully understand even now just how serious your conduct was,' the judge told him.

Layton was sitting behind Stretch in the dock and when the sentencing was completed, Dennehy leaned across the man she always called 'Gaz' and said to him in a stage whisper, 'I may be taking your life sentence but you and Stretch are idiots.'

It was a theme that she was to repeat more than once in the first month of her sentence, insisting just a few weeks after the end of her trial that Layton was also a killer. Unusually for a spree killer who pleaded guilty to her murders, Dennehy proved anxious to explain herself to the world.

In two letters to Gary Stretch's ex-wife Julie Gibbons, who was fifty-three, Dennehy claimed that her friend and accomplice Leslie Layton killed John Chapman in a 'pathetic attempt to impress' her.

The extraordinary six-page letter was handed to the *Daily Mirror* by Gibbons, who handed it on to the police.

Dennehy wrote, 'Dear Julie, thank you for your letter and your honesty. I know I am portrayed as a person without feeling but it's not the case. I will repay your honesty shortly. My crimes were not impulse nor were they without reason.'

She claimed that her murder of her lover and landlord Kevin Lee was planned, but she did not reveal her motive. Dennehy explained, 'Gaz was there in the room for the first one, I told him what I was going to do but not why, I told him to leave over and over before I did it. I told him to leave after, my path was set.'

'My crimes Julie were vengeance,' Dennehy added. 'I knew what the outcome would be, I tried my best to make sure Gary was away from me before I set about the killings. I got him a place to stay and a job. I got him a car which he insisted was in my name.'

But that was not all. Dennehy also said that she had broken off all contact with Stretch after their imprisonment, even though he had written to her five times declaring his undying love. She told his ex-wife, 'I replied to him once since your first letter, telling him how sick it made me feel to hear he claimed I was a threat to you or your family. I informed him that out of respect for you ... I no longer wish for contact, which led to another begging letter.'

In an earlier letter to Gibbons, Dennehy had said that writing 'an apology would be pointless', but denied that she forced Stretch to help her by threatening his family. He had told his ex-wife that he did not know why he had become involved in the killings, but that Dennehy was 'evil' and 'had control over him', while he was also frightened she would harm Gibbons and their three children.

Then Dennehy added her reasons for breaking contact with Stretch. 'There is something you must understand, I am incapable of harming females or children, I think that's why his lie cut so deep.'

That did not prevent her from confessing that 'Killing Kevin Lee was planned ... I kept my mouth shut in the police station, I did not take the stand either because Gary said it would harm him and no doubt he was right. He knew if I were to take the stand and lies were being chucked at me I'd lose my temper and tell it how it is, regardless of the outcome. Gary knows I react badly to lies.'

For her part, Julie Gibbons explained after receiving the letters from Dennehy, 'I'm surprised to say this but I believe every word she says. Police should investigate the letter. The families of the victims will want to know exactly what happened. It won't take any of the pain away but I hope this confession will help them get a little bit of closure. It certainly helped me. I feel like a massive weight has lifted off my shoulders. She obviously thought out what she was going to write very carefully.'

In the second letter, written from high-security women's prison Bronzefield, in Surrey, Dennehy insisted that Stretch 'went along' with her on his own but added, 'I do not wish to cause you pain, I respect and admire the strength it has taken you to survive. I took the coward's way out by not being able to restrain my hate. Under different circumstances I would have liked to have met you, maybe we could have balanced each other out ... Please stay strong and have faith in yourself, respectfully, Joanna.'

Then she added a PS. 'Again I am sorry. God I can't tell you how much I admire you!!! For your sake alone I wish I had never met Gary Stretch.'

Julie Gibbons was not the only person to pass judgement on Dennehy after her conviction and sentence. Dennehy's younger sister Maria told the BBC that she was a 'bright, happy and bookish' child, who showed no evidence whatever of violent behaviour. 'Parents always blame themselves, but they were a great mum and dad,' she went on. 'My sister turned into a monster.'

For their part, Dennehy's parents, Kevin, a security guard, aged fifty-six, and Kathleen, fifty-one, had lost contact with their daughter in the fifteen years before her arrest. But their other daughter Maria spoke for them when she said, 'It has ruined my mum completely. If you can imagine being a mother and giving birth to someone who causes a family so much hurt. It is indescribable how she is feeling . . . from one day to the next all she ever talks about is the families that Joanna has caused this to.'

Meanwhile, the father of Dennehy's two daughters, John Treanor, aged thirty-seven, who had remarried since his time with her, told the *Daily Express*, 'Jo is evil, pure and simple, that is why I took the girls as far away from her as possible.' He also said that their elder daughter, aged thirteen, was having difficulty coming to terms with her mother's killings and was afraid she might end up like her. 'She's seen her mother's face all over the news, the papers and internet. Now she's struggling to come to terms with it all.'

Treanor then told ITV's *This Morning* programme that his former partner should face the death penalty because she will 'lord it up in prison' and that life with her was 'like living with the devil'.

Significantly, he added, 'I think the punishment, a whole life sentence, is not enough – not for what she's done to those people . . . It should be capital punishment as far as I'm concerned . . . There are certain crimes that need to be punished in the right way and just serving life in prison and having your TV and your nice bunk and your warm radiator and your three meals a day, she's going to enjoy it, she's going to love it.'

John Treanor's conclusion about Joanna Dennehy is reflected time after time in the reactions to the dreadful crimes that lead to a whole life sentence, and it precisely encapsulates the argument that runs throughout this book – is being incarcerated in a prison cell for sixty years or more better or worse than the death penalty?

After all, there is no chance that Dennehy was innocent of her three murders – no chance that that an innocent woman might be put to death – for she admitted them in open court.

Dennehy's whole life sentence underlines the dilemma for a society, its judges and its legislators over whether it is indeed either 'justifiable' or 'human' treatment to sentence any man or woman to spend more than half a century in prison.

The former President of the Supreme Court in England, and a former Lord Chief Justice, Lord Phillips of Worth Matravers, suggested in 2006 – when he was still Lord Chief Justice – that judges had been pushed into longer and longer sentences in England and Wales by public opinion and politicians.

'But I sometimes wonder whether, in a hundred years' time,' he said, 'people will be as shocked by the length of sentences we are imposing as we are by some of the punishments in the eighteenth century.'

Is the whole life term the modern equivalent of the rack – rendering exquisite pain over ever-increasing periods of time? And can that truly be justified?

5

'I am bored and it was something to do'

Gary Vintner, Ian McLoughlin and Lee Newell

The courts of England and Wales have been struggling with the issue of the morality of whole life sentences for murder since 2003, when the Criminal Justice Act formalised their use by the judiciary in the wake of Parliament's decision to remove the power to instate them from politicians and, in particular, from the Home Secretary.

In Scotland, the law was changed in 2001 to ensure that a fixed minimum period should be the case whenever a life sentence was imposed – to bring Scottish law into line with the European Convention on Human Rights. That is certainly not the position in England and Wales.

In the past few years the struggle in England and Wales has become increasingly intense, with three convicted murderers sentenced to whole life terms – Douglas Vinter, Jeremy Bamber and Peter Moore – conducting a battle against them in the European Court of Human Rights.

Meanwhile, two others, Ian McLoughlin, who was sentenced to life imprisonment with a minimum period of forty years, and Lee Newell, who had a whole life sentence, took their appeal to the Court of Appeal in England and Wales. These two sets of appeals encapsulate the arguments over whether life should mean life.

Let us begin with Vinter, Bamber and Moore, who are particularly critical of whole life terms. Vinter, who is now in his early forties, cannot accept being locked up until he dies, irrespective of his behaviour or remorse.

'I'm young and fit,' he said in 2012, 'and I've maybe got another fifty years of life as a category A prisoner. Torture every single day. I actually pray for a heart attack or cancer.'

In another letter in 2012, Vinter also pointed out the irony that his whole life sentence meant that he could commit any offence whatever – including murder – while in prison as there is no further punishment available to the courts to deter him.

'I was involved in a stabbing (not fatal) on the wing,' Vinter explained. 'You see how I can admit in a letter to an offence as serious as that. It's because the judge when he sentenced me to natural life gave me an invisible licence that said I can breach any laws I want, no matter how serious, and the law can't touch me. I'm above the law. I said to the governor, don't waste any money on investigations, just give me another life sentence for my collection. They don't mean anything any more.'

Not long after he wrote that letter Vinter offended again – stabbing convicted paedophile Roy Whiting in both eyes, using a sharpened plastic toilet brush handle. Whiting was himself serving a whole life sentence at the time for the murder of eight-year-old Sussex schoolgirl Sarah Payne.

After being tried for the attack, Vinter was given an indefinite sentence with a five-year minimum term to serve in addition to his whole life sentence. There could hardly have been a better example of what Vinter called his 'invisible licence' to break any laws he chose. The further sentence was irrelevant to a man already destined to spend the rest of his life in jail.

No one would describe Douglas Gary Vinter, usually known as Gary, as being an innocent or good man. Born in 1970 in Middlesbrough, he is six feet seven inches tall, powerfully built, and given to misusing anabolic steroids. He also has a record of exceptionally violent behaviour. He committed his first murder in August 1995, when he brutally stabbed and killed fellow railway worker Carl Edon, aged twenty-two, in a trackside railway workers' cabin near Middlesbrough. Covered in blood, Vinter then drove to a local police station and gave himself up. He had stabbed Edon, who had one child and was expecting another with his girlfriend Michelle at the time of his death, no fewer than thirty-seven times. The police found Edon's body with the knife still embedded in it.

When he was interviewed by the police Vinter formally denied committing the murder, but he accepted responsibility even though he said he 'could not remember what happened'. But the jury at Teesside Crown Court convicted him of murder, and he was sentenced to life in 1996. The Home Office then ordered that he should serve a minimum of ten years and he was released in August 2005 having been on remand since Edon's murder was committed.

In the last two years of that life sentence, Vinter struck up a relationship with a young woman named Anne White, then in her thirties, whom he had met during a series of 'home visits' from prison prior to his intended release. They moved in together in Eston, near Middlesbrough, some distance from his former hunting grounds, and married in July 2006.

Even the move to another part of Teesside did not quell Vinter's appetite for violence, however. On New Year's Eve 2006, just a few months after his marriage, he was arrested after a brawl outside a local pub. By that time he had started beating his new wife, and shortly after the New Year they separated, but were later reconciled.

In July 2007, however, Vinter was recalled to jail for six months after being convicted of affray at the pub brawl on New Year's Eve, thereby breaching his right to freedom.

Anne, who had four children by previous relationships, still suffered severely when he was at home with her, and friends became deeply concerned that his abuse of her was escalating dramatically, while also realising that she was 'afraid' to leave him.

Nevertheless, Vinter behaved impeccably in prison, becoming a 'model prisoner'. Suitably impressed, the Parole Board recommended his second release in December 2007.

At the very beginning of February 2008, just a few weeks after his re-release from prison, he moved out of the family home after yet another violent argument with his wife Anne. Vinter smashed the television set and confiscated her passport – presumably so that she could never escape him.

The couple remained apart for the ensuing few days, but on the evening of 10 February, Vinter spotted her on a night out in central Middlesbrough with friends and once again turned to extreme violence. He grabbed her and bundled her into his car. He drove his terrified wife, then aged forty, to his mother's house in Middlesbrough, and repeatedly attacked her over a period of half an hour– an attack which finally ended with her brutal murder.

Vinter tried to strangle Anne with his bare hands, before losing his temper and stabbing her four times with two knives, one wound piercing her heart. He then strangled her again, this time driving the life out of his innocent wife's dying body. He left her lifeless corpse on his mother's kitchen floor.

Armed police arrested him in the early hours of the

following morning, using two baton rounds to subdue the six-foot-seven-inch bodybuilder. Vinter offered no excuse for the killing, beyond telling the police, 'Right, my name is Gary Vinter. I am solely responsible for the death of my wife. There's nobody else involved, just me. That's all I'm prepared to say.'

Shortly after he was charged, Vinter pleaded guilty to murder and, passing sentence, the Recorder of Middlesbrough, Judge Peter Fox QC, told him, 'The extreme violence which you used is described as continuing . . . You therefore fall into that small category of people who should be deprived permanently of their liberty. I therefore pass a whole life sentence.'

For his part, Vinter sneered at the White family in the courtroom around him, and smirked as he pleaded guilty.

As the local newspaper put it: 'With tears and disgust, Ms White's loved ones were asked to try and control their emotions.' That did not prove easy, and Anne White's father Jim, aged seventy-one, asked reporters outside the court after Vinter had been taken to the cells, 'Why was this convicted murderer allowed to walk free last Christmas?'

By way of explanation, the Parole Board extended its 'deepest sympathies' to Ms White's family and announced that it would be reviewing the case 'in order to identify learning points for the future'.

The murder of Anne White had a catastrophic effect on her family. Her father died of cancer a year after her death. His wife, Anne's mother Peggy White, said later, 'We have often said that he died of a broken heart.' Sixty-eight-year-old Mrs White also maintained that Vinter should have been hanged. 'What about Anne's children, my grandchildren?' she asked after his second life sentence. 'What about Mrs Edon, what about their human rights? He can never be released. He would kill again. They should throw away the key. I think people in his category should really be hanged.'

Michelle Edon, who had changed her surname to Carl's by deed poll following the death of her late fiancée, felt every bit as strongly, saying, 'I hope Gary Vinter suffers and rots in hell.' She added, 'I want to hear that he is dead. I hope one day to hear those words. I want him to suffer like he has made us suffer.' Her mother agreed: 'We will never understand why he was released from prison. He stabbed someone thirty-seven times – how could anyone think it is OK to let him back into society? And then he took someone else's life. Ruined more lives.'

It is a tragic fact that no fewer than thirty-eight of the sixty or so individuals serving whole life sentences in England and Wales killed after being released from fixed term sentences – though that has never been officially confirmed. The delicate question of releasing a man already convicted of a murder so that he can kill again lies close to the heart of the debate about whether or not life should mean life.

Douglas Vinter clearly does not believe that it should. In June 2009 he appealed against his whole life term to the Court of Appeal, but was turned down. Undeterred, in 2011, Vinter joined forces with convicted-murderer-of-five Jeremy Bamber and convicted-murderer-of-four Peter Moore – both of whom were also serving whole life sentences – to petition the European Court of Human Rights that their sentences breached Article Three of the European Convention on Human Rights which gives protection against 'inhuman or degrading treatment'.

In January 2012 the three lost their petition by four judges to three, the European Court deciding that the sentences did not breach their human rights. The then Secretary of State for Justice, Kenneth Clarke QC, made an impassioned plea to the Court, saying, 'There will always be a small number of prisoners whose crimes are so appalling that the judges rule that they should never become eligible for parole.' The European Court, presided over at that time by the British judge, Sir Nicolas Bratza, agreed.

As the *Guardian* newspaper commented, the European Court's decision was a little out of character for Sir Nicolas, because three years earlier he had argued in the Court against whole life terms. 'I consider,' he said then, 'that the time has come when the Court should clearly affirm that the imposition of an irreducible life sentence, even on an adult offender, is in principle inconsistent with Article Three of the Convention.'

Perhaps with that contradiction in mind, in December 2012 Vinter, Bamber and Moore launched an appeal against the European Court's decision. Their petition had been heard by the First Chamber of the Court, but the appeal would be heard by the more important Grand Chamber, who had granted a rare appeal.

This time the three killers won their appeal. On 9 July 2013, the European Court of Human Rights ruled that the whole life tariffs given to Vinter, Bamber and Moore did indeed breach their human rights. The problem, the Grand Chamber concluded, was that under the current system a prisoner does not get a chance to prove that they are reformed.

The Grand Chamber's seventeen judges ruled by sixteen to one that there had to be a review of the sentence and, at least, the possibility of a release. But they added that this did not mean there was 'any prospect of imminent release'.

Jeremy Bamber dismissed the decision as 'hollow' as he was still serving a sentence for a crime he insisted that he did not commit. The European Court's judges were sympathetic, suggesting that if a prisoner like Bamber was incarcerated 'without any prospect of release and without the possibility of having his life sentence reviewed, there is the risk that he can never atone for his offence: whatever the prisoner does in prison, however exceptional his progress towards rehabilitation, his punishment remains fixed and unreviewable.'

'If anything,' their judgement concluded, 'the punishment becomes greater with time: the longer the prisoner lives, the longer his sentence.'

Prime Minister David Cameron immediately announced that he profoundly disagreed with the Court's ruling, and added that he was a 'strong supporter of whole life tariffs'.

Neither Vinter nor Moore made any public comment on their victory, although both must have believed that there was now at least a chance that they might be released before the end of their lives. If so, they underestimated the decisiveness and clarity of the Court of Appeal in England and Wales.

As we have seen, the European Court's decision in July 2013 meant that four significant murder trials over the next seven months placed the judiciary in a quandary. Could a judge in England and Wales sentence a prisoner convicted of murder to life imprisonment with a whole life term? The cases involved Jamie Reynolds, Anwar Rosser, Joanna Dennehy and Michael Adebolajo.

In the first three cases, each of the judges concerned concluded that they were still perfectly entitled to sentence the offender to a whole life term, and duly did so, while in the high-profile case of Adebolajo and Adebowale, the jihadist killers of Fusilier Lee Rigby, Mr Justice Sweeney thought it prudent to wait until the Court of Appeal had reached its conclusion on the European Court's decision. The judge did not have to wait long.

In October 2013, Mr Justice Sweeney had also declined to

impose a whole life term on fifty-five-year-old Ian McLoughlin, who had admitted killing sixty-six-year-old pensioner Graham Buck on the very first day of his day-release from prison after serving twenty-one years for a murder in 1992.

Mr Justice Sweeney told McLoughlin, passing a life sentence with a minimum of forty years, 'The implementation of a whole life order within the current legislative framework in this country is in breach at the time of passing of sentence of Article Three of the European Convention,' and he therefore declined to do so.

The then Secretary of State for Justice, and Lord Chancellor, Chris Grayling MP, immediately criticised Mr Justice Sweeney's decision, saying, 'Our courts should be able to send the most brutal murderers to jail for the rest of their lives.' Not long afterwards, the Attorney General, Dominic Grieve MP, launched an appeal against the sentence, arguing that it was 'unduly lenient' – even though McLoughlin would have been ninety-nine years of age when his minimum term of forty years had passed.

Once again the confusion over the reality of whole life sentences was at the forefront of the discussion over the issue of whether life should indeed mean life. It was left to the Court of Appeal to try to clarify the position in England and Wales.

On 18 February 2014, the Court's Criminal Division responded to the argument over McLoughlin and the European Court's decision with a specially constituted Court to hear appeals on three whole life terms and the appeal from the Attorney General that McLoughlin should have been given a whole life term. The five members of the special Court were led by the Lord Chief Justice Lord Thomas, with Sir Brian Leveson, Lady Justice Hallett, Lord Justice Treacy and Mr Justice Burnett. Their decision was robust, and made it abundantly clear that judges in England and Wales could indeed continue to impose whole life orders under the terms of the Criminal Justice Act of 2003.

The Court ended up hearing appeals on only two of the four cases. The principal one was, of course, McLoughlin's, whom the Attorney General had suggested should receive a harsher sentence for the murder of Graham Buck, while the other involved Lee Newell, who was already serving a whole life term for the murder of his fellow prison inmate Subhan Anwar, and was appealing against the decision to jail him for the rest of his life.

What is not in doubt was that the facts of the McLoughlin case were shocking in the extreme. An incredibly bright child, he had nevertheless been a criminal since the age of twelve, and had been sentenced to imprisonment fourteen times before his twenty-fifth birthday, even though it was estimated by one psychologist that he possessed an IQ of 140. Then, in September 1984, at the age of twenty-six, he was convicted of manslaughter and sentenced to eight years in prison.

A man with a profound hatred of homosexuals, possibly driven by his loathing for his own bisexuality, he lost his temper with a gay man named Len Dalgatty, picked up a hammer and hit him over the head several times. McLoughlin then tied a towel round his head to dull the sound of yet more hammer blows. When he was certain that Dalgatty was dead, McLoughlin hid his body in a cupboard.

Shortly after he was released from prison after that first murder, he killed again – and once again, his motive concerned his victim's sexuality. He became convinced that his victim this time, Peter Hall, had a sexual interest in young boys, which infuriated him. McLoughlin marched the man into the bedroom of his house and stabbed Hall repeatedly until he was dead. In July 1992 he was convicted of that second murder and sentenced to life imprisonment – this time with a minimum term of fourteen years.

While serving his sentence in Littlehay Prison in Cambridgeshire, McLoughlin befriended a fellow prisoner, old Etonian Francis Corey-Wright. A wealthy man, but a convicted paedophile serving a thirty-month sentence for indecently assaulting a ten-year-old boy, Corey-Wright was released in February 2013, at the age of eighty-seven.

Five months later, on Saturday 13 July 2013, on the very first day of his unsupervised release from prison as a prelude to his eventual release, McLoughlin hitched a lift from Spring Hill Prison, near Aylesbury, straight to Corey-Wright's home in the picturesque village of Little Gaddesden in Hertfordshire. As it turned out, McLoughlin was most certainly not suitable for unsupervised release.

When McLoughlin arrived at his home in the village, Corey-Wright invited him into the house and gave him a drink, but things quickly turned ugly. McLoughlin demanded to know where he kept his 'gold and silver', but when the elderly man told him, 'In the bank,' McLoughlin picked up a kitchen knife and forced him upstairs before tying him up and stealing those valuables he could find, while also taking his bank cards and demanding their pin numbers. Corey-Wright broke free and shouted for help from the upstairs window.

Graham Buck, a neighbour of Corey-Wright, heard the cries and came across the road to help, which only served to infuriate McLoughlin still further. He marched out of Corey-Wright's front door and grabbed Graham Buck as he walked towards Corey-Wright's house. No sooner had he done so than he slashed Buck's throat with a knife. His victim managed to stagger back into his front garden but died before the paramedics arrived. Meanwhile, McLoughlin took off with a pillowcase filled with Corey-Wright's valuables.

Buck paid with his life for acting the Good Samaritan. As his wife Karen, a nurse aged fifty-five, said afterwards, 'To kill him was the most senseless, vicious act of violence and cowardice possible. His family and friends will never be able to make sense of what happened.'

McLoughlin showed little remorse, telling the police, 'I'm not sorry for what I did to the "nonce", but I'm sorry for what I did to the pensioner.' In his perverted view Buck had clearly been a homosexual.

McLoughlin's sister, Karen Baker, called him an 'evil psycho' who should hang. She told reporters outside the Old Bailey when he was convicted and sentenced to a whole life term in October 2013 that she had been terrified of her brother throughout her adult life.

'He was a ticking time bomb,' she said. 'It was when he was thirteen he started to change and began getting into trouble at school. He started burgling people's homes and stealing cars.' Then he turned to violence.

'He used to beat me,' McLoughlin's sister added, 'and put rubber balls in the fire to heat up and throw them at me. He is a horrible man and I was terrified until he got caught . . . He's had his second chance and I hope he rots in prison. He should have been hanged for what he has done in the past. A life for a life, I say.'

The sister of McLoughlin's second victim Peter Hall branded his release from Springhill in 2013 as part of his 'rehabilitation' as a 'joke'. 'This monster has struck again and been allowed to strike again,' the seventy-one-year-old said, 'because he has been freed to walk the streets just as he was with my poor brother.'

Unable to come to terms with her brother's killing, even after twenty years, she described him as 'evil' and went on, 'McLoughlin has never shown a scrap of remorse for what he did to Peter. I would be happy if they gave him a lethal injection.'

The second case the specially constituted Court of Appeal considered in their judgement on 18 February 2014 was every bit as shocking as McLoughlin's. On 19 September 2013 Mr Justice Jeremy Baker, sitting at the Crown Court in Leamington Spa, had sentenced Lee Newell, then aged forty-four and a prisoner in Long Lartin Prison in Worcestershire, to a whole life term for the killing of convicted child killer Subhan Anwar while they were both prisoners in the jail.

At the time Newell was already serving a life sentence for the murder of his fifty-six-year-old neighbour Mary Neal in Gateley Gardens, Norwich. He had tricked his way into her home, demanded money and then strangled her, hiding her body in a cupboard and getting away with just £60. That was in 1988, when he was nineteen. He had been sentenced to life with a minimum term of fifteen years, but had spent the following twenty-five years in jail because of his violent behaviour. Newell was still there when he took another life on Valentine's Day, 14 February 2013. Newell's accomplice was fellow inmate Gary Smith, at forty-eight just four years Newell's senior, who was also serving a life sentence for murder with a minimum of eighteen years for killing twenty-two-year-old Ali Hassan and dumping his naked body in a Leicestershire quarry in 1998. Smith believed that Hassan had been about to tell the police about a jewellery shop robbery he was planning.

Just before 6.00 on that Thursday evening in February 2013, Newell and Smith went to visit Subhan Anwar in his cell at Long Lartin Prison. Anwar considered the two men friends and was certainly not frightened of them. He should have been, for quite without warning, that day his two 'friends' took the twenty-four-year-old man from Huddersfield in West Yorkshire hostage. They were armed with a sharpened toothbrush and a sharpened pen.

Anwar had been in the prison for four years and had built up friendships with prisoners and officers. A member of his family later described him as 'a very young knowledgeable man. He had proven to be a model prisoner, was a wing representative, helped prisoners to be heard, was well behaved and never caused any trouble.' He was serving a life sentence with a minimum of twenty-three years for killing his partner's two-year-old baby – although he had repeatedly insisted that he was innocent.

Newell and Smith, who had been involved in taking hostages in the prison twice before in the previous six years, engaged the 'security lock' on Anwar's cell – effectively barricading themselves in. To lull him into a false sense of security, they told him they were keeping him hostage to bargain with the prison authorities, but they nevertheless tied the young man up with Sellotape.

Once they had done so, Newell used Anwar's tracksuit bottoms as a ligature around his neck and strangled him to death. It took him more than half a minute to do it. Newell then used the cell intercom to inform the authorities that Anwar was dead. Meanwhile Smith made Newell a cup of hot chocolate from Anwar's supply and sweetened it with icing sugar.

When prison officers asked why they had done it, one of the pair shouted through the cell door, 'I am bored and it was something to do.'

As the siege went on, the officers heard the pair talking behind the cell door. One was joking to the other, 'It just snapped. I wonder where he is. I bet Allah has got him.'

There was speculation in the prison that the fact Anwar

had been a child killer had made him a target for Newell and Smith. What is not in doubt is that the pair showed no emotion throughout the siege, which lasted until shortly after 8.20 that evening, and walked calmly out of Anwar's cell after the killing. They were each wearing a trophy from the dead man – Newell his watch and Smith his earring.

'There was no tension between them,' one prison officer said afterwards. 'They were horrendously calm.' Newell just laughed about the murder and refused to answer any questions. The fact that the killing might mean that he could spend the rest of his life in prison proved no deterrent whatever.

After a two-week trial in September 2013 both Newell and Smith were convicted of the murder of Subhan Anwar. But before the judge could begin his sentencing remarks both men demanded to be returned to their cells because they objected to Anwar's family members being allowed into the well of the courtroom to hear Mr Justice Jeremy Baker pass sentence. They did so, but their attitude did not deter the judge.

'One of the most chilling aspects of this case,' he told the Court out of the men's earshot, 'was the almost complete lack of emotion shown by either of you after the killing . . . you have both murdered others before, on this occasion you did so in a cold-blooded manner, having deliberately lulled your victim into a false sense of security . . . You, Newell, later laughing about what you had both done.'

Calling these 'exceptional circumstances', Mr Justice Jeremy Baker then sentenced both men to life imprisonment with a whole life term.

Of the two men, only Newell launched an appeal against his sentence, and it was this appeal, together with the Attorney General's appeal against Ian McLoughlin's 'unduly lenient' sentence of a minimum of forty years that was the basis of the landmark ruling by the Lord Chief Justice and his specially constituted Court of Appeal on 18 February 2014.

In the case of McLoughlin, the Lord Chief Justice, Lord Thomas, specifically stated in the Court's judgement that Mr Justice Sweeney had been wrong in his view that he could not impose a whole life sentence on the killer. 'It is clear that the judge did not think he had the power to make a whole life order,' the Lord Chief Justice pointed out. 'The judge proceeded on the basis of a misunderstanding of the law. It is our duty to exercise our judgement free from that misunderstanding.'

'In our judgement,' he went on, 'this was a case where the seriousness was exceptionally high and just punishment required a whole life order. A fixed term of forty years was for that reason unduly lenient. We therefore quash the minimum term of forty years and make a whole life order.'

In the case of Newell the Lord Chief Justice concluded on behalf of the whole Court that, 'The murder was premeditated and involved the use of an improvised weapon. It occurred in prison whilst Newell was serving a life sentence. The deceased took a significant time to die. There was no mitigation. This was a murder where the seriousness of the offence was exceptionally high. The judge was right in making a whole life order.'

The Court concluded firmly: 'These two cases [of McLoughlin and Newell] are exceptional and rare cases of second murders committed by persons serving the custodial part of a life sentence. The making of a whole life order requires detailed consideration of the individual circumstances of each case. It is likely to be rare that the circumstances will be such that a whole life order is required. Our decision on each case turns on its specific facts and cannot be seen as a guide to any similar case.'

The Court was of the opinion, however, that there remained the 'possibility of release' – even for a prisoner sentenced to spend the rest of his or her life in prison. The Court cited what is known as 'The Lifer Manual', issued by the Prison Service in 2010. It suggested that the criteria that allowed for the release of a whole life prisoner included: 'terminal illness, where death is likely to occur very shortly (say within three months); where the prisoner is incapacitated, being paralysed or suffering from a severe stroke; the risk of re-offending is minimal (particularly in sexual or violent cases); further imprisonment would reduce the prisoner's life expectancy; there were adequate arrangements available for care outside the prison, and early release would bring "some significant benefit" to the prisoner and his or her family.'

But the Court of Appeal also explained that those criteria 'did not represent the whole of the circumstances in which the power of release might be exercised'. In particular, the Court pointed out that the Secretary of State for Justice had powers to 'release a life prisoner on licence if he is satisfied that exceptional circumstances exist that justify the prisoner's release on compassionate grounds'.

Yet they also reiterated the view of successive Lord Chief Justices, in particular Lord Steyn, who argued, 'There is nothing logically inconsistent with the concept of a tariff by saying that there are cases where the crimes are so wicked that even if the prisoner is detained until he or she dies it will not exhaust the requirements of retribution and deterrence.'

At the same time, they quoted another Lord Chief Justice, Lord Phillips, as saying, 'If . . . the position is reached where the continued imprisonment of a prisoner is held to amount to inhuman or degrading treatment, we can see no reason why, having particular regard to the requirement to comply with the Convention [of Human Rights], the Secretary of State should not use his statutory power to release the prisoner. In our judgement the law of England and Wales,' the Court concluded, 'therefore does provide an offender "hope" or the "possibility of release" in exceptional circumstances which render the just punishment originally imposed no longer viable.'

In other words there may be light at the end of the tunnel for a whole life prisoner, but it is a very faint one, for no one, not even the Court of Appeal, can precisely define what those 'exceptional circumstances' are – as the case of Jeremy Bamber, who was convicted of killing no fewer than five members of his family, including two children, amply proves.

6

'Imprisonment is nothing'

Jeremy Bamber and Peter Moore

When Douglas Vinter won his victory at the Grand Chamber of the European Court of Human Rights, two other murderers shared his success – Jeremy Bamber and Peter Moore. Both men had repeatedly appealed their whole life terms in England only to lose, but both clearly hoped their victory in Strasbourg might see their early release. But the decision by the specially constituted Court of Appeal in London in February 2014 that 'life could still mean life' for the most heinous crimes robbed them of that chance.

But Jeremy Bamber remains the only whole life prisoner in jail in England who has always maintained his innocence. As the fifty-four-year-old, who was adopted as a six-month-old baby by the wealthy couple Nevill and June Bamber, now insists fiercely, 'Imprisonment is nothing, but to live defeated and innocent is to die daily.'

Bamber was convicted in October 1986 at Chelmsford Crown Court of killing his father Nevill, sixty-one, his mother June, also sixty-one, his married sister Sheila Caffell, twenty-eight and her six-year-old twins Nicholas and Daniel in what famously became known as the 'White House Farm Murders' in the early hours of Wednesday 7 August 1985. He was imprisoned at the age of just twenty-five, and has spent thirty years behind bars.

As Bamber puts it, 'Because I have maintained innocence I have not taken part in any rehabilitation programmes and neither can I be viewed as a prisoner who has gained atonement.' Instead, he has firmly and repeatedly proclaimed his innocence, which brings him a distinctive view of the meaning of a whole life term of imprisonment. He insists that any individual who is condemned to spend the rest of their life behind bars is living a 'social death' before adding, 'Release for me with my conviction intact means no life at all.'

'There is only one freedom and one hope for me,' Bamber explains, 'and that is the truth of my innocence will be heard in a court of law, allowing me the liberty I have been fighting for.' He believes the sheer notoriety of his multiple murder case means that it is 'unlikely that I would ever be released without my conviction being overturned in a court of law.'

'I am the only person in the United Kingdom,' he insists, 'who was given a life tariff on a majority verdict that maintains his innocence.' Bamber also believes that a whole life sentence contradicts the notion that prison is meant to rehabilitate and denies the possibility of redemption to the prisoner.

'If the state wishes to have a death penalty,' he maintains, 'then they should be honest and reintroduce hanging.'

That view is not reflected among all whole life prisoners, however. Triple murderer John Hilton told the *Guardian* newspaper in 2012, 'Whole life versus hanging: well you can make a life for yourself, a very basic life, but life is better than death – especially by hanging.' Hilton was then in his eighties, and had his whole life term set aside so that he could be released at the age of eighty-eight.

In March 1963 Hilton watched a judge at the Central

Criminal Court in Old Bailey put a black cloth on his head and sentence his co-defendant to death by hanging. He called it a 'very sobering experience, especially while on remand'. Hilton himself had been weighed and measured by the prison authorities in case he too was sentenced to be hanged.

Jeremy Bamber, meanwhile, protests his innocence still from his cell in Full Sutton Prison near York, running his own website and acting as a trusted 'peer partner' to some of his fellow inmates who find it hard to read and write.

It would be fair to say that Bamber always did, and still does, arouse very strong emotions. At his trial witnesses described him as 'arrogant'; yet the writer Scott Lomax, who published a book in 2007 proclaiming his innocence, says his friends describe him as 'gentle' and 'caring'. In recent years a number of journalists have examined Bamber's character, with two concluding that he was 'clever and strategic', and a man 'who exudes arrogance and indifference'.

What is not in doubt is that Bamber was born the illegitimate son of the daughter of a Norfolk clergyman, who had had an affair with a married army sergeant, and then put the child up for adoption at the age of six months through the Church of England Children's Society. It was then that he was taken in by Nevill and June Bamber.

The Bambers were the wealthy farmers of three hundred acres in Essex who lived in a large Georgian house at White House Farm, near Tolleshunt D'Arcy. Nevill, who was six feet one inch in height, was a local magistrate and former RAF pilot. Four years earlier, he and his wife had also adopted a baby girl, whom they called Sheila.

Bamber was sent to a local Essex primary school, but then sent away to board at Gresham's in Norfolk. His father felt it might be difficult to send him to a local school for the village children, when he might one day have to employ them on the family farm. According to author Claire Powell, who wrote about the case in 1994, this led Bamber to feel increasingly alienated from his family and their life in the countryside. One friend alleges that Bamber was sexually assaulted at his boarding school, which may have encouraged a trait of bisexuality, though neither has ever been confirmed.

Whatever the truth, Bamber became an attractive, eloquent and plausible adult, a man who managed to convince people, both men and women, to trust him implicitly.

After he attended a sixth-form college in Colchester, passing seven GCSEs, his father paid for him to take a trip to Australia and New Zealand, where he did a scuba diving course. While in New Zealand, Bamber allegedly broke into a jewellery shop and stole two expensive watches. He also boasted, according to Claire Powell, that he had been involved in smuggling heroin, while a cousin also alleged that Bamber ended up leaving New Zealand in a hurry, because his friends had been involved in an armed robbery.

What is not in question is that he went back to Essex to work in restaurants and bars, which included spending time as a waiter in a Little Chef on the A12 in Essex, but Bamber later returned home to work on the family farm. It was a decision he resented, as he was paid just £170 a week, even though he was given a car and allowed to live rent-free in a cottage his father owned in Goldhanger, just over three miles from White House Farm. It was from there that he made a fateful telephone call to the police in the early hours of 7 August 1985.

At 3.26 on that August morning Bamber rang the police and told them that his father had just telephoned him to say that his sister Sheila 'has gone crazy and got the gun'. The police told him to meet them at White House Farm.

Quite independently, Bamber and the police made their

way to the farm, but the police did not go inside the main building until 7.54 am, when they broke the back door down. They found Nevill, June, Sheila and her twin sons, shot twenty-five times, mainly at close range. Nevill was found in the kitchen where there had clearly been a struggle, June was in the master bedroom with her adopted daughter Sheila beside her on the floor, with a rifle up against her throat in what appeared to be a suicide following the murders.

There were certainly elements of insanity and rage in the brutality of the five killings. Nevill Bamber had been shot eight times in the head; his wife June had been shot seven times while sitting up in bed, the last shot between her eyes from less than a foot away; Sheila's twin boys had been massacred in their beds as they slept, Daniel shot five times in the back of the head and Nicholas three times. Sheila herself had been shot twice under the chin.

The crime shocked the nation who, at first, accepted Bamber's version of events and his sister's guilt, describing it as a 'family tragedy'. At the inquest a week later, on 14 August 1985, the police even supported his version of events and agreed that it was clearly a murder-suicide committed by Sheila.

Sheila Caffell, who had divorced her sculptor husband Colin in May 1982, had twice spent time in a psychiatric hospital being treated for schizophrenia in the months before the murders. Her sons had been placed in temporary foster care in both 1982 and 1983. Indeed, Bamber told the police she could have been upset on the night of the murders because her parents had asked her to consider placing Nicholas and Daniel back in temporary foster care as she was having difficulty coping.

At Bamber's eventual trial for the five murders in October 1986, the prosecution argued that there was no evidence whatever that this discussion had actually taken place, and that

Bamber's suggestion was part of his plan to make it seem as though Sheila had indeed been the killer. If that was so, then Bamber's plan worked for a month. Indeed, it was not until he fell out with his then girlfriend, art student Julie Mugford, that his scheme started to unravel. She told the police not only that Bamber hated his adopted parents but also that he had confessed to her that he had hired a friend to kill his family.

That was the beginning of the end for Bamber, who had been on holiday in Amsterdam as Mugford decided to tell her story. His behaviour there had already aroused some suspicions as he was alleged by a friend to have tried to sell drugs – and nude photographs of his late sister Sheila to the tabloid press.

Whatever the truth, Bamber was arrested shortly after his return from Holland, on 8 September, but was given bail five days later. At this point he promptly went on holiday again, this time to Saint Tropez in the South of France, once again demonstrating his taste for luxury and the good life. He was re-arrested on his return on 29 September and charged with all five murders.

The prosecution case against Bamber hinged on four crucial elements. First, that there was no evidence that his father Nevill had ever telephoned him that night, and if he was lying about the phone call, then Bamber must have been the killer. They also argued that the father was too badly injured to have spoken to anyone and that there was no blood on the kitchen phone. The prosecution also suggested that, even if he had made a phone call, he would surely have called the police rather than his adopted son.

The prosecution argued that a silencer was on the rifle when the shots were fired. This was based on the discovery of what they alleged was a spot of blood inside the silencer. If the silencer was on the gun, Sheila could not possibly have killed herself as she was too short to hold the gun to her throat and reach down to pull the trigger. Finally, the prosecution suggested that Sheila was not strong enough to have overcome her six-foot-one-inch-tall father in what seemed to have been a violent struggle.

With Julie Mugford as their star witness, the prosecution convinced the jury of seven men and five women, who convicted Bamber by a majority verdict of ten to two. Sentencing him to five life terms at Chelmsford Crown Court, Mr Justice Drake said, 'I find it difficult to foresee whether it will ever be safe to release into the community someone who can plan and kill five members of their family and shoot two little boys asleep in their beds.'

The five life terms carried a minimum term of twenty-five years' imprisonment. Eight years later, the Home Secretary Michael Howard confirmed that Bamber would be subject to a whole life sentence, and never be released.

In the years since, Bamber's defence team has produced a string of expert testimony to challenge each of the prosecution's arguments. They found a police log that showed that someone claiming to be Bamber's father did call the police that night, though there is no indication as to who actually made the call. They argued that the silencer may not have been on the gun during the attacks, and produced crime-scene photographs that suggested Sheila's body and the gun had been moved by Essex Police, who had restaged the crime scene because they had inadvertently damaged it. They also argued that the silencer was found by Bamber's relatives weeks after the murders in a cupboard upstairs at White House Farm – and that they themselves stood to inherit the estate if he was convicted.

Bamber has undergone a series of psychological assessments during his thirty years in prison, but no evidence of his having any form of psychopathy has ever been found. His lawyers arranged for him to undergo a lie detector test in 2007, which he passed.

In the wake of this amassed evidence, Bamber has repeatedly attempted to get his case re-opened, by petitioning the Criminal Cases Review Commission to look at the new evidence and then mounting two appeals to the Court of Appeal. The CCRC began an initial review in May 1997 and referred his case to the Court of Appeal on the basis of fresh DNA evidence about the blood on the silencer, but the Court rejected the appeal. In December 2002, in a 522-point judgement, the judges said that the more they examined the details of the case, the more they thought the jury had been right.

Undeterred, Bamber tried again, asking the CCRC to review new evidence, and even offering a reward to anyone who could help his cause. But in April 2012 they again refused to intervene. There seems little doubt that Bamber will continue his campaign to prove his innocence in the years to come, which is why the outcome of the European Court was so important to him.

Relentless in his determination to re-open his case and prove his innocence, Bamber has a large number of friends and supporters outside prison, and has formed several close relationships with women while in jail. Bamber has rarely been involved in trouble during his nearly thirty years in prison, but on one occasion defended himself from a knife attack by using a broken bottle, and he received twenty-eight stitches on his neck when he was attacked from behind by another inmate while making a telephone call.

Bamber has also launched two civil law suits while serving his sentence, both claiming that he had been denied his rightful share of the family's estate: one involving the home of his adoptive grandmother; the other focusing on the family ownership of a caravan site in Essex. He lost both cases, which, his supporters have suggested, only increased his sense of injustice.

Nevill and June Bamber's relatives have persistently dismissed his claims as ridiculous and argued that his guilt is plain for all to see. The law suits he brought against them for a share of the inheritance that they received has only served to sharpen the antagonism. In particular, June's nephew told the BBC after Bamber's appeal in 2002, 'I am obviously biased, you know I have lost five members of my family, and I would be very concerned if he should be let out, as I think he would be a threat to the public, not just to myself but to everyone else as well.'

Another family member commented, 'We are particularly saddened that Sheila's memory is constantly tarnished by Bamber. We never doubted for a second that this was the only possible decision the Court could reach and that justice was indeed done in 1986.'

Meanwhile, Essex Police's Assistant Chief Constable at the time of Bamber's arrest, John Broughton, said in 2002, 'We have never been in any doubt that the original verdict was the right and only verdict. Even with the modern technology now available, today's decision has demonstrated that the original evidence continues to stand the test of time.'

Nevertheless Jeremy Bamber steadfastly continues to protest his innocence, and his sister's guilt, on his website, which contains testimonials, details of new evidence, articles he has written and his blog, which chronicles the many twists and turns in his campaign.

The other appellant alongside Vinter and Bamber in the European Court victory was former cinema owner Peter Moore, a homosexual who was always known as the 'Man in Black', and who was convicted of killing and mutilating four men, three of whom were gay, 'for fun' in his native North Wales between September and December 1995. His case is every bit as chilling as Bamber's.

An unmarried loner, Moore was born in Rhyl in North Wales in 1940 and ran local cinemas in the 1970s and 1980s, living with his mother in Kinmel Bay, Clwyd until her death in May 1994. She doted on Moore, calling him her 'miracle son' because he had been born when she was in her forties. The loss of his mother may have triggered 'an extremely ugly change in his character' according to the prosecution at his trial for the four murders in November 1996.

It was alleged that Moore may have attacked as many as fifty men in the twenty years before his killing spree in 1995 in what the trial judge later described as 'twenty years of terror', but he had apparently never killed any of them. What is certain is that Moore was fixated on gay men.

With a fascination for the wartime German Nazi party, he would haunt gay meeting places across North Wales, dressed in Nazi-style caps and leather boots, while carrying a large knife or truncheon to terrorise his victims. 'The Man in Black', as Alex Carlile, the QC for the prosecution, put it at his trial. 'Black thoughts and the blackest of deeds.' The QC also told the Court, 'He thought it gave him the dominating and overbearing appearance he sought to frighten his victims and for his own sexual gratification.'

A tall man with mousy hair and a greying moustache, Moore hardly looks a threatening killer, yet his total lack of empathy for any other human being sets him apart. One of the police officers who interviewed him after his arrest explained, 'I could not believe how dispassionately he was talking. He was talking the way you and I would talk about going down to town to buy a newspaper or a pint of milk.'

Moore concealed his true self in the persona of a friendly

businessman who would help the local residents by running a Saturday morning 'cinema club' for their children. Moore would entertain the children with film and then treat them to snacks and popcorn in the cinema's little snack bar. Many local parents would drop their kids off into the care of Moore and then go off to do their shopping, picking them up again afterwards. It was an ideal arrangement. To them, Moore appeared to be nothing more than an affable and trustworthy local businessman – 'an upstanding member of the community', as one put it.

In fact it was just part of the subtle disguise that Moore had assumed in public for more than twenty years, hiding himself in plain sight, and disguising his true personality – that of a man who was both deeply manipulative and intensely calculating.

His mother's death in 1994 may have tipped Moore over the edge, but whatever the reason, he killed for the first time in late September 1995 with a £25 hunting knife that he had bought for himself as a birthday present. His victim was Henry Roberts, a fifty-six-year-old retired railwayman who lived alone in a crumbling cottage on the island of Anglesey off the Welsh coast. Though he chose to live in squalor, Roberts was comparatively well off as the result of a large redundancy payment and family inheritances.

Like Moore, Roberts was interested in Nazi memorabilia and sported a Nazi flag on the wall of his cottage, which lay just off Moore's route home from one of his cinemas.

When the retired railwayman failed to turn up at his local pub for three days a friend went to look for him at his cottage and found him lying face down near an outhouse outside. His trousers were round his ankles and he had been stabbed in each buttock. But those were certainly not his only injuries. Roberts' body was covered in stab wounds – fourteen to the front and thirteen to the back in an attack 'of frenzied and sadistic viciousness' as the prosecution put it at Moore's trial. But he had died as a result of just one of the stab wounds – to the heart. Roberts' swastika flag was missing.

Less than a month later Moore went trawling for another victim in a Liverpool gay bar. He came across a drunken young drug addict named Edward Carthy, who was twenty-eight and 'a disaster waiting to happen' according to the prosecution at Moore's trial. The young man wanted the cinema owner to drive him to his home in Birkenhead for sex, but instead Moore drove him into a forest in North Wales. When Carthy realised he tried to jump out of the van Moore was driving, but failed. 'I think he got a bit frightened, actually,' his killer said laconically afterwards. Moore stabbed him four times, killing him, and left Carthy's body in the forest.

After his arrest in December 1995 Moore led police to the spot where he had dumped the young man's body in the forest. What they found were Carthy's remains, badly decomposed and mutilated by animals which had severed an arm and bitten off his head. Moore showed not a trace of concern or remorse, however, looking on stony-faced, his eyes flat and disengaged as the police gathered the remains.

By now Moore had developed a taste for killing, and his desire to kill was escalating rapidly. Before the end of November he had killed a third time, but this time the victim was clearly not gay. Keith Randles was a forty-nine-year-old divorced father of two daughters who had recently lost his job in middle management, but who had found work as a traffic safety officer looking after some roadworks on the A5 road to Anglesey.

On 30 November Randles went to buy some fish and chips for supper, and then returned to the caravan he was living in beside the roadworks to spend the rest of the evening quietly.

It did not turn out to be as quiet as he had hoped, because later that night, once again using the A5 as his route home, Moore knocked on the caravan's door and dragged Randles outside while stabbing him repeatedly until he died. Unlike Roberts or Carthy, his two previous victims, there was no sign that Moore knew Randles; it was the spontaneous attack of a man bent on murder, no matter the cost.

After his arrest Moore told the police that Randles had pleaded for his life, asking him what he was doing, and why. 'For fun,' Moore told him as he continued the killing, with his victim looking 'nonplussed' as he put it.

'Would you say at that point he accepted the inevitable?' a detective asked.

'No, he carried on screaming,' Moore replied.

Then, when asked if he enjoyed it, Moore added chillingly, and once more with an absolutely stony face, 'There was a certain enjoyment from it, but the enjoyment wasn't sexual. Like everything it was a job well done.'

As trophies Moore took Randles' video recorder and his mobile phone.

Just over two weeks later, Moore killed for the fourth time, but this time returning to his preference for a gay victim. On the evening of Sunday 17 December, thirty-five-year-old crematorium worker and father of two Anthony Davies, who lived near Colwyn Bay with his wife Sheila, told her that he was going to visit his aunt who had just been discharged from hospital with a broken leg. It was about 11 pm, and the story was a subterfuge to get out of the house and meet other gay or bisexual men.

When Davies had not returned by 4.30 the following morning Sheila Davies phoned her husband's aunt, who told her that Tony had left her more than three hours before. In fact he had driven to Pensarn Beach, a local gay meeting place for men looking for casual sex. There he encountered Peter Moore who had been 'cruising around', as he told the police later, almost certainly intent on finding another gay man to kill.

Later Moore told the police that he had watched Davies get out of his car, light a cigarette and then walk to the water's edge. When he got to him he found him with his trousers round his ankles. Nothing could have been more provocative to the conflicted Moore.

'I just took the knife out and stabbed him,' he told the police. 'I think he screamed or shouted a bit.'

When the police finally searched Moore's house, they found Davies' duffel bag, while his keys were in the fish pond. Moore never neglected to keep some trophies which he always craved from his victims to help him to relive the details of the killings.

Peter Moore's spree of four murders in barely three months might have gone undetected had the police not been persuaded to open a confidential 'tip line' for information on the murders aimed at the gay community. Within four days of the killing of Anthony Davies the line had received a series of anonymous calls suggesting that Moore had been, and still was, violent towards homosexuals. One man even told the police that he had been taken to Moore's home six months earlier and been tortured, but had never admitted his ordeal to anyone because of his shame.

When detectives visited his home on 21 December 1995, they found a treasure trove of sexual equipment, including handcuffs and rubber gags, a long black truncheon and his customary black leather uniform – and they also found trophies from three of his victims.

An unrepentant Moore was to tell them over the next two days the details of how he had committed the murders and confessed that they had not found his second victim, Edward Carthy, whose body he had dumped in the woods.

'I used the same knife on them all,' he explained.

When the detectives asked why he bought the knife in the first place, his response was every bit as matter of fact.

'To kill somebody. With the sole intent of killing somebody.'

Then Moore explained that killing for him was 'a relief from stress'.

'I don't feel any remorse for what I've done.'

Not long afterwards he also confessed to a whole string of 'mostly sexual' attacks during the 1970s and 1980s. Criminal psychologists suggest that stabbing can sometimes be a substitute for sex in both straight and gay relationships, and there is little doubt that Moore was both hypnotised by his own latent homosexuality and yet simultaneously appalled by it.

In spite of his confessions, however, Moore pleaded not guilty at his trial, which began on 11 November 1996. He claimed instead that a gay lover called Alan, whom he had nicknamed Jason after a character in the *Friday the Thirteenth* series of films, had 'wielded the knife', while he watched.

When prosecuting barrister Alex Carlile QC asked why he had confessed to the police about the killings, he said: 'I led them up the garden path and back because I wanted Jason to get away.'

'Do you see Jason here?' the prosecutor asked, looking round the courtroom.

'No,' Moore replied.

'That's because he doesn't exist.'

'He does exist,' Moore insisted. 'He's still out there ... I don't think he will ever stop.'

Maintaining the fiction that 'Jason' existed, Moore nevertheless agreed that he was fascinated by knives and had assaulted men with them over the years during his attacks on gay and bisexual men. He also confessed that he kept hand-cuffs and a truncheon in his car 'on the off chance' of meeting a man he could assault.

'You're a bad man,' the prosecuting barrister suggested to him, 'aren't you? And you like other bad men?'

'Yes,' Moore agreed.

The jury did not believe a word of Moore's fantasy about a gay lover called Jason who had actually committed the crimes, and took just two hours and thirty-five minutes to convict him of the four murders.

Mr Justice Kerr had no difficulty in sentencing him to four life terms.

'I consider you to be as dangerous a man as it is possible to find,' the judge told him. 'You are responsible for four sadistic murders in the space of three months. Not one of the victims had done you the slightest of harm; it was killing for killing's sake.'

'At no stage,' the judge went on, 'have you shown the slightest remorse or regret for the killings, or for the twenty years of assaults that preceded them.' As to the question of release, he added, 'I don't want you or anyone else to be in the slightest doubt as to what I shall say . . . in a word, never.'

The judge was as good as his word and recommended to the Home Secretary that he impose a whole life order on Moore, which was confirmed in 1997.

Outside Leeds Crown Court after the verdict and sentenc-ing Janine Ingrams, the twenty-six-year-old daughter of Keith Randles who had been dragged from his caravan and murdered by Moore, called the killer, who had been wearing a black shirt and tie in the dock, 'an evil man'.

'Justice has been done,' she said, 'and the best place for this person to be is where he is going for the rest of his life and that is in prison. Nobody deserves to die in the way that my father and the other men died.'

Unashamed, Moore had his solicitor read a statement from him after the conviction.

'I knew from the start,' Moore insisted, 'that nobody could win in this matter – not the deceased, the relatives, nor myself – nobody.'

To call Moore's view bizarre would be an understatement, but it did serve to underline his arrogance and the fantasy world that he had come to inhabit, a fantasy world that included his right to consider himself some kind of victim in these brutal, callous and premeditated killings.

Moore's arrogance and determination to 'work the system' was evident within four years when, in 1999, he won nearly £13,000 compensation from a couple he claimed had stolen the contents of his home, including his prized set of garden gnomes. He claimed his neighbours had abused his offer for them to become caretakers of his property by selling his belongings at car boot sales.

The following year, in July 2000, Moore was not so fortunate when he lost his fight to win £160,000 in damages from North Wales Police, after accusing them of failing to protect his home following his arrest in 1995. A district judge agreed his case should be struck off the list, on the grounds that Moore had no realistic chance of winning at trial. Moore appeared in Court flanked by heavy security but did not bother with legal representation. He was clearly intent on causing the maximum inconvenience to the prison authorities and proving to himself that he could.

It was a view sharpened still more when he launched an appeal against his whole life sentence in 2008, to be told by the Court of Appeal that he would indeed spend the rest of his life behind bars. That decision only fuelled his desire to prove his omnipotence and join Bamber and Vinter's appeal to the European Court, which provoked fury among the relatives of his victims and the police.

The mother of Edward Carthy said, as Moore's European case began, 'The thought of him having the cheek to think he can get out. He's just not going to get out because he's destroyed how many families? He's destroyed ours, I know that. My husband was never the same again . . . He went into shock, drew into himself and wouldn't talk about it. It horrified him.'

The reaction was every bit as strong when Moore won his appeal in July 2013 in Strasbourg, which found that a whole life term was 'degrading and inhuman'. Detective Constable Dave Morris, for example, who had arrested Moore in 1995, said bitterly when the Court in Strasbourg found in Moore's favour, 'There are other people here whose rights have been infringed. The rights of his victims have been overlooked in this matter and not just the victims, the victims' families as well.'

Those words were reflected in the Court of Appeal's decision not to reconsider the whole life terms that applied to Peter Moore, any more than those of Jeremy Bamber and Douglas Vinter in the light of their European victory.

1. Jeremy Bamber: Convicted of murdering his adoptive parents, adoptive sister and her 6-year-old twins in 1986. He is the only lifer to still maintain that he is innocent of his crimes.

25 AUG 15

JEREMY BAMBER
A5352AC
HMP C 2-39
WAKEFIELD
WF2 9AG

DEAR MR WANSELL,
    SORRY FOR THE DELAY IN WRITING
TO YOU — I'M ALWAYS SO BUSY.
    DURING THE PAST TEN YEARS
I WORKED EXTREMELY CLOSELY
WITH DR GRAINGER WHO GAINED
HER PHD FROM SCHOOL OF LAW
KINGS COLLEGE LONDON. PERHAPS
YOU MIGHT CONTACT HER PROFESSOR
ELAINE PLAYER TO SEE IF SHE
COULD ASSIST YOU. THE PHD
WAS ON THE WHOLE LIFE TARIFF
AND I GAVE HER ACCESS TO ALL
THE DOCUMENTS FROM MY CASES
IN THE UK AND EUROPEAN COURTS.
THE PHD IS AN INCREDIBLE
PIECE OF WORK, THOUGH IT
MAY NOT BE AVAILABLE FOR ANYONE

2. Letter from Jeremy Bamber: A never-before-seen letter sent to me by Bamber just last year from his cell.

TO READ — I DON'T KNOW HOW
THESE THINGS WORK.
YOU ASK ME THREE QUESTIONS
AND I DO UNDERSTAND WHY
THE ANSWERS MIGHT BE ONES
THAT MIGHT GIVE SOME INSIGHT
INTO THIS ISSUE.
  BUT —
OF THE 50 OR SO PRISONERS
WHO HAVE WHOLE LIFE ORDERS
I'M THE ONLY ONE CONVICTED
ON A 10:2 MAJORITY VERDICT.
I'M ONE OF THE FEW TO HAVE
BEEN SET A TARIFF OF 25
YEARS BY THE TRIAL JUDGE
AND LORD CHIEF. JUSTICE,
AND NOT GIVEN THIS WHOLE
LIFE ORDER FROM A JUDGE,
BUT FROM AN M.P.
I'VE HAD PAROLE HEARINGS
SCHEDULED MY FIRST IN 2002

3

I'VE WON IN THE EUROPEAN
GRAND CHAMBER THAT MY
WHOLE LIFE ORDER WITH NO
POSSIBILITY OF A REVIEW WAS
A BREACH OF MY HUMAN RIGHTS.
I BELIEVE I'M THE ONLY ONE
WITH A WHOLE LIFE ORDER WHO
HAS CONSISTANTLY MAINTAINED
INNOCENCE. I WAS THE
FIRST UK PRISONER TO
BE ALLOWED TO TAKE A
POLYGRAPH TEST, I TOOK.
4 OVER 110 MINUTES WIRED
UP AND PASSED WITHOOT A
SHADOW OF DOUBT. I HAVE
33 PSYCHOLOGY ASSESSMENTS
ALL STATING THAT I HAVE NO
PERSONALITY DISORDERS OR
TRAITS OF PSYCHOPATHY., I HAVE.

NOW DISPROVEN WITH OFFICIAL
PROSECUTION DOCUMENTS
PREVIOUSLY HIDDEN BEHIND
PUBLIC INTEREST IMMUNITY
ORDERS (Pii) THAT EVERY
PIECE OF PROSECUTION EVIDENCE
USED AGAINST ME AT TRIAL WAS
MANUFACTURED, MADE UP OR
MANIPULATED IN SOME WAY TO
MY DETRIMENT. I'M NOT A
MURDERER AND ESSEX POLICE
PROVED THAT THEMSELVES
WHEN DCi KENNEALLY COMPLETED
IS REPORT ON THE CASE DATED
6TH SEPT 85 STATING THAT
"THE EVIDENCE INDICATED THAT
CHEICA WAS RESPONSIBLE"
A REPORT ESSEX POLICE STILL
WANT TO CONCEAL, BECAUSE
IT PROVES MY INNOCECE.
  SO I'M SORRY I CAN'T HELP
      YOURS SINCERELY

3. Joanna Dennehy: Serial killer found guilty of stabbing three men to death in the 'Peterborough Ditch Murders'. Dennehy was the first woman sentenced to life in prison by a judge.

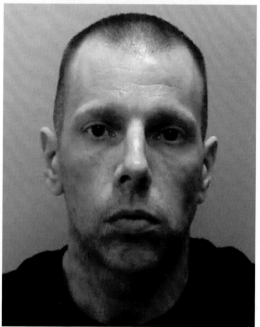

4. *Above* Ian McLoughlin: Committed murder while on day release from prison, where he was already 21 years into a life sentence for a previous murder.

5. *Left* Lee Newell: Was serving life for a killing when he and another prisoner, Gary Smith, strangled a fellow inmate to death.

6. *Right* Sidney Cooke:
The convicted paedophile
nicknamed 'Hissing Sid'.

7. *Below* Danilo Restivo:
The hair fetishist who killed
Heather Barnett in 2002 and
comforted her children once
they found her body.

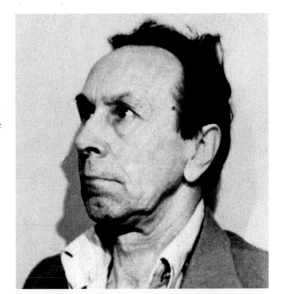

7

'Selfish, self-pitying and grotesquely violent'

David Oakes and Daniel Restivo

Another case that confirmed just how determined the Court of Appeal in England and Wales was to protect the right of the English judiciary to pass a whole life sentence on the most heinous murderers concerned a vicious, bullying, former nightclub bouncer and unemployed builder named David Oakes, aged fifty, who lived part of the time in a static caravan near Braintree in Essex. His crime also shocked the nation and the Court.

In July 2005, when he was still only forty-four, the swaggering, bald-headed Oakes, who had a reputation in the local area for being a man who would resort to violence at the slightest opportunity, started a relationship with a round-faced, cheerful, outgoing thirty-two-year-old woman named Christine Chambers. She already had three children with her previous partner, a close friend of Oakes called Ian Flitt. These three were Levi, Gary and Abigail, but Chambers went on to have another daughter with Oakes, called Shania, who was born in October 2008. Chambers and her children lived in a plain, white-painted, semi-detached house on the outskirts of Braintree.

Never exactly conventional and, indeed, distinctly stormy,

the relationship between Oakes and Chambers began to break down in the first months of 2011. There were fights between them, he dragged her out of her house by the hair on several occasions and attacked her repeatedly – all because Oakes sensed that she might be the one person who would not be bullied by him into doing exactly what he wanted. By the end of March the couple had broken up completely, but that did not stop Oakes harassing Chambers.

As a result, Chambers made an application to the Court for a non-molestation order, and on 21 April 2011, on the basis of a number of allegations of Oakes's persistent violence towards Chambers, the order was made. It did not deter Oakes for one moment. If anything, it made the man who had a gunshot for a ringtone on his mobile phone even angrier, so determined was he to show that he controlled his partner and their now two-year-old daughter Shania. In the seven weeks after the non-molestation order was granted, Oakes lost control completely.

In spite of the order, and repeated police warnings to Oakes about his breaches of it, which included a ruling that he could not come within one hundred yards of his partner and their daughter, his violent threats continued. In one week, Chambers received no fewer than a hundred arrogant, bullying text messages from Oakes, many of them threatening to kill her. Finally, just before midnight on the evening of 5 June 2011, he decided to act.

Oakes left his caravan and arrived at Chambers's house carrying a blue holdall containing an axe, a bottle of petrol, a Stanley knife, some scissors and a pair of pliers, as well as a length of wire threaded through rubber tubing that could be used as a garrotte. He was also carrying a double-barrelled twelve-bore shotgun together with cartridges for it. Oakes had bought it from a 'friend' for £300 just a few days earlier.

Most significant of all, this was the evening before Oakes and Chambers were due to go to court to confirm the custody arrangements for their daughter Shania.

At about 11.55 on that June evening Oakes let himself into Chambers's house with a key that he had kept from the time that he had lived there and walked up the stairs to the bedrooms where she and her daughters were asleep in bed. Oakes turned the lights on, waking everyone, including ten-year-old Abigail and her two-year-old stepsister. He then subjected his former partner and her two daughters to one of the most terrifying and brutal ordeals it is possible to imagine.

When Christine Chambers told Oakes to 'get out' of the house, he opened the holdall and took out the axe. He then showed her the shotgun and said he would burn the house down and that he had petrol in the holdall as well as a lighter to do the job. Oakes then punched ten-year-old Abigail in the eye and hit her with the butt of the shotgun, but when she tried to use her mobile phone to get help, he snatched it from her and broke both it and her mother's phone.

Oakes then ordered his former partner to cut off chunks of her hair with the pair of scissors he had brought along in the holdall. He made her remove her top and walk about without a bra, before insisting that she hug and kiss him, and say that she loved him. For her part, Christine Chambers pleaded with him not to touch her children, saying that she would do anything he wanted. It did nothing to placate Oakes whatever – quite the reverse.

By now in an unimaginable rage, Oakes proceeded to threaten Chambers with a knife before telling her that he would blow her ten-year-old daughter's leg off with his shotgun and rip off her nipples with pliers. At one point he put his gun into Abigail's mouth, but removed it, and her mother shouted, 'Run, run, save yourself while you can!' In a panic the girl managed to climb out of her bedroom window, drop down on to a flat roof beneath, and then jump down a further ten feet to the ground below. No sooner had she got there than she ran to her father, who lived near by, for help.

Ian Flitt later remembered that his daughter banged on the window to wake him up and then started screaming, 'He is there at the house with a gun!' Flitt called the police, and armed officers arrived outside not long afterwards. Inside Christine Chambers's house, however, things were rapidly disintegrating as Oakes's anger showed no limits. The arrival of armed police made no difference whatever. He continued to subject his former partner to an 'attack of horrifying violence', as the Court of Appeal was to put it later.

Using the axe he had brought with him, Oakes cut deeply into Chambers's scalp, and then – using the Stanley knife – proceeded to disfigure her dreadfully. He was clearly consumed with the thought that if he could not have her then no other man would. He cut a deep incised wound into her left eyebrow, to which he applied superglue, and a Y shaped laceration to the bridge of her nose. He also all but cut off the lower part of her left ear.

Even that was not enough for Oakes. He slashed both sides of her face, and used the Stanley knife to cut her from her lower abdomen to the vulva. She was then shot in the left thigh, and while lying on the ground in the upstairs of her house, he shot her again, this time in the right knee. It was only after that inconceivable torture that Oakes killed her, shooting her in the left side of her chest.

A few minutes later, Oakes raised his shotgun again and shot his two-year-old daughter Shania from point blank range in the left side of her forehead, just above her left eyebrow, killing her, though not instantly – and not until after she had been forced to watch the vicious, prolonged and remorseless attack on her mother.

In the wake of the defenceless child's pointless killing, there was a stand-off between the armed police outside Chambers's house and Oakes, which lasted until 5.45 am on 6 June 2011 when Oakes turned the shotgun on himself in an attempt at suicide. He failed. The gun's powerful recoil skewed the barrel as he pulled the trigger, and resulted in a severe wound to the left side of his face, but he survived. The police took him to hospital, where he was later arrested and charged with the murders of Christine Chambers and their daughter Shania.

When it came to Oakes's trial at Chelmsford Crown Court in April 2012, however, Oakes version of events was quite different. He pleaded not guilty to both charges of murder and maintained that it was Christine Chambers' fault that she had died.

Nevertheless, the jury heard prosecuting counsel, Orlando Pownall QC, say that Oakes, 'fuelled by jealousy, frustrated by the fact that his relationship with Christine Chambers was over and that he would only, in the future, have limited access to Shania, deemed that he would kill them and kill himself.' Describing Oakes as 'violent and domineering', Pownall also pointed out that Chambers had been a 'doting mother'.

When Oakes took the witness stand in his own defence, however, he told a completely different version of events. He insisted that Chambers had shot their daughter and that he did not have the shotgun at the time it was fired.

'It's like time was in slow motion,' he told his defence barrister. 'I went through the bedroom door and Chris is on her knees and she's swinging the gun towards me and I grabbed the gun. I'm hitting and kicking her – I don't care at that point.'

'I'm not sure if I've shot Christine,' Oakes went on. 'I'm trying to stop her and get to my baby and then I feel a passing out sensation.' It was a tissue of lies, but it did not end there.

Oakes also maintained that he had arrived at the house much earlier in the evening, and that Chambers had attacked him with a pair of scissors after an argument about money.

'I slapped her around the face and she hit her head on the bedpost or the fireplace which made her bleed,' he told the jury, then adding that she had been acting 'like a lunatic' and hitting her own head against the bathroom wall.

Oakes even claimed that in the last hour and a half of her life he and his partner had been getting on well. 'I thought we were going to have sex,' he said, before explaining that he had given the shotgun to Chambers three days earlier at her request.

'I wouldn't kill my family, I didn't intend to either,' he told the jury.

They were not convinced, not least, perhaps, because Oakes barely sat in the dock during his two-week trial, saying he did not attend the Court as a result of the 'physical discomfort' he was suffering after the shotgun wound to his face, and that he could not bear to hear the details of his daughter's death.

'It's the stress of going through it,' he told the judge, Mr Justice Fulford. 'I've seen first-hand [what happened] and I can't go through the pictures of my baby again and again.'

In spite of his protestations of innocence, the jury convicted Oakes on both counts of murder.

Passing sentence on 12 May 2012, Mr Justice Fulford told the defendant – who by now was in the dock of the court – that he was a 'bullying and controlling man who had frequently inflicted serious violence on Christine Chambers during the course of their five- or six-year relationship, killed his partner and young daughter simply because he was unable to accept that Ms Chambers could no longer bear to be with him and wanted to start a new life.'

The judge added, 'Ms Chambers had, for her part, made it clear that she wished to treat the defendant generously. She recognised that he was important to Shania and that contact between father and daughter ought to continue.'

That was not the way that Oakes had interpreted the three weekends a month access that was the likely outcome of the custody hearing they were both to attend on the morning that he killed his daughter and her mother. As Mr Justice Fulford put it, Oakes reaction 'was purely selfish, self-pitying and grotesquely violent'.

'Instead of thinking about his daughter whom he has claimed to love,' the judge went on, 'he concentrated on himself alone and most particularly his desire for revenge and his determination, that he had expressed quite clearly on more than one occasion in the past, that no other man was going to be Christine's partner or was going to act as Shania's father. He resolved that if the family was at an end, then they would pay for leaving him with their lives. And worse still, he decided that their last hours of life would be terrifying, and in the case of Christine Chambers, extremely painful.'

Pointing out that Oakes had carefully planned the murders and arrived at Chambers's house complete with a holdall filled with weapons that he intended to use against her, the judge continued, 'Drink and drugs may well have played their part, but this defendant knew exactly what he was doing, particularly having clearly prepared and planned these deaths for a not insignificant period in advance.'

But it was the torture inflicted on Christine Chambers before her death that drew Mr Justice Fulford's gravest condemnation.

'Two final aspects of this terrible history need emphasising,' the judge told the Court, whose public gallery included members of the Chambers family. 'First, it is apparent that before she died, Christine Chambers would have been in agony. The injury to her head and the shotgun wound to her knee would have been excruciatingly painful. I am certain that Oakes delayed delivering the fatal gunshot wound as an act of deliberate sadism. She had made him suffer by ending the relationship . . . and this was his revenge.'

The second aspect was Oakes's treatment of his baby daughter, Shania, who had been asleep in her cot when he first burst into the house and began to attack her mother. He had taken the trouble to lift her out of the cot and wake her up so that she could witness the attack on her mother.

'Throughout, she would have been aware of her mother's cries and tears,' the judge concluded. 'In my judgement the defendant allowed his daughter to see at least part of what he was doing and she would have seen the appalling injuries to her mother. The next door neighbour heard Shania crying for at least five minutes after Christine Chambers had been shot. That little girl must have been terrified. He then put the barrel of the twelve-bore shotgun against her head and pulled the trigger. No civilised, decent human being could ever describe that as being the result of love.'

Mr Justice Fulford concluded by passing a whole life sentence for the two murders, and added, 'The defendant will never be released from prison.'

That was certainly not how David Oakes saw it, however. Barely five months later, his legal team brought an appeal against his whole life sentence to the Court of Appeal in London. They argued that the fact that the by now fifty-one year old would be condemned to spend the rest of his life in prison was 'grossly disproportionate' to the crime. They also argued that the whole life sentence was incompatible with Article 3 of the European Convention on Human Rights. The hearings were held on 10 October 2012, and the Court released its decision on 21 November 2012.

Led by the Lord Chief Justice, Lord Thomas, the Court of Appeal took the opportunity to outline its view about the Vinter, Bamber and Moore appeal to the European Court of Human Rights, and Oakes's attempt to piggyback on it.

They also dealt – exceptionally firmly – with Oakes, and his appeal against his whole life term. The specially convened Court, which included Lady Justice Hallett, Lord Justice Hughes, Lord Justice Leveson and Lady Justice Rafferty, used the Oakes case to underline again the Court of Appeal's support for whole life sentences – regardless of what the European Court might say about them.

Dismissing any suggestion that the gruesome murders of Christine Chambers and her daughter were anything but 'sadistic', the Court concluded, 'It seems to us clear that Oakes did not simply explode into violence as a result of the stresses and strains of the breakdown of his relationship. Rather, he decided to revenge himself on Christine Chambers.'

'He did not merely plan to kill her and their daughter,' the Court went on, 'but he planned and then carried out his deliberate intention to make the death of his former partner the most terrifying and agonising ordeal that he could envisage, and this was exactly what he did. He was utterly merciless, and took pleasure at her prolonged suffering. Thereafter, quite deliberately, and in cold blood, he deliberately executed their daughter, as she was screaming with fear at witnessing what he had been doing to her mother.'

There had been ample opportunity after the murder of his former partner, the Court argued, for Oakes to allow a moment of compassion for their daughter – but he turned it down. 'We agree with the judge that there was not a shred of mitigation,' the Court concluded. 'The analysis made by the highly respected judge is not open to criticism. There is no reason to interfere with this sentence.'

In a supreme irony, by the time David Oakes learned that his appeal had been refused he had been given another sentence, but this time a medical one. He had been diagnosed with a terminal cancer that had spread from his lungs. 'We used to write,' his father said when he broke the news of his son's illness. 'He was still my son, despite being a killer.'

David Oakes died on Tuesday 12 February 2013, less than two years after he had viciously murdered his former partner and their daughter. The day before, he had been taken from Frankland Prison to a local hospital, and he died within a matter of hours.

As Ian Flitt, Christine Chambers' former partner, told one reporter the next day, 'His death is probably the best thing for everybody concerned, including him. He was a monster, but I remember him being my best mate as well.'

In their judgement on the Oakes murders, the specially convened Court of Appeal also considered three other recent cases that had attracted whole life sentences, but – in stark contrast to the case of Oakes – they did not confirm any of them as appropriate.

The Lord Chief Justice, Lord Thomas, was at pains to describe the reasoning behind whole life terms, not least because the Court of Appeal was well aware that the European Court would be considering the issue in just a few months' time, at some point in 2013.

At the outset, Lord Thomas carefully summarised the background to the whole life term. 'Whatever the judicial views about the whole life minimum term, it was incorporated in express legislative terms in the 2003 Act,' he said. 'This statutory provision reflects the settled will of Parliament. Simultaneously, the legislation removed the possibility of imposing it from the executive and placed it full square in the hands of the judiciary, we emphasise, as a *discretionary* element of sentencing.'

He then went on to say that it was 'reserved for the few exceptionally serious offences in which, after reflecting on all the features of aggravation and mitigation, the judge is satisfied that the element of just punishment and retribution requires the imposition of a whole life order. If that conclusion is justified, the whole life order is appropriate: but only then. It is not a mandatory or automatic or minimum sentence.'

That meant the whole life sentence was 'not incompatible' with Article Three of the European Convention on Human Rights, he said firmly.

The other three defendants appearing before the Court of Appeal had also been given whole life sentences by the judge in their original trials, but the Court saw fit to replace each of those sentences with shorter minimum terms, while taking some pains to point out that this did not mean that any of the three would be released once their minimum terms had been served. In doing so, the judges reaffirmed their view that life should only mean life in 'exceptionally serious offences'.

One of the three men concerned was the Sicilian-born, Bournemouth-based hair fetishist, Danilo Restivo, who was aged fifty at the time of his appeal, and had escaped justice for a full ten years before being arrested and tried for the exceptionally ugly murder of Heather Barnett, who lived across the road from him in Dorset, where she worked from home as a seamstress.

Barnett, a single mother aged forty-eight, lived with her three children in Bournemouth when she was killed on 12 November 2002. At 8.30 am she had driven her children to school, then returned and parked her car outside her house about ten minutes later. When the children come back from school shortly after four that afternoon, her son Terry, aged fourteen, along with his sister Caitlin, aged nine, discovered her body.

Barnett had been hit on the head, most probably with a hammer, though the murder weapon was never found. There were at least ten lacerating blows, causing skull fractures, while it was also clear that she had fought with her attacker, as there were defensive wounds to her left hand.

It turned out that Restivo had visited Barnett six days earlier using an excuse that he wanted her to make some bedroom curtains for him as a surprise Christmas present. After that visit she told some friends that she thought he might have taken the key to her house, but she was not certain. What is certain is that there was no forced entry into her home when her children got back from school and found her body.

What made the murder quite exceptional was the mutilation that her body had been subjected to over a period of time after her death. Her throat was cut from ear to ear, she had been cut down her spine and both her breasts had been cut off. The zip of her jeans was unfastened and her underwear and part of her pubic hair was exposed. A hank of cut hair was found in the palm of her right hand which lay over her stomach near her groin. This hair came from someone else, but the victim's own hair was cut – some was placed in her left hand, and some left on the floor beside her.

After the discovery of her mutilated body in the bathroom, and desperately upset, Barnett's children ran into the street to look for help. Restivo, who had been watching from his house across the road, then emerged with his then girl-friend to help them. Quite calmly and deliberately, he comforted them, even though he knew perfectly well that it was he who had killed their mother. It was an act of the most wretched disingenuousness, for behind his caring face lurked the foulest killer.

Unsurprisingly, the police quickly concluded that Restivo could have been the killer as he was the first person on the scene. Indeed, they took him in for questioning, only to release him without charge after three days. One reason for his release was that he produced a bus ticket timed at 8.44 on the morning of the murder to prove that he had been on his way to a computer course at the time. Another was that the police regarded him as 'bumbling' and therefore possibly not competent enough to commit such a vicious crime without leaving any forensic evidence.

The police investigation revealed that the killer had left very few traces at the crime scene. Their Luminol tests, for exam-ple, showed a trail of bloody shoe-prints that ended suddenly, which they concluded might mean that the killer was clever enough to change his shoes before leaving Barnett's house that morning. The detectives clearly wondered whether the apparently harmless and slow Restivo could have managed that subterfuge.

Even though the dead woman's son told them that his mother's keys had disappeared after Restivo's visit on 6 November, and he was found to have soaked the trainers he had worn on 12 November in bleach – possibly to remove any traces of blood on them – he was dismissed as a prime suspect partly because of the bus ticket and his unthreaten-ing manner.

After Restivo's release the investigation to identify Heather

Barnett's killer stalled. It was not until March 2004 that it was to start again in earnest – when it emerged that he was a suspect in the murder of a sixteen-year-old girl named Elisa Clap in southern Italy in 1993. Restivo was placed under close surveillance using electronic tracking and listening devices, and as a result the police heard Restivo being spoken to as a child by his parents on the telephone. He was also observed making regular visits to a local beauty spot where he took a close interest in women there on their own.

On 12 May 2004 the police surveillance team became alarmed, because although it was a warm day Restivo was seen wearing waterproof over-trousers. A uniformed patrol car was ordered to stop and search Restivo. In his car they found an identical change of clothing, filleting knife, scissors, a balaclava helmet and more than one pair of gloves. The following month a local schoolgirl identified him as the man who had cut her hair on a bus in the town without her permission and without her initially noticing that he had done so.

But Restivo was not arrested. Indeed it was not until November 2006, more than two years after the beauty spot incident, and four years after Barnett's murder, that he was finally rearrested and his home searched. It was then that the police found a lock of hair and discovered that the trainers he had worn on the day of Barnett's murder had minute traces of blood on them. The problem was it could not be identified as hers.

Once again, Restivo was released without charge, and it was not until 2008, when new techniques revealed a blood-stained towel left at the murder scene had a DNA match for Restivo, that he was to be taken in for questioning again. Even then, he claimed to have left the towel on his visit to order some curtains from Barnett on 6 November 2002.

Once again, it was decided that there was still insufficient evidence to justify his prosecution for murder.

It was not until the body of sixteen-year-old Elisa Clap was finally discovered in the loft of the Church of the Most Holy Trinity in Potenza, Italy in March 2010 that the case against Danilo Restivo strengthened decisively. She had disappeared in September 1993, and was well known to Restivo, whom she had 'taken pity on' before going missing. The Italian investigators found that Clap's bra had been broken in exactly the same manner that Heather Barnett's had, while her trousers had also been damaged and disarranged in the same way.

Every bit as tellingly, Clap's hair had been cut shortly after she had been killed and her body placed in the loft, where remnants of her hair were left with it. The last person to see her alive had been Restivo.

It was the similarity between the two cases that finally convinced the police and the Crown Prosecution Service in 2011 they should proceed against Restivo. Two months after the discovery of Clap's body he was arrested and charged with the murder of Heather Barnett – almost a decade after the crime had been committed. The Italian case played a central part in Restivo's trial, once the judge, Mr Justice Burnett, had ruled that the foreign case could be mentioned as part of the prosecution's case against him, even though – at that point – Restivo had not been convicted of the Clap murder. (That was not to happen until several months later.)

At the opening of Restivo's trial at Winchester Crown Court in June 2011, prosecuting counsel Michael Bowes QC told the jury, ' . . . the circumstances in which Elisa Clap was killed so closely resemble the circumstances in which Heather Barnett was killed that you can have no doubt that both of the killings must have been the work of one person – Danilo Restivo.' He described her killer as 'depraved' and 'callous'.

The jury then heard one psychiatrist's assessment of the reasons for Restivo's actions and, particularly, those parts of his life that may have led him towards a hair fetish and anger at women. The psychiatrist referred to an occasion when Restivo had responded aggressively to bullying when he was thirteen; that he had admitted to voyeurism as a teenager; and that from the age of fifteen he liked to touch and smell the hair of women he came across in public, for example on a bus, and had started to cut it secretly.

The prosecution's psychiatric expert then offered the jury a motive for Restivo's killing. He suggested that the Sicilian, whose family had moved to Potenza when he was a child, may have decided to kill a mother in circumstances that would leave her children to 'fend for themselves' as he felt he had been forced to do himself. This meant he had directed the anger he felt at his own mother's treatment of him on to Heather Barnett and her children. The psychiatrist also maintained that his habit of cutting hair was sexually driven and sadistic, and the murder itself was a sexually sadistic act. Nevertheless, he also concluded that Restivo was mentally fit to stand trial.

Indeed, Restivo did not claim 'diminished responsibility' at his trial, instead he simply pleaded that he was innocent of Barnett's murder and mutilation.

During his trial in June 2011, the jury heard evidence from two local schoolgirls in Bournemouth who had come across Restivo's fetish for cutting the hair of young women. One, Holly Stroud, who had been seventeen in 2003, told the Court that he had cut her ponytail while travelling on a bus around 8 am on 13 March 2003: 'I first thought my hair had got caught on the bus seat, so turned around and was expecting a child from my school teasing me, what I saw shocked me because it was a grown man.' It was not until later that she realised her hair had actually been cut. A year later she identified Restivo from a set of photographs the police showed her of possible suspects. Another local girl, Katie McGoldrick, who was fifteen at the time, also told the Court that she had felt her hair being tugged while travelling on a bus in Bournemouth. It too had been secretly cut.

For his part, Restivo maintained that he had started cutting hair in Potenza at about the age of fifteen for a bet. 'I started liking it,' he told the jury, 'and I kept doing it. The problem was that I liked touching the hair and also smelling it. It was not a sexual attraction.' But the jury did not believe him. They clearly saw the fetish for what it was – a means of sexual arousal.

The schoolgirls' evidence about his hair fetish, together with the similarity between Restivo's behaviour in Bournemouth and in Italy, clearly weighed heavily with the members of the jury. On Wednesday 29 June 2011 they found him guilty, and the following day he was sentenced to life imprisonment – with a whole life term – not least because the judge concluded firmly that he must indeed have killed Elisa Clap.

Sentencing Restivo on Thursday 30 June Mr Justice Burnett told him, '. . . you have not been convicted of that murder and I do not sentence you in respect of it. But it is important background, because I approach this sentence on the basis that you had killed before. It would be quite unrealistic to pretend that you had not.'

The judge then told him, 'You are a cold, depraved and calculating killer,' and went on to describe the killing of Heather Barnett as 'inhuman depravity'.

'I can find no mitigation in this case, none has been advanced on your behalf,' he added. As he spoke some members of the jury, who had returned to hear the sentencing, wept – just as they had done when they had heard the impact statement read to the Court on behalf of the victim's son and daughter.

At the end of his remarks, Mr Justice Burnett said simply, 'You will never be released,' before telling the prison officers in the dock beside him, 'Take him down.'

Restivo received his sentence without a trace of emotion showing on his face.

Outside the Court, Heather Barnett's sister, Denise Le Voir, told waiting reporters that her sister 'would have been horrified by the cruel and callous way Danilo Restivo designed her murder and mutilation so that her children would find her body on return from school.'

Ben Barnett, Heather's brother, added, 'Restivo has already had eight years of freedom that my sister never had. I've thought about the death penalty, but I think it's too good for him. It seems like the easy way out. I think he's going to have a miserable rest of his life in prison.'

But it was Heather Barnett's daughter Caitlin Marsh, by then eighteen, who had found her mother's body together with her elder brother Terry, who was by then aged twenty-three, who made the most dramatic and revealing statement about her mother's murder. She said that her life had 'changed forever' as a result of the killing, and the 'horror' of their discovery of their mother's body.

'It was at that moment,' Caitlin said, 'that I felt as if my heart had been ripped out. I was in a state of complete and utter shock and it took months before I accepted the truth.' Explaining that her brother had now become her 'protector', and the only person she could fully trust, she added, 'I used to have nightmares and flashbacks reminding me of the events of 12 November 2002. I also don't like going into bathrooms. I used to think that someone might be waiting for me. Now I just hold a fear of what's behind the bathroom door.'

Having decided to sit in Court throughout the trial, in order to look Restivo in the eye – which provoked no reaction whatever from the defendant, who remained impassive – Caitlin Marsh explained how she felt when she saw the killer sitting just yards away. 'I feel a great anger at him,' she said. 'Without him she'd still be here. How could he intrude into our safe and happy family home and then take everything from us in such a horrific and callous way? I still have no explanation for why this happened to Mum. What did she do wrong? Why was Mum the victim?'

Detective Superintendent Mark Cooper, who led the investigation, agreed with Caitlin Marsh. 'This was a horrendous and brutal murder,' he said, 'and I cannot even begin to describe him.'

But the judge's decision to allow the Italian case of Elisa Clap's murder into Restivo's trial in Winchester led Edward Fitzgerald QC, who had defended him, to raise the case at the Court of Appeal in the autumn of 2012, and it formed the principal reason for the Court's decision to remove his whole life term.

'We note in particular,' the Lord Chief Justice, Lord Judge, noted in their decision, 'the extensive preparation for the killing (which included careful measures to avoid detection) and the display of sexual perversions and sadism, not least the appalling mutilation of the body, when the appellant knew perfectly well that it would be found by the victim's children.'

The Court also pointed out that Restivo was capable of what it called 'brutal hypocrisy' in the expressions of 'concern and assistance' that he had offered to the children after their mother's body was found.

Given those circumstances, which some, including the judge at his trial, felt fully justified the harshest possible sentence, the Court of Appeal nevertheless decided that instead of being condemned to spend the rest of his life in jail, they would reduce his whole life term to one of a minimum of forty years, although they were at pains to point out: 'We think it highly improbable that it will ever be safe for Restivo to be released from custody.' Even if he were to be released, which would not be possible under the Court's ruling until 2051, Restivo would be seventy-nine years of age.

The decision to lower his sentence provoked a melancholy reaction from Heather Barnett's brother Ben, who had said that he hoped Restivo would have a 'miserable rest of his life in prison'.

'I am not criticising those who have made this decision,' Mr Barnett explained, 'they must do as the law provides, however distasteful this is for all concerned.' But Mr Barnett felt that life should have meant life in his sister's case, as it would have given Restivo an opportunity to reflect on what he had done, although he concluded sadly, 'Somehow I doubt that this would ever have been the case.'

The English judicial system was not finished with Restivo, however. In February 2014, the Home Secretary decreed that he should complete the remainder of his life sentence in Italy, where he had now been convicted of the Clap killing in his absence, and transfer the estimated cost of his imprisonment – some £5m – to the Italian Government.

But Restivo, by then aged forty-one, whose wife still lives not far from the scene of Heather Barnett's murder, claimed he had the right to a family life in England. He launched an appeal in a special Immigration Court, and so far remains in the high-security Full Sutton Prison, near York.

As we know, however, Oakes and Restivo were not the only whole life prisoners dealt with by the specially convened Court of Appeal in the autumn of 2012.

8

'Only for the most heinous of crimes'

Michael Roberts and David Simmons

One of the other cases dealt with by the specially convened Court of Appeal in the autumn of 2012 involved an intensely wicked young man named Michael John Roberts – who became known as the 'Bermondsey Rapist' between 1988 and 1995 while in his twenties. He earned the title with a string of brutal sexual attacks in his native Bermondsey in south London, where he had spent his entire life when not in prison. It was an old-fashioned close-knit community on the south side of the Thames, and Roberts was very much a part of it.

Tall, thin-faced, with scruffy stubble and piercing blue eyes beneath a shock of ruddy brown hair, Roberts was born in April 1966 and quickly developed into a violent, aggressive teenager and then a young man who had launched a spree of burglaries and brutal sexual attacks on the elderly before he reached the age of twenty-five.

Indeed, Roberts committed his worst crimes even before the police became fully aware of his existence as a vicious predator. It was not until 1995, at the age of twenty-nine, that he was first convicted of a sickening attack on an elderly male pensioner near his south London home, and sentenced to six years' imprisonment.

One of his neighbours at the time remembered that Roberts was frequently violent towards his girlfriends, and had been equally violent towards two longer-term female partners. 'You heard him because they was always fighting,' the neighbour explained. 'He had the kids screaming – he used to smash the place up. It sounded like wardrobes were coming down the stairs.'

Little did the neighbours or police know that Roberts had also been committing a string of frightening, degrading attacks on elderly women in the area – all of which took place before his 1995 conviction. In the years between 1988 and 1995, Roberts's attacks created an atmosphere of fear among elderly people in his south London community, although at the time the police had no idea whatever of his identity.

His period of imprisonment in the late 1990s did nothing to lessen Roberts's appetite for violence or crime, and in 2005 he was again convicted of robbery and committing grievous bodily harm on another elderly male pensioner in south London, once again not far from his home. This time he was given a life sentence – though not a whole life sentence – for the crime, allowing the parole board to decide when he might be released.

It was while Roberts was in prison for the 2005 attack that the police opened a 'cold case review' of the attacks committed by the 'Bermondsey Rapist' between ten and seventeen years previously. Improvements in DNA testing meant that the police then identified him as a potential suspect, as they had a record of his DNA in the wake of his 1995 conviction.

They rapidly matched it to the samples taken from the operation to try to track down the man also known as the 'Praying Rapist' – who had been known to cross himself and utter parts of a Catholic prayer during his sexual attacks. Yet few local people in Roberts's part of south London could have imagined that this belligerent local burglar could also be guilty of crimes of quite such sexual depravity.

Roberts's first victim was attacked in December 1988, when he was just twenty-two. She was a fifty-seven-year-old spinster and virgin, who suffered from a degree of disability, and had returned home on Boxing Day after spending Christmas with her family. She found a male intruder in her house.

He demanded to know where she kept her money and jewellery and proceeded to hit her repeatedly, inflicting a series of horrific injuries, including a broken jaw and a fractured eye socket. He also left her with a deep cut above her right eyebrow, while her left breast and shoulders were bruised. There were defensive injuries on both her hands, because she had fought him in an effort to defend herself, but it was to no avail. Her thighs were bruised, with dried blood smeared over the entire surface of her thighs and lower legs.

The ugly truth is that Roberts also raped her, forcing her thighs apart during a prolonged sexual assault. The majority of the blows to her head were caused by his clenched fist, while the injuries to her jaw and eye sockets were caused by separate impacts, possibly by punches or blows from a soft heeled shoe. The injuries above her right ear were more consistent with kicks to her head. It was a merciless attack on a mature, single and vulnerable woman who had done nothing whatever to provoke it. She did not even know Roberts.

Roberts struck again nine months later. This victim lived just a few yards away from his first. She was a seventy-seven-year-old, frail woman with advanced arthritis. On this occasion, however, Roberts was known to his victim. About ten days before the attack, he had suddenly appeared in her sitting room, claiming that he had been chased out of a local pub, but before he could attack her she called out to a neighbour and Roberts ran off.

The false start did not deter him. On 11 September 1989 he again entered her sitting room, demanding to know where her money and jewellery were kept. Roberts also instructed her not to look at him and then ordered her to take off her clothes, threatening her with his fists if she refused. He made her lie on the bed, and then attempted to rape her. But his victim protested volubly, saying she was a single woman who had never had sexual intercourse and did not want to have it now.

Roberts completely ignored her. He then tried to make her kneel on the floor but she told him she could not do so because of her arthritis, so he ordered her back on to the bed, before making her remove her dentures and suck his penis. Roberts then left, taking £5 from her handbag in the kitchen.

Less than a month later Roberts found a third elderly female victim. On 7 October 1989 he attacked her in her flat just over 300 yards from his latest address. Moments after her nephew had left her at the flat door, he rushed in, grabbed her from behind and put his hand over her nose and mouth. He then pushed her into the sitting room and ordered her not to speak, explaining that he could be violent. Desperate to protect herself, his elderly victim told him her nephew would be coming back at any moment, but Roberts ignored her, telling her that she was lying. Indeed the lie served only to make him angrier.

As Roberts had done in the two previous attacks, he demanded to know where she kept her money and jewellery, and then ordered her to take off her clothes. When she refused he started to pull her dressing gown off and, because she was not strong enough to stop him she took off the rest of her clothes herself, as she was clearly terrified. Roberts then proceeded to assault her sexually, eventually forcing her into the bedroom, where he committed a series of repulsive sexual acts against her. By now his victim was shaking and crying, her body bruised and her shoulders heaving with fear. She begged him to leave, but he refused. Desperate to bring an end to the ordeal, which had already lasted almost three hours, she persuaded him to allow her to make him some tea, hoping that might bring him to his senses. It did not.

After taking a drink from a tap in the kitchen Roberts returned and once again attempted to rape her before forcing her to masturbate him. This was followed by a third rape attempt and ejaculation. When he was finished Roberts attempted to remove every trace of his presence in the flat, before finally cutting the telephone cord before he left.

Unable to identify her attacker, and with no leads from the other two attacks, Roberts's attempts to eradicate any trace of his presence from his third victim's flat worked. The police were no nearer finding him than they had been in December the previous year and so, emboldened by his 'success', he struck again.

Towards the end of February in 1990, five months after his last attack, Roberts chose another victim, once again someone living within walking distance of his own flat, and close to the home of his previous victim. He had clearly been watching her for some time, planning his assault. This time she was an eighty-four-year-old woman, living alone in a ground-floor flat. Even more distressingly, she was barely able to walk, due to a recent hip operation, a fact that Roberts must have been aware of.

When she was found, on 2 March 1990, by her 'home help', her injuries were so serious that she was unable to speak or describe anything of what had happened to her.

A medical examination revealed that her upper jaw had been fractured in one place, and her lower jaw in two. The left side of her face was severely swollen, blackened and bruised. But this time there was no evidence of sexual assault, although her telephone cord had been cut.

The police were still completely in the dark about who might have committed these four merciless attacks and, as a result, the local community in Bermondsey was left in a state of shock and fear, which took more than a year to dissipate as the attacks stopped.

When Roberts was eventually arrested for the attack on an elderly male pensioner in 1995, no connection was made with any of his attacks of elderly women, and he certainly did not confess to having committed them. Instead he accepted his six-year prison sentence and served his time without complaint.

It was not until 2005, when he robbed a second elderly man and was sentenced to life imprisonment – though not a whole life term – that the police began to suspect that he may indeed have been the 'Bermondsey Rapist', who had committed the four attacks starting fifteen years earlier.

It was at this point that Roberts was examined by a number of psychiatrists, all of whom concluded that his mental condition was extremely dangerous. They recorded a long history of drink and drug abuse, not to mention obsessive compulsive disorder and depression, and said he should be regarded as having a personality disorder which could, in legal terms, be called a 'psychopathic disorder'.

The psychiatrists concluded firmly that Roberts could not be seen as anything other than 'a danger to the public' and that any treatment for his condition, even after 'the most arduous efforts' was not assured, simply because treatment 'is notoriously unsuccessful'.

Had those psychiatric reports been conducted after Roberts's conviction in 1995 the possibility that he was indeed the 'Bermondsey Rapist' might have been considered, but as it was, no such examinations took place. But one aspect of his 1995 arrest and conviction did come back to haunt him – his DNA.

Not long after Roberts's conviction in 2005, the 'cold case review' discovered that his DNA matched that found at the crime scenes in Bermondsey and, as a result, officers visited Roberts at Wandsworth Prison in south London where he was beginning his life sentence.

When they arrested him for the 'Bermondsey Rapist' attacks, Roberts told them, 'You are having a joke, aren't you?'

But it was not until December 2011 that Michael John Roberts finally stood trial for the four attacks that took place twenty years earlier. He was charged with three counts of rape, four counts of burglary, two counts of indecent assault, two counts of causing grievous bodily harm, and one count of buggery. But he denied them all, protesting his innocence repeatedly from the dock. Tragically, none of his elderly victims had survived to see him brought to trial.

Roberts was still proclaiming his innocence after the jury convicted him on all counts on 20 December 2011 at Southwark Crown Court, and he was shouting in protest at Judge Stephen Robbins when he started to pass sentence on 12 January 2012. That did not prevent the judge reaching a firm conclusion.

'I'm quite satisfied that you are a danger to society, therefore I do sentence you to imprisonment for the rest of your natural life,' Judge Robbins told him. 'Your utter depravity knows no bounds, these are very grave offences.'

Roberts became only the second person ever to be given a

whole life term of imprisonment without having committed a murder. The other was a man named Stephen Ayre in 2006, whose case we shall come to.

'You terrified a whole community of south London,' Judge Robbins went on. 'People in south London had been living in fear that they might be your next victim.'

As for the four victims, the judge concluded: 'Your actions blighted the remaining years of their lives. Their homes should have been their safest refuge, where they could expect to live their lives undisturbed and in peace. You must have distilled complete terror and fear that one can only imagine.'

It was a view shared by the son of one of the Bermondsey victims, who made an 'impact' statement to the court, in which he described his mother's reaction. 'My mother was once a cheerful and kindly person who never used to worry about anything,' he explained. 'That was until the night when she was brutally assaulted. She said later that she thought that night was going to be her last. How anyone can attack a defenceless female in her own home, who is disabled, words fail me.'

The Metropolitan Police knew that only too well. Detective Inspector Nathan Eason, who led the 'cold case' investigation, said forcefully, 'Michael Roberts is a sexual predator who preyed on vulnerable women in the late eighties and early nineties. 'Unfortunately none of his victims lived to see him being brought to justice today but the family members of the victims have expressed deep satisfaction with the judgement handed down today. They take huge satisfaction from the fact that he will never devastate other lives.'

But Michael Roberts's whole life sentence was not destined to last. At the same specially convened hearing of the Court of Appeal just nine months later, in October 2012, he launched an appeal against his whole life term.

The then Lord Chief Justice, Lord Judge, on behalf of the Court, acknowledged the seriousness of Roberts's crimes, and the brutal effect his attacks had had on his elderly victims, pointing out that he had shown no pity or remorse. 'These offences,' Lord Judge said, 'together with some of his earlier convictions, confirm that he was cruel and ruthless and a real and continuing danger, especially to vulnerable people.'

But Lord Judge went on to point out that among the cases where whole life orders had been imposed, 'none could be found in the context of sexual crime where one or more of the victims had not been murdered.' That meant, he explained, that without seeking to trivialise the ordeals of Roberts's four elderly victims, his being handed a whole life order was a mistake, as that sentence should be 'reserved for cases where the criminal went even further'.

'It is regrettably possible to envisage, and there have been cases,' Lord Judge explained, 'where dreadful sexual assaults have been followed by murderous violence.' The central issue, he added, was that a whole life order should be 'reserved for the most exceptional cases'. The Lord Chief Justice then revealed that the Court was not suggesting that a defendant could now be subject to a whole life sentence only if he or she had been convicted 'of at least one murder'.

Given the circumstances, he concluded, the Court had decided to quash the whole life sentence, and in its place substitute a life sentence with a minimum term of twenty-five years – meaning that Roberts could not even be considered for release until he was at least seventy. But Lord Judge added, finally, 'On the evidence before us at the moment it seems highly improbable that he will, after the expiry of twenty-five or thirty or more years, or indeed ever, be safe for release.'

The fact that Roberts had never been convicted of

murder brought him at least the possibility of release, no matter how remote that possibility might be. Yet the irony is that Scotland Yard suspected, but could not prove, that he was linked to the 1990 murder of sixty-eight-year-old Irene Grainey in south London, who was sexually attacked and stabbed to death with a kitchen knife on 31 May 1990. Her body had lain undiscovered for six weeks at her council maisonette in Rotherhithe, and her murder remained unsolved.

Only too aware of the possibility that he might be linked to the Irene Grainey murder, Michael Roberts has remained studiously silent ever since his appeal against his whole life sentence succeeded.

But Roberts was not the only whole life prisoner to be treated more leniently by the specially convened Court of Appeal in their judgement published on 21 November 2012.

David Martin Simmons was aged forty at the time of his appeal eight years after sentencing. The delay was attributed to the confusion over whether a whole life sentence had ever been specifically designated by the judge in his case.

On 17 February 2004 Simmons had pleaded guilty to two charges of rape and false imprisonment and on 9 December 2004 Judge Foley sentenced him to life imprisonment on each of the two counts, but did not add a fixed 'whole life' term.

Shortly after he was sentenced, Simmons was transferred from prison to Broadmoor Special Hospital, where he spent the next six years before being transferred back to Bristol Prison in 2010. When he got to Bristol, however, he was told, allegedly for the first time, that in the absence of any specific term of life sentence, he was now being regarded as a whole life prisoner. Not surprisingly this came as a profound shock to Simmons, and he asked for leave to appeal against a sentence he did not know he had.

Like Roberts, Simmons had not committed murder, although he clearly presented a grave danger to women, and to prostitutes in particular. This may have influenced the judge's decision to give him a life sentence, while not indicating that it should be a whole life term. Nevertheless, the details of Simmons's case certainly justified his life imprisonment.

Just after midnight on 25 August 2003 Simmons, who was then aged thirty-one, offered a young prostitute a lift in his car, which she accepted. But almost immediately after she had climbed into the passenger seat he produced a knife and held it to her throat. Simmons then drove to an industrial estate. He tied her hands behind her back and blindfolded her, before pushing the passenger seat right back so that she was forced to lie almost flat. He then removed her shoes, her jeans and her knickers, before putting his fingers inside her. Then, using a condom, Simmons climbed on top of her and unsuccessfully attempted to penetrate her without achieving any kind of climax.

Frustrated, Simmons then used great force to penetrate her vagina and ejaculated inside her. He removed her from his car, washed her vagina and anus with wine, before putting her jeans back on, tying her to the passenger seat and driving her, still blindfolded, to another industrial estate. There Simmons pulled her out of his car and put a jumper over the back of her head, using part of it in her mouth as a gag and then securing it there with a rope. He then told his young and helpless victim that he was going to 'slit her throat', but had to get a bigger knife to do so. She was utterly terrified and in desperate fear for her life, but Simmons never returned, and eventually she managed to attract the attention of a security officer on the industrial estate and the police were called.

Simmons had something of a reputation for attacking

prostitutes and, as a result, was interviewed several times by the police after this attack. He told them that he had indeed been with a prostitute that night and had agreed a price for certain sex acts, before adding that he had 'lost the plot', although he did not remember exactly what had happened. But he denied that he had ever threatened her or done anything against her will.

In fact Simmons had a number of previous convictions for assaulting women, including two in 2000, one for an indecent assault and one for robbery. Those offences had many similarities to this new case. In one, the victim was a working prostitute when he forced her to perform oral sex on him and then masturbate him. He also threatened her with a knife to her throat, and inserted his fingers into her vagina. In the other case, Simmons grabbed another woman in the street from behind, told her that he had a knife and that he would kill if she did not shut up. He then robbed her.

On 17 February 2004, when Simmons finally arrived in Court over the attack in the previous August, he pleaded guilty to the charges of rape and false imprisonment, and on 9 December 2004 Judge Foley sentenced him to life imprisonment on each count. But Simmons had refused to communicate with the prison authorities or to attend any interviews between pleading guilty and his sentence, which may have led the judge to pass a life sentence.

In his sentencing remarks, the judge said he was satisfied that Simmons posed 'a significant risk to women', and added that it was the wish of the Court that he 'could not be released until (he) ceased to be such a risk', because he was a man of 'unstable character likely to commit similar offences' and 'a danger'.

Judge Foley added that the Court was not required to specify a period 'if it is of the opinion that no period should be specified', and said he was satisfied that a life sentence was appropriate because of the seriousness of the offences and Simmons's history of offending.

The prosecution in Simmons's appeal in the autumn of 2012 accepted that the whole life sentence he had ended up with was inappropriate, and the specially convened Court of Appeal agreed. Lord Judge explained on behalf of the Court, 'As it seems to us, profoundly disturbing as this offence certainly was, it was not an offence of the extreme level of seriousness to justify a whole life order.'

The Court substituted a minimum term of just ten years for Simmons's whole life sentence, although they were at pains to point out that by quashing the whole life term they were 'not suggesting for one moment that Simmons will be safe to be released at the conclusion of the ten year period'. Lord Judge went so far as to conclude, 'We note that it has been necessary for him to spend time in Broadmoor Hospital, and we suspect that his release is most unlikely.'

Nevertheless, it represented a remarkable turn of events for a man who could have been facing another thirty or more years in prison without a realistic possibility for release. Whether David Martin Simmons will ever see life beyond a prison cell or a secure hospital ward is a matter for the prison or hospital authorities – but there is now at least the possibility that he might.

Throughout their lengthy judgement on 21 November 2012 about the cases of Oakes, Restivo, Roberts and Simmons, the Court of Appeal went to considerable lengths to point out that each man was dangerous, before adding, 'on the available evidence, likely to remain dangerous for the indefinite future. At present it is difficult to see how it will ever become safe for any of them to be released from custody.'

They also took pains to explain their views about the concept of a 'whole life term' using case law in England and Wales that had been built up over the previous decade. It is a judgement worth reading in full, for it presents the finest and most coherent argument on both sides of the debate, while still coming down firmly in favour of the principle of a 'whole life term' remaining in force.

In particular, Lord Judge went to considerable lengths to represent the views of many senior judges on the issue. He explained, for example, that every civilised country embraces the idea encapsulated in Article Three of the European Convention of Human Rights, which says, 'No one shall be subjected to torture or to inhuman or degrading treatment or punishment.' But he went on to add that every civilised country also 'embraces the principle that just punishment is appropriate for those convicted of criminal offences'. Lord Judge concluded that the issues that related to 'just and proportionate punishment' should be the subject of 'rational debate and civilised disagreement'.

The Lord Chief Justice pointed out that one of his senior colleagues, Lord Justice Laws, had expressed his doubts about whole life terms of imprisonment in a 2007 judgement, in which he said: '. . . a prisoner's incarceration without hope of release is in many respects . . . a sentence of death. He can never atone for his offence. However he may use incarceration as time for amendment of life, his punishment is only exhausted by his last breath . . . The supposed inalienable value of the prisoner's life is reduced, merely to his survival: to nothing more than his drawing breath and being kept, no doubt, confined in decent circumstances. That is to pay lip-service to the value of life; not to vouchsafe it.'

That was a similar view, he went on, to that expressed in the European Court of Human Rights in the case of

Gary Vinter, but, on the other hand, there were certainly some eminent judges who took a fundamentally different view.

An earlier Lord Chief Justice, Lord Bingham, certainly did. In passing judgement on the Moors murderess Myra Hindley's appeal for release from prison in 1998, Lord Bingham stated firmly, 'I can see no reason, *in principle*, why a crime or crimes, if sufficiently heinous, should not be regarded as deserving life-long incarceration for purposes of pure punishment.' He then concluded, 'Successive Lord Chief Justices have regarded such a tariff as lawful, and I share their view.'

Myra Hindley's appeal was dismissed in the Court of Appeal, and was also dismissed in the House of Lords – then the highest Court in England and Wales, though it has since been succeeded by the Supreme Court.

In the House of Lords, Lord Steyn agreed with Lord Bingham that some crimes 'would be sufficiently heinous to deserve life-long incarceration for the purposes of pure punishment'. He added, 'There is nothing logically inconsistent with . . . saying that there are cases where the crimes are so wicked that even if the prisoner is detained until he or she dies it will not exhaust the requirements of retribution and deterrence.'

It was a fierce judgement, but one widely subscribed to by a succession of the most senior judges in the country, a fact which Lord Judge pointed out in the November 2012 Court of Appeal judgement on Oakes and the others.

In particular he pointed to a 2009 judgement by Baroness Hale, now Deputy President of the Supreme Court, in which she observed, 'I do understand the philosophical position, that each human being should be regarded as capable of redemption here on earth as well as hereafter. To those who hold this view, the denial of the possibility of redeeming oneself in this life by repentance and reform may seem in-human. I myself was brought up in that tradition. But ... that is not the only tenable view of the matter. ... there are many justifications for subjecting a wrongdoer to a life in prison.'

Lord Judge concluded by saying that the judges were, after all, only carrying out the 'settled will of Parliament' which removed the possibility of imposing a whole life sentence from the politicians and placed it in the hands of the judges as a 'discretionary element of sentencing'. There was no escaping the fact, he concluded, that the Court of Appeal in England and Wales had persistently argued in favour of the whole life term for the most heinous offences, no matter what the European Court of Human Rights might say.

Yet the Court of Appeal can make controversial decisions – even where the most heinous of crimes are involved. It cer-tainly did so in the case of American David Francis Bieber, who killed a serving police officer and attempted to murder two others on 26 December 2003 in Leeds, Yorkshire. The incident lasted for just eight seconds, but it reverberated throughout the criminal justice system for several years and came to epitomise the complexities of the argument about whole life terms.

The case of David Bieber was the very first time that a judge rather than the Home Secretary imposed a whole life term of imprisonment, but to understand its significance we need to go back to the beginning.

9

'He kills coppers'

David Bieber

It was a grey, dull Boxing Day in 2003 and two traffic officers from West Yorkshire Police – PC Ian Broadhurst, aged thirty-four, who had been married for just two years, and PC Neil Roper, aged forty-three – were out on a perfectly routine patrol in Leeds, when they encountered a monster intent on killing them both.

The two men had been put together as partners just a few months earlier and had become close friends. They had even had breakfast together that morning with Broadhurst's mother Cindy, and were in good spirits. 'He was my mate, not just a policeman,' Roper was to say later of Broadhurst. 'He was just a genuine fella that got on with everybody.'

'Boxing Day is generally a quiet day,' Roper remembered, and as a result the officers were spending their time on patrol looking for stolen cars, or 'anybody that is doing something that draws our attention'. In the short time since they had joined forces the two constables had developed an almost uncanny ability to spot stolen vehicles – and this day immediately after Christmas would be no different. Yet it would cost Broadhurst his life.

In their easily identifiable police car, they were touring the border between the Gipton and Oakwood areas of Leeds in south Yorkshire when they spotted a car parked down an alley at an unusual angle – and outside a post office. A large man, with a dark moustache and dark hair, was sitting in the driving seat reading a newspaper.

'I just basically saw this black 3-series BMW parked up on the causeway in a – how can I put it – a peculiar position,' Roper recalled. 'We went slowly past the passenger side of the vehicle. I looked in and saw this white man reading a *Racing Post*.'

Broadhurst and Roper instinctively thought the car might have been stolen and radioed in to the control room to check. Their instinct had been right. The BMW had been stolen. The two officers climbed out of their police car and walked towards the car and its driver, but as they did so Roper became increasingly nervous. The man was huge and well-muscled. The two officers politely asked him to get out of his car and join them in their police car. He was then asked to sit in the back, while they sat in the front.

'In the police car there is a button that you press which gives you the facility to record anything that's being said in the car,' Roper explained later, and a record of what happened next was caught on the tape. The man from the BMW confidently told the two officers that he was from Leeds, but that he had been born in Canada, and added, 'Just to let you know – I did not steal the car.'

His dismissive, almost arrogant, attitude did nothing to calm Roper's nerves, and he decided that the safest thing was to handcuff the man, who was now clearly a suspect in a case of car theft. So Roper, the older of the two officers, got out of the police car and called another officer on his personal radio before he climbed into the back to handcuff him.

This left PC Ian Broadhurst alone with the suspect in their police car. Moments later, another uniformed officer,

PC James Banks, arrived and PC Broadhurst also got out of the police car to join his two colleagues. None of the three officers was armed in any way – apart from their truncheons.

'I said to James,' Roper recalled, '"When I'm cuffing him, can you just watch my back?" But then, as I've looked forward, I've just seen this gun coming up to my face.'

'He's got a gun!' Roper shouted at the top of his voice, but at that very moment the man in the back of the police car fired four shots in the space of three seconds. The shots were all recorded on the tape inside Broadhurst and Roper's police car.

Roper was hit in the shoulder and stomach, but somehow made it to a nearby building and radioed for help.

'I've been shot twice,' he told the control room. 'I don't know about Ian, he's down on the floor.'

Broadhurst had been shot in the chest and had slumped to the pavement.

The fourth bullet hit PC Banks, but he was saved from injury by the simple fact that the bullet had ricocheted off his police radio.

Five seconds later, and with Roper and Banks now taking cover, the man in the back of the police car got out and calmly walked across to Broadhurst's prone body. He shot him one final time, in the head, executing a defenceless serving policeman on duty without the slightest sign of panic or remorse.

Even more terrifying, the tape-recording from the police car revealed PC Broadhurst pleading for his life. As the man pointed his revolver at his head, he is heard saying, 'No don't, don't. Please, please no.'

It made no difference whatever. The young officer was dead, and his killer simply ran off down the alley, abandoning his stolen car. Minutes later he hijacked a car at gunpoint outside a nearby betting shop and disappeared.

What had started as a perfectly ordinary traffic incident over Christmas suddenly became a national tragedy. PC Broadhurst was the first British police officer to be killed while on duty for seven years, and his murder sparked a frantic, nationwide manhunt for his executioner. Yet all the police truly knew about the killer was that he was armed and ruthless.

Detective Chief Superintendent Chris Gregg, the senior detective on call that day, remembered exactly what happened. 'It was as cold-blooded an execution as you can imagine,' he said later. 'This was a dangerous criminal who was on the run.'

The only evidence DCS Gregg had that might help to establish his identity were two newspapers and a half-eaten chocolate bar, all of which had fingerprints on them and which he had left behind in the stolen BMW.

Those fingerprints yielded no match to anyone in the police database, but a videotape from the inside the post office showed the driver inside the shop just minutes before the shooting. That, at least, gave the police an image of the man they were looking for. And there was also the recording of the man's voice in Broadhurst and Roper's police car.

An audio expert, Dr Peter French, was called in to analyse it. 'He'd made a claim during the course of the arrest that he was, in fact, Canadian,' French explained. But to his trained ear it was clear that the man was American, not Canadian, and came from the southern states of America, although Dr French could not be sure exactly which of the southern states. He suggested to the police that the accent might be found in 'Georgia, Alabama and, of course, Florida'.

Then, in an effort to pin down the identity of PC Broad-hurst's killer, the police made a series of appeals to the public for their help to identify him. They got it.

'We received an anonymous phone call, from a man who said, 'I know an American guy. He has a gun and he has a black BMW.' DCS Gregg recalled, 'He just gave us the name Nathan. And a mobile phone number. Through that mobile phone number we tracked down a man using the name Nathan Wayne Coleman.'

The police now had a name, and some idea of where he had been living, but they knew little else about him. They were soon to discover that he was a very dangerous man indeed, but that his name was not Nathan Wayne Coleman. It was David Francis Bieber, then aged thirty-seven, a 220-pound professional bodybuilder who had been on the run from a charge of conspiracy to murder in Florida for the past eight years.

'He could've been a model. He was a good-looking guy,' recalled Bobby Ammons, who grew up with Bieber in Fort Myers, Florida. 'The kinda shape he was in is phenomenal. Of course, he drove around in, you know, a nice car. And he always had money.' Bieber had also become addicted to steroids as a teenager, desperate to become an American Marine.

By the age of eighteen, in 1984, Bieber had transformed himself into a muscle-bound hunk, but one with no appetite for authority. After joining the Marines he rapidly realised that taking orders was not for him, and after just two years he was discharged from the service. Bieber turned to body-building full time, entering professional contests and winning them. But he also developed a sideline in selling the steroids he had become addicted to illegally.

Spending more and more time at the gym, Bieber had encountered fellow bodybuilder Markus Mueller, a German immigrant to the United States and as large and muscled as he was. The two men had become friends. Mueller had a small career as an actor, playing heavies in low-budget movies, but he also had a sideline in importing steroids from Europe – illegally.

In October 1994, Mueller and his girlfriend, Danielle Labelle, were arrested on drugs charges, and both pleaded guilty. What did not emerge in Court, however, was that Bieber was also part of their operation. Indeed he had ambitions to take over from Mueller and run the entire business himself. As it turned out he also wanted Mueller's girlfriend Danielle. They started an affair, and after just a few weeks got married.

When she spoke on Fox Television's show, *America's Most Wanted*, Danielle explained, 'I was seeing both Markus and David. I loved Markus but David was just fun to hang out with.'

Just after noon on 10 February 1995 this love triangle came to the attention of the Florida police, when Markus Mueller's dead body was discovered. He had been shot in the head and in the stomach. The body was found by Bieber's wife – Mueller's former girlfriend – Danielle Labelle, and it was she who called 911.

In fact it was Bieber who had driven her to Mueller's house – ostensibly to collect something she had left there when they were still together – and he was still there with her when the Florida detectives arrived, looking relaxed and as if nothing unusual had happened. The reason was that he had arranged for a hitman to kill Mueller, and thereby provided himself with a perfect alibi for the time of the murder.

The detective in charge of the case, Barry Futch, quickly concluded that Bieber was behind the murder. 'He had two reasons for knocking Markus off,' he said afterwards. 'One was the steroid business. And two was Danielle. So he just decided to get rid of him. And then he would have the girl and he would have the drugs ... I told him that day, "You know you're involved in this. And we're gonna prove it.'"

Bieber was to go to great lengths to make sure he was never caught, just as he was later to make sure that Danielle did not tell the world that he had arranged for the killing of her former partner, and had stolen thousands of pounds worth of illegal steroids from Mueller after the killing. It was to take the Fort Myers' police several months to unravel the grim reality behind Mueller's murder – but when they finally contacted him, David Bieber realised that the game was up and promptly disappeared.

While the Florida police had been examining his alibi, Bieber had been setting about giving himself a completely fresh identity. He did so by visiting a cemetery in Georgia and finding the grave of a six-year-old boy named Nathan Wayne Coleman who had died in 1975. Using a technique outlined in Frederick Forsyth's best-selling thriller *The Day of the Jackal*, Bieber bought a copy of the child's birth certificate and got himself a passport using the dead child's name.

In the autumn of 1996, Bieber, now known as Nathan Wayne Coleman, left the United States and came to England, arriving through the Kent coastal town of Ramsgate on a channel ferry on 26 September, where he used his fake passport to obtain a six-month visa to remain in the United Kingdom.

The drug dealer and bodybuilder was not worried about the time limit. He had already planned to marry a British woman, which would allow him to stay in the country indefinitely, and in March 1997 – shortly before his visa expired – he did indeed marry British girl Denise Horley in Cumbria.

This then was the man that West Yorkshire Police were searching for in the wake of the killing of PC Broadhurst, and it did not take them long to find out more.

DCS Gregg discovered that Coleman/Bieber had been living in England for the past seven years, working as a night-club bouncer, while sustaining his addiction to steroids and bodybuilding. But he had also become a heavy gambler, spending about £300,000 in the three years leading up to the Boxing Day shooting in 2003. Gregg also learnt that Bieber had divorced Denise Horley in May 2002 and that this vain, over-muscled man, who wanted to become known as a gangster, had been living on the edge of the law for years, longing for what he called 'respect'.

On 28 December 2003, two days after the killing of PC Broadhurst, Gregg's team of officers raided Bieber's apartment. He was not there, but he had left substantial amount of evidence behind. 'We found items in there which we knew were connected to the shooting,' Gregg said. 'Whoever had this flat had got an interest in gambling. A gun-cleaning kit was under his bed. There was a bulletproof vest.'

Meanwhile, Coleman/Bieber was popping up on security cameras around Leeds; in particular he had been to several banks, withdrawing £2,900 in cash over a series of visits.

Then the police got another tip from a member of the public. The manager of a storage warehouse in Leeds recognised the name of Nathan Wayne Coleman, and told them that he had a unit there. When the police arrived to examine it, they made a second discovery. It contained hundreds upon hundreds of 9mm bullets, as well the means for creating home-made bullets, including gunpowder and cartridge cases.

The warehouse's video-surveillance footage revealed that Bieber had been there recently, apparently arming himself.

'It showed this character going in with one bag and coming out with another,' DCS Gregg explained. 'And we thought that rucksack was probably packed with ammunition. We were very, very concerned that now there is a man on the run, he is dangerous, and he has killed one cop and shot another. He is probably realizing that he's going to be facing the rest of his life in jail. What has he got to lose?'

At the same time as they were searching the warehouse, the police had submitted the fingerprints they had found in the BMW on Boxing Day to the FBI in the United States, having found no match on any British database. On 30 December 2003 they discovered that they belonged to the man originally known as David Bieber.

The American authorities told the Yorkshire police a great deal about David Bieber, not just that he was wanted for conspiracy to murder, but also that he had disappeared completely in 1996. This knowledge made the British police even more anxious to locate their suspect – in case he tried to leave the country again to escape another crime.

Ironically, on the very day that the Yorkshire police heard from the FBI about the true identity of their suspect, a member of the British public finally found him.

Vicky Brown, a night receptionist at the mock-Tudor Royal Hotel in Gateshead, in the north east of England, recognised a man who had checked in at 3.00 that afternoon, calling himself 'Mr Harris, from 2 Law Street, Notts', as the man she had seen in newspaper stories about the manhunt for the killer of PC Broadhurst.

Indeed Vicky Brown remembered exactly what Bieber looked like. 'Very big, very tall,' she said, 'and he looked quite broad. He was wearing this black, woolly hat pulled right down over his ears, and a big pair of old-fashioned glasses'. She called the hotel owner at home and he telephoned the police.

A team of officers arrived at the Royal Hotel shortly before 2.00 in the early hours of 31 December, 2003, New Year's Eve. Bieber was in a front bedroom upstairs, alone and – the police assumed – prepared to shoot his way out. After all, he had nothing to lose. But this time Bieber was not facing three unarmed officers, he was confronting a fully armed police team, including marksmen with high-powered rifles.

'When he first came to the door, we didn't actually see him,' one of the arresting officers said later. 'The door opened by about an inch, an inch and a half, and then slammed shut quickly after that.' For several minutes there was tense silence, but the police knew that Bieber could not climb out of the window, and that his only way of escape was through the room's front door.

In the end Bieber decided against committing what would have been certain suicide in a shoot-out with the police, and opened the door, dressed in his underpants, with his hair dyed an extraordinary shade of ginger. His first words were, 'You wouldn't shoot an unarmed man, would you?'

Under the bed in Bieber's hotel room the police found the 9mm pistol that had killed PC Broadhurst – fully loaded with fourteen rounds of ammunition – along with another 205 home-made bullets. Bieber refused to utter a single word to the officers in his hotel room after his first question at the entrance. Indeed, from the moment of his arrest and removal to a local police station under armed guard he said nothing.

But when Bieber was brought for trial on one count of murder and two of attempted murder at Newcastle Crown Court in late November 2004, almost a year after his arrest, he comprehensively broke his silence about the killing of PC Broadhurst, testifying in his own defence before the jury, and denying that he killed him.

Towards the end of his eleven-day trial, Bieber admitted being on the scene when PC Broadhurst was murdered – but insisted that the actual shooter was a friend of his from Florida, whom he refused to name. Bieber also denied being in the police patrol car with Broadhurst and Roper.

To refute Bieber's extraordinary denial, the prosecution, with the help of West Yorkshire Police, tracked down one of the telephone gambling companies that Bieber used frequently and asked their voice expert to compare the two recordings. He found the two voices 'very similar' in pronunciation. That evidence, together with the fingerprints found in the BMW that matched Bieber's from the United States, clearly convinced the jury of six men and six women. It took them less than three hours to reach a verdict of guilty.

On 2 December 2004, the trial judge, Mr Justice Moses, told Bieber he had shown 'no remorse or understanding of the brutality' of his crime. He went on to condemn his 'cool and detached approach' in attempting to explain away the evidence against him, and emphasised that both PC Broadhurst and PC Roper had treated him with 'conspicuous fairness and consideration'.

'You repaid their courtesy by killing PC Broadhurst and attempting to murder PC Roper,' Mr Justice Moses went on. In particular he drew attention to the fact that there was no need whatever to shoot PC Broadhurst a second time, in the head.

'You had already disabled him and he was defenceless,' the judge concluded. 'You could have escaped then but you chose to wait and fire a second shot at point-blank range . . . It must be acknowledged that he might have died as a result of your first shot, but you made certain of his death. To shoot and kill an officer in such circumstances, doing no more than trying to serve us all, is an attack on all of us.'

An emotionless Bieber, who stood unblinking in the dock, was given three life sentences, and Mr Justice Moses exercised the power the judiciary now had – under the Criminal Justice Act 2003 – to recommend that he should never be released.

The ever-arrogant Bieber had no intention of taking his conviction, or his sentence, lying down, however. He immediately instructed his legal team to launch an appeal, which was heard almost two years later, on 24 October 2006. At the Court of Appeal Bieber failed to secure the right to appeal against the conviction, but he was granted leave to appeal against his whole life sentence.

Two more years passed until Bieber's second Court of Appeal hearing – this time on his whole life sentence. The result was something of a victory for Bieber.

On 3 August 2008, the Court of Appeal, led by Lord Phillips, then the Lord Chief Justice, decided to replace Bieber's whole life term with a fixed term of thirty-seven years. It meant that he would have to remain in prison at the least until 2041 and the age of seventy-five, and even then there was no certainty that he would be released immediately. But there was now at least a glimpse of freedom for this merciless killer of a policeman.

It was a decision that surprised some in the judiciary, and infuriated both PC Broadhurt's family and the British Police Federation.

The Federation's chairman, Paul McKeever, bitterly condemned the three Court of Appeal judges' decision. In a letter to Lord Phillips, he said, 'Granting an evil, calculating killer any kind of dispensation is criminal and leaves the judiciary with blood on its hands. The decision to surrender to the appeal of this cold-blooded murderer is nothing but unforgivable. I urge you to do whatever is needed to reverse this travesty of justice.'

Explaining that his heart 'goes out to PC Ian Broadhurst's family' he went on, 'This is shockingly disrespectful to his memory and illustrates the utter travesty of our criminal justice system, where the rights of a cop killer outweigh the rights of a fallen officer's family, friends and colleagues. David Bieber is a monster with no consideration for life.'

PC Broadhurst's mother, Cindy Eaton, told one newspaper, 'I feel cheated and let down on behalf of my family. I brought them up to believe that for every choice you make there is a consequence and you live by it. I don't see Mr Bieber in any other light. He chose to do what he did and this is the consequence. I don't think he has any rights. We can never go back to the life we had. He has no idea about our pain.'

The fact that the Court of Appeal's decision might have been influenced by Bieber's legal team's argument about the European Court's suggestion that a whole life term might be 'inhuman' only served to heighten the sense of injustice that the Federation and PC Broadhurst's family felt.

Meanwhile, Detective Chief Superintendent Chris Gregg said, 'As a police officer one of the most frustrating things is when killers who have shown not one ounce of compassion for their fellow human beings start trying to have the shield of human rights drawn around them.'

Privately, Bieber was not intending to wait until he was seventy-five before leaving the English prison system. Even before the Court of Appeal's decision to quash his whole life term, he had been planning escape attempts, some of them involving the use of firearms. In one he had asked a former inmate, who had become a friend, to organise a helicopter to send down a revolver on the end of a rope which he could use against any prison officer that attempted to prevent him being lifted up and out of the prison on the same rope.

In one of four other known attempts, Bieber arranged for a gun to be smuggled in to a prison wedding, which he intended to use to hold at least one prison officer hostage to leverage his release. In another he faked high blood pressure to encourage the prison authorities to allow him out of prison to visit a hospital near by, having arranged for a gang of armed men to snatch him from the prison officers' hands. The prison authorities did not fall for his scheme.

Bieber discussed getting false passports and driving licences with another former cell-mate who had also been released, as well as plans to travel to Scotland, and later Ireland, where he would undergo plastic surgery to disguise his appearance still further. None of these plans succeeded – after his former cell-mate sold the story to the media.

In 2010 Bieber was suddenly moved from the high-security Full Sutton Prison near York to the equally high-security prison at Belmarsh, south-east London after the Serious Organised Crime Agency received information that there was a 'serious threat' that he might attempt to escape. Typically, Bieber reacted by launching an appeal for a judicial review against the move, claiming that it was 'unlawful'. The claim was rejected in May 2011.

That did nothing to lessen Bieber's sense of his own importance. After the quashing of his whole life term he launched a series of four legal appeals – all of them brought using public funds under the legal aid scheme and costing the taxpayer at least £12,000. He argued that he should not be categorised as a 'high security risk'.

On 22 July 2014 at Newcastle Crown Court, Mr Justice Mostyn pointed out, 'Since his incarceration, Bieber has occupied himself by making numerous applications to the

High Court about the conditions in which he is being held.'
Each one of Bieber's previous legal challenges, the judge
added, had been designed to make sure that 'his life is a little
more comfortable' in prison.

On Bieber's behalf, however, his barrister argued that the
director of high security, who took the decision as to his
security clearance, had failed to disclose all the information
he took into account when making his decision. He insisted
that Bieber's human right to a fair hearing had been violated.

In a handwritten document submitted to the Court, Bieber
himself demanded that he be given more access to certain
prison facilities – including the gym – and that he be removed
from a secure underground unit. The unit, one of only three
in the country, houses twelve of the most dangerous prisoners and is sealed off from the main jail and guarded round
the clock.

Bieber argued that there is 'no reason why I should be
subjected to this environment', claiming that he now exhib-
ited 'model behaviour'.

In the most extraordinary passage of his document, Bieber even complained about the 'horrible effect' the 'foolish
and disproportionate violence' of his shooting had had on
him as well as the victim. It was the first time an 'exceptional-
risk' inmate had challenged their status.

Dismissing the claims as 'completely untenable', Mr Justice Mostyn declared, 'The offence here was at the upper end
of bestial. For someone to have committed such a grievous
crime he must have no control when he has normal human
contact.' He added, 'It is therefore perfectly reasonable to
suppose that somebody who has committed a crime as grave
as this, and who has accepted in no respect at all the reason
for his incarceration, would make every effort to escape from
prison at the first opportunity.'

Bieber is now categorised as one of only two 'exceptional risk' prisoners in prison in England and Wales, because of his determination to escape. It is all the more surprising then that his whole life term should have been quashed, given his propensity for violence and his utter contempt for the judicial system.

The Court of Appeal's decision to quash Bieber's whole life term underlines the confusion that haunts the system for the worst of the worst offenders in England and Wales.

To some members of the Court it would seem that the execution of a serving police officer on duty could not be described as sufficiently 'heinous' as to justify a whole life term. Indeed the Court has notably not insisted on a whole life term for other killers of on-duty police officers.

There could be no better example than Britain's most famous police killer, Harry Roberts, a carpenter and armed robber from Essex who was convicted of killing three police officers in 'cold blood' at Braybrook Street in Shepherd's Bush, west London, on 12 August 1966 at the age of thirty. Roberts was never sentenced to a whole life term of imprisonment for his crimes. Instead he was given life imprisonment with a minimum term of thirty years. His killings came just eight months after the official abolition of the death penalty in England and Wales in 1965.

At his trial in December 1966 Roberts pleaded guilty to killing two of the police officers, while his two fellow robbers denied all the charges against them. All three were convicted of the murders of the three officers and sentenced to thirty years each.

The trial judge, Mr Justice Glyn-Jones, commented that the killings were 'the most heinous crime to have been committed in this country for a generation of more'. John Duddy, who was convicted alongside Roberts, died in prison in 1981, while the other robber, Jack Whitney, was released in 1991 (after just twenty-five years), only to be beaten to death at his home in Bristol eight years later.

In spite of his thirty-year term, Roberts went on to become one of the country's longest-serving prisoners, spending almost half a century behind bars before his eventual release in November 2014, at the age of seventy-eight. Interviewed in 2008 in prison, the grey-haired Roberts explained that he had changed in the more than forty years since he had committed the crime.

'I am not that person any more,' he said.

Speaking of his victims' families, he went on: 'Of course I regret it. If anyone had killed my mother I would never have forgiven them, and I totally understand why the families of the policemen could never forgive me and wouldn't want me released. But I feel I have served my time.'

Commenting on the length of his sentence, and his continued incarceration long after his thirty-year minimum term had been completed, Roberts was careful to be non-committal. 'I don't think it's political,' he said. 'I think it's more to do with civil servants fearing what the papers would say if I did do something again. I think that's what it is, but it's ridiculous. I'm just not interested in anything like that any more. I want to get out of prison and just try to make something of the last few years of my life.'

Roberts did not always felt like that. In his first two decades in prison, he made no fewer than twenty-two escape attempts. 'It was a hobby for me,' he said. 'I knew I wasn't coming out for a long time, so I had nothing to lose.' In one attempt his mother smuggled a pair of bolt cutters into the prison in her bra. 'We cut through part of the fence, but there wasn't time to finish the job, so we planned to go back the next night. What we didn't know was that there was an informer on the team who grassed us up before I could escape,' Roberts remembered.

Eventually Roberts gave up the struggle to escape. 'I decided the best way to get out was to stay clean and do my time,' he said.

His plan succeeded because in 2001 he was moved to an open prison and allowed to work daily at a nearby animal sanctuary in Derbyshire. But on 1 October 2001 he was recalled to a closed prison in the wake of allegations that he was involved in drug dealing for the prisoners, was actively engaged in other criminal activity and had made veiled but violent threats while working outside the prison.

In 2009 the *Mail on Sunday* newspaper revealed that a string of secret complaints against Roberts had been made by other workers at the animal sanctuary, who alleged that attacks on their animals after he returned to a closed prison had been co-ordinated by Roberts, and that he had subjected them to threatening telephone calls and promised the 'tearing limb from limb' of anyone who tried to block his release. The newspaper also disclosed that in December 2006 the Parole Board had written to Roberts, in the wake of these allegations, saying that it would not be recommending his release. For his part Roberts firmly denied the allegations.

The relatives of Roberts's police victims felt strongly that he should die behind bars. The sister of one of the plain-clothed detectives he killed said: 'Harry Roberts should never be released. There will never be enough time to make up for the terrible thing that he did. He is a dangerous man and, despite the time, he should remain in jail.'

The Metropolitan Police Federation agreed. Peter Smyth, the then chairman, commented, 'There are some evil acts for which there is no forgiveness, Every police officer still considers these awful murders to be one of the most awful events in our history.' He added, 'There is no death penalty and we fully accept that, but there are some crimes where life should mean life and that includes the murder of a police or prison officer in the course of their duty.'

Nevertheless, late in 2014, eight years after their decision not to recommend Roberts for release, the Parole Board changed its mind and recommended that the seventy-eight-year old should indeed be freed. In November 2014 he left the prison system, although still on licence should he reoffend. Since then Roberts, temporarily at least, has disappeared into obscurity.

Significantly, four other murderers who have killed serving police officers while on duty have also not been sentenced to a whole life term of imprisonment – suggesting that, whatever the Police Federation might urge – the judiciary does not regard the killing of a single police officer as a sufficiently heinous crime to warrant the Court's most severe penalty.

In 1993, for example, the Jamaican-born gangster Gary Nelson, now forty-three, shot and killed Ghanaian-born father of four and nightclub bouncer William Danso at his flat in Clapham. Hearing gunfire, PC Patrick Dunne, aged forty-four, who was attending a minor domestic dispute near by, went into the street to intervene but was shot and killed. Not convicted of the killings until 2006, Nelson has been told that he must serve life imprisonment with a minimum of thirty-five years – not a whole life term.

In another case, the illegal Algerian immigrant Kamel Bourgass killed Detective Constable Stephen Oake in January 2003 when Oake and other officers tried to arrest him in the wake of a plot to flood the London Underground system with the deadly poison ricin. Bourgass has been told that he must spend a minimum of thirty-seven years in prison as part of his life sentence, but again there was no whole life term.

In November 2005, two Somalian brothers, Mustaf and Yusuf Jama killed Woman Police Constable Sharon Besh-enivsky during the course of a Post Office robbery in Bradford. Yusuf was arrested shortly afterwards, while his brother Mustaf fled back to Somalia, only to be extradited to England in 2007 after an undercover operation to locate him. Both men were sentenced to life imprisonment and to serve a minimum term of thirty-five years, not a whole life term.

Ikechukwu 'Tennyson' Obih, a Nigerian, stabbed and killed PC John Henry in Luton, Bedfordshire, when Henry attempted to arrest him after Obih had stabbed a window cleaner in the town shortly after 7 am on 11 June 2007. Diag-nosed as a paranoid schizophrenic, Obih was sentenced to life imprisonment with a minimum term of twenty-five years, once again not a whole life term.

Just one man has been sentenced to life imprisonment with a whole life term by a judge for killing a police officer since 2003, and his name is Dale Cregan. The Manchester gangster killed not one but two female officers in September 2012. As we shall see, his case may help to define the nature of exactly what makes a 'heinous' crime.

10

The One-Eyed Gangster

Dale Cregan

Brought up among the neat rows of red-brick terraced houses in Droylsden, just east of Manchester's city centre, Dale Cregan was a villain from an early age. Born in June 1983, he had become a cannabis dealer while still at school, and by his early twenties had graduated to cocaine. But he was not just a drug dealer, he was also a hard man, a man with an appetite for extreme violence and a member of a criminal underworld that had spread like a malign infection throughout Manchester during his life time. Cregan was a man who gloried in his role in armed robbery, drug dealing and money laundering in the city and its suburbs.

The thin-faced Cregan, whose wiry body concealed the viciousness in his heart, also cut a threatening figure as his left eye had been so badly injured that he had replaced it with a black glass one, giving him a look of particular malevolence. He would tell his friends that he had lost the eye during a fight with a man with a knuckle duster on one of his regular trips to Thailand, but the police believe it was forcibly removed by a member of a rival gang in Manchester as a punishment for Cregan disrespecting them. That was the company he kept and flourished in.

Indeed, it was a fight between two rival gangs in east

Manchester that launched Cregan on the killing spree that would see him kill not one, but two, unarmed uniformed women police constables on a bright September day in 2012.

Cregan's journey to those killings began in his native Droylsden, in a pub called the Cotton Tree just five months earlier. It was there in early May 2012 that a fight broke out between two of Manchester's crime families, the Shorts and the Atkinsons – a fight over the Premier League success of the east Manchester team of Manchester City at the expense of their south-west Manchester counterparts, Manchester United.

There had been a feud between the two families since 2001. It started when one of the younger members of the Atkinson family, Leon Atkinson, hit David Short in the face for 'looking at him'. That ignited a sustained, violent tension between the two families.

'We had another fight after that,' Leon Atkinson admitted later. 'I had a fight with one of their nephews . . . two of their nephews. My brothers had fights with his cousins or nephews.' But the feud escalated significantly in September 2003 when Leon Atkinson's father Francis reportedly had his left knee cap 'blown across' a pub.

Not long afterwards David Short was run off his bike and his throat was cut, though he survived. The Short family become convinced that the man they called Leon Atkinson's 'right-hand man', Dale Cregan, was responsible for the attack. Even so, an uneasy truce had been called when Leon Atkinson and David Short shook hands in Manchester's Arndale Centre in 2008. 'We just said there was no use in fighting,' Atkinson was to say later.

But the war between the two families broke out again with a vengeance four years later with the row about football on that Sunday evening of 13 May 2012. It began when Theresa

Atkinson – the 'matriarch' of the crime family – threw a bottle at a member of the Short family, Raymond Young, who promptly slapped her in response.

Mrs Atkinson warned him fiercely, 'I'm going to get my boys – you're all dead.'

The telephone records show that she did indeed call her son Leon and another son a few hours later, and they also showed that the following morning Leon Atkinson spoke to his mother again before contacting Dale Cregan.

Twelve days later, on Friday 25 May, the Short family and their friends once again gathered at the Cotton Tree pub in Droylsden. The Atkinson family had been planning their revenge for just such a moment. With the Shorts all inside the pub, and due to remain there until midnight, Cregan and two other men, Luke Livesey and Damian Gorman (known as Scarface), pulled up outside in a stolen car.

Moments later a man wearing a black woollen balaclava as a disguise entered the pub and let off a volley of seven shots using a self-loading revolver. He killed twenty-three-year-old Mark Short outright and wounded three other men, narrowly missing a fourth. By sheer chance the head of the family, David Short, was in the toilet during the shooting, and emerged unscathed, only to have his son die in his arms.

The gunman was Dale Cregan, who promptly disappeared from view while the police tried to piece together what had happened. Eventually, Cregan was one of several Manchester criminals arrested and questioned about the murder of Mark Short, but without clear proof he was released on police bail in early June.

By that time Cregan was living in fear of what the Short family might do to him, his partner Georgia Merriman and their four-year-old son in response. But as May turned into June, and then July and August, Cregan decided to prevent the opposing crime family taking any revenge whatever – he resolved to kill David Short.

'I couldn't get him out of my head,' Cregan said later. 'I thought if I kill him, maybe I will get a rest. He threatened my whole family. He told me, "The gloves are off." So I was always going to kill him.'

Even though the police issued forty-six-year-old David Short with three official 'danger to life' warnings during those months, the crime family boss did nothing particular to protect himself. Indeed, he remained at his home address and went about his daily business as usual. That proved to be a fatal mistake – a mistake brought on both by his overconfidence that his own family would always protect him and his certainty that no one would dare to attack him.

On Friday 10 August 2012, Dale Cregan proved him wrong. He and his friend Anthony Wilkinson emerged from a van parked outside Short's house in Clayton, Manchester, and burst in, chasing him through the house and out into the back garden while firing at least nine shots in the process. Cregan killed the crime family patriarch during the chase, but to make sure he was dead he then shot him in the head three times and threw a hand grenade under his body which duly exploded – effectively dismembering his fatally injured body.

Ten minutes later a second grenade was thrown at a house in nearby Luke Road, Droylsden, the home of a woman named Sharon Hark, although this time no one was hurt. The hand grenade was to become Cregan's grim calling card, as WPCs Fiona Bone and Nicola Hughes were to discover a month later.

But the murder of David Short did not prick Dale Cregan's conscience. As he told Dr James Collins, a consultant forensic psychiatrist, 'The night I shot David Short I had the best sleep of my life.'

He also told Dr Collins that Short had threatened to rape his sister and his son, and then to set the four-year-old boy on fire. It was his dread of reprisals, rather than the thought of killing David Short, that had preyed on Cregan's mind. He was later to confess that he had been having fantasies about killing Short for years.

'I could not get him out of my head,' Cregan told the psychiatrist. 'It was on my mind constantly, I could not put the thoughts away. When I was having my fantasies I used to think of stabbing him repeatedly, smashing his head with a hammer and cutting his head off. If I'd had time I would have cut his head off and his arms and legs. I thought if I killed David Short all these thoughts would go away. I did feel better after killing him. I felt better for a couple of days, but all the thoughts came back. The paranoia was so bad that I used to sit in the house on my own.'

To try to escape his paranoid fears, Cregan had gone on holiday to Thailand before he killed David Short, only to be arrested as he got off the plane at Manchester airport when he returned on 12 June 2012 on suspicion of the killing of Short's son Mark. Tragically, three days later the police had to release him on bail while they continued gathering evidence against him. It was while Cregan was on police bail that he shot the head of the crime family.

At the beginning of August, the police had decided to re-arrest Cregan, but when they went to his house he was not at home, having taken his family on holiday to a hotel in Bowness in the Lake District. With the police still searching for him, Cregan killed David Short and was then moved around North Wales and the North of England by a series of accomplices, many of whom were being sought by the police.

At one point he stayed at a hotel and spa in Anglesey, but as the days passed he clearly developed an overwhelming grudge against Greater Manchester Police for not offering protection to him, his wife and son in the wake of the murder of Mark Short. It was a grudge that would lead to more murder.

In sharp contrast, Anthony Wilkinson surrendered himself to the police not long after the David Short killing. But surrender did not suit Cregan's view of himself or his importance in Manchester. Instead he decided to cement his celebrity in the local neighbourhood, which had protected him for more than four weeks, allowing him to visit local pubs and shops with impunity. He resolved to do so by committing a crime so vicious and brutal that it would ensure him fame in the Manchester underworld.

At 10.14 on the clear, fresh Tuesday morning of 18 September, 2012, Cregan, using a false name, called the police and said that someone had thrown a concrete slab through the window of his house in the midst of a burglary and had run off across the nearby fields in Mottram, Manchester. When the police told him that they would be sending officers to investigate, he said calmly, 'I'll be waiting.'

The by-now bearded Cregan had planned for the arrival of two uniformed officers whom he intended to kill. He had armed himself with at least one hand grenade and the same Glock pistol that he had used to kill David Short, although this time loaded with an extended magazine to accommodate more bullets.

Two female police constables, WPC Fiona Bone, aged thirty-two and WPC Nicola Hughes, aged twenty-three, were dispatched to the address Cregan had given to the police, a vacant council house with its windows painted with whitewash so that no one could see inside.

Irrespective of the fact that the officers were women, and clearly unarmed, Cregan carried on with his plan. As the two climbed out of their police van and approached the front door of the house, he opened it and emerged brandishing the self-loading pistol. He then fired all thirty-two bullets in the magazine at them within a period of just thirty-one seconds, in a cold-blooded and utterly ruthless attempt to end their lives.

One of Cregan's first shots hit WPC Hughes in the back, as she turned away from danger, only to leave her paralysed on the ground near the front door. He then pursued her younger companion WPC Bone, firing some twenty shots at her and killing her. At one point she had bravely tried to use her Taser gun to subdue Cregan, only to be killed before she could do so as a bullet penetrated her body armour and hit her in the heart.

Cregan then returned to WPC Hughes, who was lying defenceless, unable to move, outside the house. He shot her in the head no fewer than three times, but he did not even leave matters there. Cregan then took one of his signature hand grenades and exploded it near her body, causing her yet further dramatic injuries. Both officers had been shot at least eight times.

Having achieved his dream and guaranteed his notoriety in Droylsden, Cregan obviously realised that he would be unlikely to escape detection – even though he had considered taking a car ferry to Ireland. Desperate to avoid being caught up in a shoot-out with armed police, he drove himself to Hyde police station in Manchester in a stolen BMW, casually phoning his girlfriend on his mobile phone as he walked into the station and waited at the front desk to be arrested. Wearing a pair of blue shorts and a grey hoodie, he looked for all the world like a man without a care in the world.

When a constable leapt over the front counter, recognising him instantly as the man wanted for the Short murders, Cregan said calmly, 'I'm wanted by the police and I've just done two coppers.'

When asked if he was armed, he simply replied, 'I dropped the gun at the scene and I've murdered two police officers. You were hounding my family so I took it out on yous.' He still had his mobile to his ear as the officer began to handcuff him, carrying on his mobile phone conversation with his girlfriend, seemingly oblivious to the two murders he had just committed in cold blood.

It was the final public act of a vainglorious, ruthless killer, though Cregan did admit to the officers who formally arrested him later that afternoon, 'Sorry about those two that have been killed, I wish it was men.'

He may have meant it, though I fundamentally doubt it, as Cregan had more than enough time to abort his attack when officers Hughes and Bone arrived at his door. It is far more likely that the ever-vain Cregan was being facetious. That certainly fits in with the description of him by a leading psychologist.

Elie Godsi, a consultant criminal psychologist, said after his arrest that Cregan displayed all the characteristics of a psychopath and may have killed the PCs because 'he wanted to go out in some sort of distorted blaze of glory'. He added, 'In the criminal underworld there are not only people taken out because of turf wars and disputes . . . there is also a very strange moral code where people mustn't be offended, you must save face . . . Perhaps in some circles the murder of police has some sort of kudos attached to it.'

'Grandiosity is central to the behaviour of psychopaths,' Godsi went on, 'because usually their lives are quite pathetic, empty and meaningless . . . so they have to create a very distorted sense of their own self-worth. The other side of that is that other people are not important to them.'

Sir Peter Fahy, the then Chief Constable of Greater Manchester Police, also believes that Cregan wanted to be seen as a 'folk hero' by the criminal underworld by killing police officers before his inevitable capture for the Short murders.

'I do think that was part of his plan, trying to get the hero status,' Sir Peter said after Cregan's arrest. 'He handed himself in because he feared that if he engaged with police officers, he would have been shot. That's why he desperately got into the car and raced to the station.'

But there were elements of envy as well as fear among the people around Cregan in his neighbourhood in Manchester. As one local resident put it later, 'People like Cregan were living a lifestyle that was far beyond most people's means. Trips away, decent cars, I mean it was pretty obvious what people are up to when you go to school or the nursery in the morning and someone turns up in a four-by-four with a blazing suntan.'

Violence, drugs and an insatiable appetite for local celebrity were among the ingredients that helped to turn Cregan into the killer of two innocent policewomen and two local gangsters. He may have had psychopathic elements to his personality, but he was also self-obsessed and manipulative, a bully who liked nothing more than to have people live in fear of him. He could not bear to go unnoticed.

That helps to explain why Cregan pleaded not guilty to four murder charges and three attempted murder charges when his trial opened at Preston Crown Court on 4 February 2013. Relishing in the extraordinary security at the Court, which included around 150 armed officers at a cost of some £5m, and the fact that the prosecution would have to lay out in detail the brutal reality of his crimes before the families of the victims, Cregan preened in the dock. He wanted the world to know who he was and what he was capable of.

Wearing a yellow sweatshirt, Cregan sat impervious to anything around him as the prosecution opened their case against him before the Honorable Mr Justice Holroyde. It was not until four days into the trial – significantly, after the prosecution had detailed his ruthless killings of the two policewomen – that Cregan changed his plea from not guilty to guilty in respect of their murders. But, equally significantly, he did not change his plea in respect of the killings of Mark and David Short; there was still his reputation as the leading hard man among the Manchester underworld to be embellished.

It was to be more than two months, after the full extent of his involvement in the killings of the Shorts had been revealed in Court, before Cregan changed his plea a second time and admitted those murders as well. The extraordinary publicity the trial received and the attention that was paid to his part in it helped to feed Cregan's vanity and his image as a hero in the underworld community.

Finally, on 5 June 2013, the jury retired to consider their verdict after a seventeen-week trial. The only issue for them in Cregan's case was whether he was to be convicted of the attempted murder of Sharon Hark in the wake of his killing of David Short on 10 August 2012 – as he had by now pleaded guilty to the four murders he was charged with initially.

But there were his accomplices and co-defendants to consider, none of whom had pleaded guilty at the outset, including Leon Atkinson, who had been with him when Cregan killed David Short, and Luke Livesey and Damian Gorman, who had gone with him to kill Mark Short in the Cotton Tree pub.

Seven days later, on 12 June, the jury returned the first of the verdicts – ironically clearing Cregan of the attempted murder of Sharon Hark. The following day Mr Justice Holroyde delivered his sentencing remarks. They provide an eloquent explication of Cregan's crimes, but the judge was also intent on explaining to the Court the detailed reasoning that lay behind the sentences he was about to pass on the gangsters in the dock in front of him.

Dealing with the assassination of Mark Short first, Mr Justice Holroyde told Cregan, 'I have no doubt that you intended to kill him, not merely to cause him serious injury . . . you were trying to kill as many persons as you could.'

Turning to the killing of Mark's father, David, the judge went on, 'I have no doubt that you had been planning to kill David Short ever since he had escaped death at the Cotton Tree. I have no doubt that you were determined to carry out that plan and murder the man you hated whilst you were still able to do so.' The judge added that the fact Cregan was on police bail at the time was 'an aggravating feature'.

Examining the killings of WPC Hughes and WPC Bone, Mr Justice Holroyde was withering in his condemnation of Cregan's murderous scheme. 'You lured two female officers to their deaths by making a false report that you had been the victim of a crime. I have no doubt that you were expecting one or more unarmed officers to attend, and that is what happened. You had armed yourself with at least one grenade, and with a self-loading pistol to which you had fitted an extended magazine containing thirty-two rounds. PC Fiona Bone and PC Nicola Hughes were sent in response to your call for help, performing their public duty for the public good.'

The judge pointed out that their good intentions had no impact whatever on Cregan's evil intent, not least because he could clearly see from his position within the house that they were unarmed female officers, and that the element of surprise he had over them as a result enabled him to shoot them without their having any chance whatever to defend themselves or take cover.

Every bit as significantly, Mr Justice Holroyde then pointed out that Cregan's use of a hand grenade was something that the 'Criminal Courts in this country had never encountered before', and was, therefore, an exceptional 'aggravating feature' of the crime.

'The crime of murder ends one life but ruins many more,' he went on. 'The harm you have caused, and the pain, anguish and misery you have inflicted, extend far beyond those who were killed and injured by your individual and collective acts.'

Looking sternly across the courtroom to the dock, Mr Justice Holroyde paused and added, 'I have seen no sign of any real remorse or of any compassion for your victims. None of you has shown any sign that you care at all for the death and injury you have caused to your immediate victims or of the immense harm you have done to many others. Self-interest has been the motivating force for each of you.'

But Mr Justice Holroyde took considerable pains to explain that life imprisonment with a whole life term was reserved for the 'few most exceptional offences', in which the judge is satisfied that the 'element of just punishment and retribution requires the imposition of a whole life order.'

'It is important that you the defendants, and the general public, should understand what that means in practice,' he went on. In one of the most precise and careful descriptions of sentencing the most dangerous and vicious offenders, and what exactly a life sentence for murder meant in the wake of the 2003 Criminal Justice Act, the judge carefully explained what a minimum term meant.

'If the court specifies a minimum term, you cannot be released until that minimum term has expired,' Mr Justice Holroyde said. 'But even then you will not automatically be released. You will not be released unless and until the Parole

Board are satisfied that it is safe to release you into the community. That time may never come. Even if you are released on licence, that is not the end of your sentence. You will remain subject to the conditions of your licence for the rest of your life. If you reoffend, the Secretary of State has the power to order that you be returned to prison to continue to serve your life sentence until it is thought safe to release you again.'

The judge then went on to address the principal offender in front of him, Dale Cregan, and he made it abundantly clear from the outset that he felt his crimes were exceptionally serious and therefore warranted the harshest treatment.

'Parliament has provided a non-exhaustive list of categories of murder which will normally be regarded as being exceptionally serious,' Mr Justice Holroyde told him. 'One of those categories includes the murder of two or more persons where each murder involves a substantial degree of premeditation or planning. There can be no doubt that at least three of your crimes come within that category, but the full enormity of your offending extends even further.'

'First, because I have no doubt that your guilty pleas were cynically timed to suit your own purposes, and did not reflect any regret for what you had done. Secondly, because in your case the overall sentence which must be imposed is dictated by the exceptional seriousness of your crimes. The aggravating features which I have mentioned lead inescapably to the clear conclusion that your offending is so exceptionally serious that the Court must order that the early release provisions shall not apply to you.'

Cregan stood impassively in the dock as the sentence was passed, although there were gasps and muffled cheers from the public gallery when they heard that he would never be released from prison. But he smiled and shook hands with some of his fellow defendants when he was eventually led down to the cells.

Mr Justice Holroyde then went on to sentence his accomplices, the nine other defendants. Luke Livesey, aged twenty-eight, and Damian Gorman, aged thirty-eight, had been found guilty of the killing of Mark Short at the Cotton Tree – though they had pleaded their innocence. Both were sentenced to life imprisonment with a minimum term of thirty-three years.

Anthony Wilkinson, aged thirty-four, who had taken part in the killing of David Short alongside Cregan, had pleaded guilty during the trial to murdering him, although he was cleared of the attempted murder of Mrs Hark on the same day and cleared of causing an explosion with a hand grenade. He was sentenced to life with a minimum of thirty-five years.

Meanwhile, Leon Atkinson, aged thirty-five, together with Ryan Hadfield, aged twenty-nine, and Matthew James, aged thirty-three, had been cleared of the murder of Mark Short in the Cotton Tree and the attempted murders of three others in the pub. Francis Dixon, aged thirty-eight, was acquitted of the murder of David Short and the attempted murder of Mrs Hark as well as causing an explosion with a hand grenade. They received no sentence.

Finally Mohammed Ali, aged thirty-two, was found guilty of assisting an offender – Dale Cregan. He was sentenced to seven years' imprisonment.

Outside Preston Crown Court, the families of both young women police officers explained to reporters how devastated their lives had been by their murder. Bryn Hughes, Nicola's father, said simply, 'Our lives will never be the same again,' and that his family would 'live with what Cregan has done every single hour of every single day for the rest of our lives.'

Speaking about Cregan himself, Hughes added, 'He has

lost nothing, He had already committed two murders and was destined for a lifetime behind bars.' The family on the other hand were left with 'a life barely worth living without her'. But he did not call for the reinstatement of the death penalty.

Alongside him outside Preston Crown Court, Paul Bone, Fiona's father, explained that he had been told that it gets easier with time, 'but at this moment every Tuesday lunchtime is difficult as that is when our lives changed forever'. He expressed his pride in his daughter's achievements, and her service as a police officer, but he too declined to call for the reinstatement of the death penalty.

In the wake of Cregan's sentencing one friend of his family admitted, 'He knows he'll never be freed from prison, and the enormity of what he did is starting to dawn on him. He is praying he dies early. He told his family, "I'm not going to kill myself but I wish I had cancer." He's sorry for what he did. Whether anybody believes it or not is another matter.'

Cregan's mother Anita reflected that sentiment when she told the *Manchester Evening News* later, 'Can I just take this opportunity to say sorry to the police and policewomen's families? That shouldn't have happened. I mean it from the bottom of my heart, my heart goes out to them. I've cried for them, but I didn't bring him up that way.'

So ended one of the most dramatic criminal trials in modern history, and certainly one of the most expensive, but it was certainly not the end of the story of Dale Cregan. No sooner had he been taken to the cells than he made sure that the world would hear more and more about him.

By then in Full Sutton Prison, near York, Cregan was demonstrating no remorse. Like David Bieber before him, he was demanding that he should be released from the solitary confinement that the prison authorities had decided was the best place for him. They had done so for his own protection, as there were persistent, and apparently well-founded, rumours in the jail and among the underworld community in Manchester that a £20,000 payment was on offer to any offender who blinded Cregan's right eye permanently, thereby rendering him blind for life.

Cregan ignored the threat and went on hunger strike, this time to support his demand that he be relocated to Strangeways Prison in Manchester so that he could be nearer to his family. By August 2013 he had achieved his transfer, but still Cregan refused to collaborate. He maintained his hunger strike in Strangeways, where he was again kept in isolation for fear of an attack by a fellow prisoner, and was eventually placed in the prison's hospital wing.

In early September 2013, Cregan was transferred again, this time to Ashworth Secure Hospital on Merseyside, which houses prisoners deemed to be criminally insane. Moors Murderer Ian Brady was continuing to serve his sentence there. Brady had been on permanent hunger strike for several years, insisting that he wanted to bring his own life to an end.

By the time Cregan arrived at Ashworth he was reported not to have eaten for five weeks and was just lying on his bed all day every day without talking to anyone, be they inmates or staff. 'His head has gone,' reported a police source. 'He can't take it any more, he's not cocky any more, what a difference in attitude.'

But Ashworth did not suit Cregan either. Within a matter of weeks of his arrival he was in a fury with the authorities because the hospital banned everyone from smoking. 'He thought it was going to be a holiday camp in there but it has not panned out like that,' one source commented as Cregan was about to be transferred again. 'He is pleased he is going back to prison because he thinks he will be around prisoners who are more like him. But he does not want to be kept in solitary.'

Cregan was reported to have told one friend, 'I'll do my time standing on my head. I just want to be on a regular wing.' Such was his apparent ability to influence the authorities that he was transferred back to Strangeways in Manchester in February 2014 after barely six months in Ashworth.

He has always had his friends within the police service, however. In December 2014 WPC Katie Murray, a serving officer with Greater Manchester Police, was sentenced to two years and nine months' imprisonment for supplying information about the hunt for Cregan, while it was going on, to her lover Jason Lloyd, a drug dealer and associate of Cregan's.

There can be little doubt that Dale Cregan positively relishes his reputation as the whole life prisoner who killed not one but two unarmed policewomen. It burnishes his preening vanity and brings him the notoriety he craves. More frighteningly, however, it also brings him an 'invisible licence' to kill again in prison as there is nothing left for him to lose. That very fact underlines the dangers behind a whole life sentence – no matter how 'heinous' the crimes he has committed – and places a great burden on the prison officers and staff, not to mention the other inmates who are in prison alongside him.

It is perhaps significant that Cregan has, so far, declined to appeal against his whole life term of imprisonment.

What 'Life Means Life' Feels Like

Robert Maudsley, Sidney Cooke and Charles Bronson

One man who knows exactly what it means to be sentenced to spend the rest of your life behind bars – and the 'invisible licence' it gives to kill in prison – is sixty-two-year-old Robert John Maudsley, a wild-eyed, long-haired Liverpudlian, who killed one man before he was imprisoned and three more once in custody.

Now living in a specially constructed cell, Maudsley has spent a large part of the past thirty-two years in solitary confinement in what is effectively a two-roomed cage, with bulletproof windows and a team of six prison officers dedicated to looking after him. He is allowed just one hour of exercise outside a day, and never in the company of other prisoners – both for his protection and theirs.

Maudsley's two-cell unit bears an uncanny resemblance to the one featured in the film version of Thomas Harris's novel *The Silence of the Lambs*, but it was created more than seven years before the film itself was released. A visitor has to pass through no fewer than seventeen locked steel doors to reach the unit, which is approximately five and a half metres by four and a half metres. The only furniture is a table and chair, both made from compressed cardboard, and the lavatory and sink are bolted to the floor. The bed is a concrete slab with a mattress.

A solid steel door opens into a small cage within the cell, encased in thick Perspex, with a slot at the bottom through which prison officers pass food and other items. During his daily hour of exercise, he is escorted to the yard by at least three officers. As the *Observer* writer Tony Thompson noted in 2003, 'It is a level of intense isolation to which no other prisoner, not even Myra Hindley, has been subjected.'

The effect on Maudsley has been to drive him into a severe depression. 'My life in solitary is one long period of unbroken depression,' he has said. It also illuminates the dilemma that lies behind the 'lock them up and throw away the key' approach to the incarceration of those who have committed the most heinous crimes – for it reveals the effect it can have on those who receive a whole life sentence.

Maudsley has made no secret of his views, even to the extent of writing to *The Times* newspaper several times about his treatment. 'It does not matter to them whether I am mad or bad,' he has said. 'They do not know the answer and they do not care just so long as I am kept out of sight and out of mind.' Now with a pale prison pallor and wispy, thinning hair, Maudsley also said, 'I am left to stagnate; vegetate; and to regress; left to confront my solitary head-on with people who have eyes but don't see and who have ears but don't hear, who have mouths but don't speak.'

'Why can't I have amazing pictures on my walls in solitary rather than the dirty damp patches I currently have?' Maudsley wrote. 'Why can't I possess or purchase postage stamps so I can maintain contact with my family, friends, people who contact me etc; why can't I have hand-held electronic games in my cell; why can't I have toiletries? With the open toilet that blocks up here it certainly does smell like a sewer.'

In another letter he asked, 'Why can't I have a budgie instead of the flies and cockroaches and spiders I currently have? I promise to love it and not eat it.'

With an exceptional IQ, he has repeatedly asked for access to classical music tapes, a television set, pictures and toiletries, as well as the budgerigar. Some of his requests have been granted. He gained access to postage stamps, for example, but his conditions in the first decade or more of his time in his Perspex cell have left him with a residue of anger as well as depression.

'If the Prison Service says no,' he wrote in another letter, 'then I ask for a simple cyanide capsule which I shall willingly take and the problem of Robert John Maudsley can easily and swiftly be resolved.'

There are those within the Prison Service who see Maudsley as a problem that cannot be solved in any other way than his exceptional confinement, in view of the outstanding danger he presents to other prisoners whom he may come into contact with.

But not everyone shares that view. Professor Andrew Coyle, now Emeritus Professor of Prison Studies at the University of London, and a former prison governor himself, asked me when I discussed the issue with him, 'Do people really know or understand what "throw away the key" really means?'

In a speech in the United States in 2014, Professor Coyle quoted from a United Nations report to the General Assembly, which said bluntly, 'Prison regimes of solitary confinement often cause mental and physical suffering or humiliation that amounts to cruel, inhuman or degrading treatment or punishment . . . Solitary confinement should be imposed, if at all, in very exceptional circumstances, as a last resort, for as short a time as possible.'

Professor Coyle also cited an example from his own experience as a prison governor in Scotland's maximum security prison with a prisoner named Thomas McCullough. In 1970 McCullough had been convicted of murdering two people and was ordered to be detained indefinitely in the Scottish Secure Psychiatric Hospital. But in 1976 McCulloch and another patient broke out armed with an axe and a knife. In the course of their escape they killed another patient, a member of the nursing staff and a policeman.

When they were caught, both men were sentenced to life imprisonment, and McCulloch was kept in a specially constructed suite of three rooms – a cell where he slept at night, a living area and a workroom. Three prison officers were present within the suite and directly supervised his movements at all times, and a further team of three rotated their duties with them.

'At the outset,' Professor Coyle told me, 'it seemed likely that he would never be released. But as the years passed the prison staff worked with McCulloch so successfully that he was eventually transferred to lower security prisons and in 2013 was released from prison entirely – although he will remain under supervision in the community for the rest of his life. McCulloch is now living anonymously in the Highlands of Scotland.'

Professor Coyle is convinced that other whole life term prisoners could benefit from the same treatment as McCulloch, but acknowledges that there will always be those who deny it.

There is no doubt, however, that the reasons for Robert Maudsley's solitary confinement lie in the nature of his crimes, and the legend that grew up around them. In particular, they revolve around the myth that he was alleged to have eaten part of the brain of one of his prison victims –

earning him the nicknames of 'Hannibal the Cannibal' and 'Spoons'. The reality is that Maudsley did no such thing, as at least one prison officer who worked with him for almost twenty years has explained repeatedly. Nevertheless, the legend lives on, repeated regularly whenever his name is mentioned. That is not for one moment to diminish the heinous nature of Maudsley's crimes, nor to dismiss his need for the most severe of penalties. It is simply to suggest that his story is considerably more nuanced than is often told.

Maudsley's story began with a deeply disturbed and abused childhood, which enraged him. In 1979, during his last murder trial, his defence team argued repeatedly that when he sank into the violent rages that became commonplace, he was often thinking of his parents, and how much he wanted them dead.

'When I kill I have my parents in mind,' Maudsley has admitted himself. 'If I had killed my parents in 1970 none of these people would have died. If I had killed them then I would be walking around as a free man without a care in the world.'

One of twelve children, he was born in Liverpool in 1953, and spent most of his early life in an orphanage. He reportedly found the orphanage relatively pleasant compared to staying at home with his parents – but he was retrieved by them at the age of eight.

'All I remember of my childhood is the beatings,' Maudsley has said. 'Once I was locked in a room for six months and my father only opened the door to come in and beat me, four or six times a day. He used to hit me with sticks and or rods, and once he bust a .22 air rifle over my back.' Maudsley was eventually rescued by social services and placed in a series of foster homes, while his father told the rest of the family that he was dead.

During the late 1960s, Maudsley became a rentboy in

London, and often suffered sexual abuse at the hands of older men, which induced in him a hatred of paedophiles, as well as giving him a serious drug habit. He sold himself to men to support this drug abuse, and he made repeated suicide attempts. Maudsley also spent extended periods in psychiatric care during those years, sometimes telling his doctors that he could hear voices telling him to kill his parents.

In 1973, Maudsley killed one of the men who picked him up for sex. John Farrell, a labourer, produced several pictures of children he had abused, which provoked Maudsley to fly into a rage and garrotte him with wire. Declared unfit to stand trial, he was sent to Broadmoor Special Hospital for the criminally insane. He remained there for four years before killing again – the murder that gave him his nickname and created his legend.

In 1977, at the age of just twenty-four, Maudsley and another Broadmoor patient, John Cheeseman, took another patient, David Francis, a convicted paedophile, hostage and proceeded to barricade all three of them into a secure room in the hospital. Over the next nine hours Maudsley and Cheeseman tortured Francis, before finally garrotting him and holding his body aloft so that the staff could see him through the spyhole in the door. According to legend, Francis's body was found with his head 'cracked open like a boiled egg' and with a spoon hanging out of it.

In reality, Maudsley did not eat any part of his victim's brains. One prison officer who worked with him explained that Maudsley had, in fact, made a makeshift weapon by splitting a plastic spoon in half to create a rough pointed weapon. He then killed his fellow Broadmoor inmate by ramming it into his victim's ear, penetrating the brain. Inevitably, the plastic spoon blade was covered in gore, which was alleged to be 'his brains'.

Ironically after this second murder – even though the crime was committed in a secure psychiatric hospital – Maudsley was declared fit to stand trial. He was convicted of manslaughter and sent to Wakefield Prison instead of Broadmoor. But within a matter of weeks of arriving there, Maudsley killed again. The rage he had felt for years exploded, and he set out to kill seven people in one day. He managed two.

One Saturday morning in 1978 he lured fellow prisoner Salney Darwood, who had been imprisoned for killing his wife, into his cell. Maudsley proceeded to tie a garrotte around his neck and swing him round the cell, smashing his head repeatedly against the walls. He then hid Darwood's dead body under his bed and went out in search of other victims, but none could be persuaded to go into his cell. Frustrated, Maudsley crept into the cell of fifty-six-year-old Bill Roberts who was lying face down on his bunk. He attacked his head with a serrated home-made knife as he lay there, killing him in a matter of minutes.

His anger satiated, Maudsley calmly went to a nearby prison officers' office, put the home-made knife on the table and announced to the officers present that they would be 'two short when it comes to the next roll-call'. Convicted of both murders and sentenced to life imprisonment – though not, at that time, a whole life term – Maudsley was sent back to Wakefield, where he was not allowed to mix with other prisoners. It was the Home Secretary who later decreed that Maudsley should never be released, and serve a whole life term.

Sent to Parkhurst Prison on the Isle of Wight for a time in the early 1980s, Maudsley worked with a prison psychiatrist for three years, who came to believe that his patient was making progress at controlling his anger and depression. The treatment was discontinued, however, and Maudsley was sent back to Wakefield, where the prison authorities constructed his first special cell in 1983. He was incarcerated there for more than a decade before being transferred to another specially constructed secure unit at Woodhill Prison near Milton Keynes.

Maudsley's elder brother Paul has said repeatedly, 'As far as I can tell, the prison authorities are trying to break him. Every time they see him making a little progress they throw a spanner in the works.' At one point at Woodhill, for example, he was again reported to have made progress, even to the extent of playing chess with his special group of prison officers, and being granted access to books and music. Nevertheless, Maudsley was eventually returned to the glass cage at Wakefield – before being moved to another specially constructed secure unit.

'All I have to look forward to is further mental breakdown and possible suicide,' was how Maudsley put it not long after his return to Wakefield. That certainly seems to have proved the case. In the thirty-two years he has spent in almost constant solitary confinement, Maudsley's health is reported to have declined, while his mental condition also appears to have deteriorated. There are even suggestions that he has grown his hair and fingernails to excessive lengths, much as the billionaire American Howard Hughes did in the last years of his life.

In 2012 the *Daily Mirror* reported that Maudsley was in poor health and required two visits from a doctor every day due to the severe weight loss he was suffering as a result of the medication he was taking to control his violent mood swings.

One of his fellow inmates at Wakefield, Charles Bronson, a former professional fighter with a reputation for extreme violence himself, even wrote about Maudsley in his 2007 book *Loonyology*. Bronson declared, 'I know about Bob. I've seen him go mad, I know what's happened to him.' Bronson also alleged that during his one-hour period of exercise each day, which he takes individually as he is not allowed to come into contact with fellow prisoners, Maudsley paces around his separate prison yard – twenty feet long by twelve feet wide – a stooped figure with his eyes fixed on the ground and sporting a long grey beard. 'Maybe the untold solitary years have made him madder,' Bronson concluded.

Whatever the exact truth, it is a frightening portrait of the damage that extremely prolonged periods of solitary confinement can inflict on a prisoner. One woman who befriended him in letters during his time at Wakefield, and then visited him on a number of occasions, found him friendly, and reported, 'Everyone concentrated on the crimes he committed twenty-five years ago. It's as if they are living in a time loop and no one is prepared to look at him as he is now.' Those views were expressed more than a decade ago.

The probable truth now is that Robert Maudsley's health and mental condition have deteriorated so severely that he is left as little more than a husk of a human being with no realistic chance that he will do anything other than die in prison. The question Maudsley raises, however, is whether his fate is what a civilised and humane society actually desires for those who are deemed the 'worst of the worst offenders' for their heinous crimes.

Another inhabitant of Wakefield Prison, who helped to bring the jail its nickname of the 'monster mansion', received treatment not appreciably different from Maudsley's and for distinctly similar reasons.

Convicted paedophile Sidney Cooke is now eighty-eight years old, and was born in April 1927 in Stroud, Gloucestershire. He has been in prison with only a nine-month break since his initial remand in custody for the gang rape and manslaughter of fourteen-year-old Jason Swift in November 1985, a period of thirty years, and he too is in exceptionally frail health having suffered a series of strokes. Cooke is mostly confined to bed in Wakefield, although he can sometimes be seen being pushed around in a wheelchair.

Cooke has been called 'Britain's most notorious paedophile', and known by the nickname 'Hissing Sid' as a result of his unusual speech pattern, but he was not convicted until he was in his late fifties. As a result he has spent all his later years in prison after a period of at least twenty years committing crimes against children and teenagers without being detected.

Starting out as a farm labourer, Cooke found a job working in a fairground in the 1960s, a career that allowed him to travel the country in pursuit of boys. To help him do so, he set up a children's version of a 'Test Your Strength' machine, which formed a familiar part of many travelling fairs. There seems little doubt that throughout this period he sexually attacked many boys.

By the 1970s Cooke, and a group of paedophiles later described in the media as the 'Dirty Dozen', began taking young boys off the streets and drugging them, before raping and abusing them in group orgies. By the mid-1980s, the group had acquired a flat on the run-down Kingsmead estate in Hackney, east London, where they took their young male victims, and sometimes tortured them.

In November 1985, a group led by Cooke each paid £5 to gang-rape fourteen-year-old Jason Swift at one of their orgies. After his body was found in a shallow grave by a dog-walker, an investigation led to the arrest of Cooke, along with three accomplices – Leslie Bailey, Robert Oliver and

Steven Barrell. Cooke was sentenced to nineteen years at the Central Criminal Court in Old Bailey for the manslaughter of Swift.

Jason Swift's half-brother, Steve, said after the verdict that he was disgusted that Cooke had only received a similar sentence to somebody who kills someone else in a pub fight. He felt it was far too short. 'At the very least, part of the sentence for men who attack children should be castration,' he said. 'Their pleasure is boys. Take away that pleasure and they have nothing left to live for . . . But as far as I'm concerned he can never pay his debt to society. The debt of Jason's life was too great.'

Shortly afterwards, his accomplice in the 'Dirty Dozen', Leslie Bailey, confessed to the prison authorities that Cooke was among those who had murdered seven-year-old Mark Tildesley in Wokingham, Berkshire, on 1 June 1984. The boy had disappeared while visiting a funfair in Wokingham that evening, having been lured away with the promise of a fifty-pence bag of sweets. His bicycle was found chained to railings near by.

Cooke contradicted Bailey's story completely, insisting that in fact it was Bailey who had been the ringleader of the gang that killed Tildesley, and who were believed to have killed at least nine other victims. Bailey himself was murdered in prison in 1993.

In 1991, the Crown Prosecution Service declined to prosecute Cooke for Tildesley's murder as he was already in prison for the manslaughter of Jason Swift. Cooke's sentence was reduced to sixteen years on appeal in 1989, and he was paroled nine years later in April 1998. Cooke's parole caused huge public outrage, and even he admitted that he might reoffend. During his time in prison, he had refused to take part in any rehabilitation scheme.

As a result of the public controversy over his release and police fear for his safety, Cooke was forced to live in a suite of cells at Yeovil police station in Somerset during his period of freedom. The Home Office provided him with a TV, washing machine, microwave and small cooker. But on 26 January 1999, he was arrested again and charged with committing eighteen sex offences between 1972 and 1981. They included the repeated abuse of two brothers and the rape of a young woman.

At his trial on 5 October 1999, Cooke pleaded guilty to sexually abusing the two brothers on ten occasions in 1972 and 1973. He also admitted five counts of indecent assault and five counts of buggery, but he firmly denied the remaining eight charges, which were four counts of rape, three further counts of indecent assault, and one of buggery, all in 1981. The judge ordered them to lie on file. In defence of his actions, Cooke claimed that he was sexually abused as a child, and that when he abused the two boys he thought he had 'behaved naturally'.

On 17 December 1999, Cooke received two life sentences and the judge told him that he would only be considered for release after he had served at least a five-year jail sentence. That would have come at the end of 2004, but Cooke is still behind bars today. At the time, the director of the National Society for the Protection and Care of Children insisted, 'He should never have been freed after serving his last sentence. We certainly hope he will never be given the opportunity to hurt a child again. The children who were abused by Sidney Cooke suffered some of the vilest and cruellest sex offences imaginable.'

Aware of his reputation as a 'loathsome paedophile', Cooke retired to the security of Wakefield with some relief. In the words of a senior police officer who dealt with him,

'He certainly does not want to face the public. He is well aware of their reaction to him – and is in some fear of that. He spends a lot of his time watching television. He reads the papers. He cleans his accommodation, he sends out for food, he has his own money. He generally busies himself living under supervision.'

Within a matter of years, however, Cooke suffered the first of a series of strokes, and his health began to deteriorate rapidly.

Sidney Cooke was never sentenced to a whole life term of imprisonment, nevertheless it seems highly likely that he will end his life in jail as he will never be fit enough to be released – in spite of the fact it is difficult to see how he can now present a risk to society, given his physical condition. But there is no sign whatever that Cooke is being considered for parole. In that respect he represents one of the conundrums of the current sentencing regime – a prisoner who probably would be eligible for parole, if there were somewhere that he could go which could provide security and care.

Yet Cooke also epitomises an increasing trend among prisoners subject to long periods of imprisonment, which raises the question: do the Prison Service and prison officers within it have the necessary skills and training to cope with older inmates whose medical, physical and emotional needs present quite different challenges to prison staff who are used to dealing with younger prisoners? The ageing population that is affecting the National Health Service also affects the Prison Service and the small group of prisoners who have been sentenced to a whole life term – or are effectively serving one as a result of the heinous nature of their crimes.

A third prisoner apparently destined to spend the rest of his life in Wakefield Prison is the man often described as 'Britain's most violent inmate', former bare-knuckle fighter

Charles Bronson, who is now known as Charles Salvador. He too has never received a whole life sentence and is still only sixty-three, but his reputation would seem to make it highly unlikely that he will ever be judged to present no risk to the general public, and therefore eligible for release on licence.

A distinctly larger-than-life character in every sense, Bronson was born Michael Gordon Peterson in Luton, Bedfordshire, on 6 December 1952, and has spent almost his entire adult life as a prisoner. He has served forty years behind bars, and thirty-six years of those years in solitary confinement, since he was first sentenced to seven years for armed robbery in 1974 as a young man of twenty-two.

But Bronson has used his period in jail to create a distinctive reputation for himself, both as a prisoner and to the wider public, writing a string of eleven books, including his life story, holding a series of art exhibitions of his work as a painter, which won him several awards, creating his own Appeal Fund, and even being featured in a 2008 film about his life, called simply *Bronson*, in which he was portrayed by the actor Tom Hardy.

Bronson's website states boldly: '40 years, not out. Not a murderer, sex offender, not a terrorist. NOT A DANGER TO THE PUBLIC. 40 years served it is time to free Charles Bronson.' But Bronson is intelligent enough to add: '(This can be disputed into what life imprisonment means. Should Bronson be in prison for life on the definition of life in prison?)'

What cannot be denied is that Bronson's reputation for violence and non-cooperation during his many years as a prisoner is without parallel in the British prison system.

A bright, gentle child, according to his aunt, Michael Peterson – as he then was – had nevertheless begun to get into trouble with the law by the age of thirteen, and at nineteen only narrowly escaped his first prison sentence for a smash and grab raid. He was given a suspended sentence on the grounds that the judge felt that he deserved one more chance. That was in 1971, but the chance did not last long.

In 1974, the young Peterson was imprisoned for seven years for his part in an armed robbery at a post office in a suburb of Ellesmere Port, Cheshire, during which he stole £26.18. He was imprisoned at Walton Gaol, and his long history of violence in prison began. Peterson soon ended up on the punishment block after attacking two prisoners, and was then transferred to Hull Prison in 1975. Refusing to work, he smashed up a workshop after an altercation with a prison officer and was sent to the punishment block.

Within a matter of weeks he attacked another prisoner with a glass jug, and was charged with unlawful wounding; a further nine months were added to his original sentence. By now his reputation as a highly dangerous inmate preceded him, and he spent the years between 1975 and 1977 switching from prison to prison, though almost always being kept in isolation from his fellow prisoners. It was not until he came into contact with the London gangsters Ronnie and Reggie Kray that he seemed to calm down slightly, describing them as 'the best two guys I've ever met', although Reggie Kray in turn called meeting Peterson 'the most frightening visit I ever had'.

The calm did not last long. Peterson was moved to Wandsworth after threatening to kill a prison officer, only to spend four months in isolation after being caught trying to dig his way out of his cell. The governor wanted him transferred again, but only Parkhurst on the Isle of Wight was willing to accept him. There he attacked a prisoner with a jam jar and was again charged with grievous bodily harm. Peterson attempted suicide and attacked another prison officer and was eventually sectioned under the Mental Health Act 1959.

As a result, in December 1978, Peterson found himself in Broadmoor, where he all but killed a child sex attacker and was reunited with Ronnie Kray. Then, in 1982, he launched his first rooftop protest after escaping to the top of the hospital and tearing off roof tiles. Not long afterwards he did it again, causing £250,000 worth of damage in a three-day protest before he was talked down by his family. Another rooftop protest followed, and Peterson then started an eighteen-day hunger strike.

Even given his own mental problems, Bronson found the experience of life in Broadmoor very disturbing. 'I witnessed them running into walls, using their heads as rams,' he wrote later. 'I've seen them fall unconscious doing this. They stabbed themselves with pens, needles, and scissors. One even blinded himself in one eye and another tore out his own testicle. There was one just kept trying to eat himself, biting his arms, legs and feet.'

Bronson was eventually moved to Ashworth Special Secure Hospital, home to Moors Murderer Ian Brady, in June 1984, where he lapsed into another brief period of calm. So calm, indeed, that he was granted release on licence – but not before another rooftop protest and being moved again from prison to prison.

'I'd been certified mad because of my violence,' Bronson has said, questioning his time in Broadmoor and Ashworth. 'I was still violent – but they are now certifying me sane. Where's the sanity in that? Isn't the system just as crazy?'

After his release in 1987 Peterson embarked on his short-lived career as an illegal bare-knuckle boxer in the East End of London on the advice of Reggie Kray. It was then that he changed his name from Michael Peterson to Charles Bronson

– even though he had never actually seen the American actor whose name he chose.

On 7 January 1988, his sixty-ninth day of freedom, Bronson was arrested in the wake of a jewellery shop robbery and was remanded in custody again, only to plead guilty in June 1988 and receive another seven-year sentence. His prison career, with all its violence, resumed again as though nothing had happened. In 1989, for example, he ran riot in the nude, clutching a spear he fashioned out of a broken bottle and a broom handle, and was transferred again. In 1991 he was stabbed in the back by two fellow prisoners, but refused to discuss any element of the attack with the police and, after a long period of recovery, was again released on licence from prison in November 1992.

This time his period of freedom was even shorter – fifty-three days. Bronson was arrested and charged with conspiracy to rob and once again remanded in jail, but in February 1993 the case was dropped and he was released. Just sixteen days after that, however, he was arrested and remanded, once again on robbery charges. It was while he was on remand that he took a civilian librarian hostage and demanded an inflatable doll, a helicopter and a cup of tea from police negotiators. He released the hostage after being disgusted when the man he was holding broke wind in front of him.

On Easter Monday 1994, Bronson took a deputy prison governor hostage, but was eventually overpowered. Then, in 1996, he took a prison doctor hostage, but was again over-powered. A matter of months later an Iraqi hijacker bumped into him in the canteen and did not apologise. After brooding in his cell, he took two Iraqi hijackers, along with another inmate, hostage in a cell. Bronson then forced the Iraqis to tickle his feet and call him 'General', before demanding a plane to take him to Libya, two Uzi sub-machine guns, 5,000 rounds of ammunition and an axe. Eventually he agreed to release the three men, but another seven years were added to his sentence, later reduced to five on appeal.

Nothing changed. There were more hostage incidents – notably one involving a prison art teacher named Phil Danielson in January 1999. Bronson targeted Danielson because he had mildly criticised one of Bronson's own drawings. Bronson tied him up with computer cable and put him on a pool table in the recreation hall while he danced around with a makeshift spear made out of a pool cue with a home-made knife taped to the tip, while telling Danielson he was going to kill him. Ironically, it was Danielson who had first interested him in art. The siege lasted forty-four hours before he finally released his hostage, who was left traumatised by the experience. In its wake, Bronson received a discretionary life sentence with a three-year minimum tariff for the incident.

Once again he appeared to calm down, although for a time he was placed in the glass cage cell that Robert Maudsley had occupied for more than a decade. Eventually both men were transferred to a newly conformed Close Supervision Centre in the Special Security Unit in Wakefield.

The period of calm meant that Bronson became due for a parole hearing in September 2008, but this was postponed after his lawyer objected to a one-hour interview, requesting instead a full day to deal with the case. Bronson had been claiming he was a reformed character since 2000, rather over-looking the fact that in that eight-year period he had attacked two prison officers, been sprayed with CS gas for refusing to exercise, and spat at a prison governor. The hearing finally took place on 11 March 2009. Parole was refused shortly afterwards, on the grounds that Bronson had certainly not proved that he was a reformed character.

Little has changed since then. In 2013, he was moved to Woodhill Prison near Milton Keynes and on 28 February 2014 he hit the governor over the head several times and was moved again. Then, on 17 May 2014, he attacked prison officers at Full Sutton in Durham after Arsenal – his least favourite football team – had won the FA Cup final. At the end of 2014, still unrepentant, Bronson admitted causing the prison governor at Woodhill actual bodily harm and was sentenced to two more years of imprisonment within his discretionary life sentence.

Bronson's many years in prison have had a dramatic effect on him. 'My eyes are bad due to the years of unnatural light I have had,' he has said. 'My vision is terrible; I have to wear shaded glasses even to read. Years of solitary have left me unable to face the light for more than a few minutes. It gives me terrible headaches if I do . . . Years of loneliness in small cells have left me paranoid about people invading my space. I now can't stand people getting too close, crowding me. I hate people breathing on me and I hate smelly bodies coming near me. Mouths to me are simply for eating – never for kissing . . . A man needs a routine to cope with such an extreme situation. For me it is my push-ups and sit-ups. I also pace the room and count each step.'

Bronson is also clearly searching for some sense of his own true identity. Nowhere could that be clearer than in his personal life and his appetite for changing his name to assume a new and different identity.

Bronson met his first wife, Irene, in 1971, and eight months later, when she was four months pregnant, they married at Chester Register Office, only to divorce five years later. The couple had a son, Michael. Nevertheless, in 2001, Bronson married again, this time in Woodhill Prison. His new wife was Fatema Saira Rehman, a Bangladeshi-born divorcee who had seen his picture in a newspaper and begun writing to him before visiting him ten times in prison. For a short time, Bronson converted to his wife's faith of Islam, and insisted that he be known as Charles Ali Ahmed.

After four years, however, the couple divorced, and she subsequently described him repeatedly in the harshest terms. In one newspaper interview, for example, she said, 'He fooled me – he is nothing but an abusive, racist thug.' Bronson immediately went back to using his bare-knuckle boxing name.

In August 2014, however, Bronson changed his name again, this time by deed poll, insisting that in future he must be known as Charles Arthur Salvador – in a tribute to the artist Salvador Dali. In a statement on his website, Salvador said, 'The old me dried up . . . Bronson came alive in 1987. He died in 2014.' He also announced that he was renouncing violence. 'It's non-violent all the way. It's a peaceful journey from here on . . . Coz my heart is at peace and my mind is set on art.'

There are some in the prison system who doubt that Bronson's transformation will last any longer than his conversion to Islam. Yet he seems destined to see out the rest of his life in prison. He may claim to hate it, but there is also something in his incarceration that feeds his rage, and the conviction that he is the victim, not those whom he has attacked or taken hostage. There is also an element of self-pity in him that turns into a form of narcissism, fuelling his constant desire for notoriety and attention.

Now offering T-shirts for sale on his website, and claiming he wants to be released, the reality is that Bronson has taken eleven hostages, fought with twenty prison officers – leaving one 'covered in blood and squealing like a pig', to use his own words – and staged nine rooftop protests, including one lasting forty-seven hours that caused £500,000 of damage. In total, it has been estimated that Bronson has cost the state more than £5 million in prison costs, court appearances and criminal damage during his time inside.

As one member of the Prison Officers' Association has put it, 'The only reason he hasn't been even more violent in recent years is because he's been kept completely isolated. Every time he's been put back among other prisoners, he's committed another act of violence.'

Like Robert Maudsley and Sidney Cooke, Bronson has never been sentenced to a whole life term of imprisonment, but has already served more time in prison than they have, and he is still only sixty-three. But he presents the same question to British society and, of course, the Parole Board. Will it ever be safe to release him? Indeed, could he survive in the world beyond the prison walls? He has never known how to use a computer – his website is run by his supporters – and has never even possessed a mobile phone.

Should the new Charles Salvador be left forever to rot behind bars, as a form of retribution for his repeated acts of violence, or should he be released on licence to see if he can survive in a world that he really does not know, in an attempt to redeem his repeated violent crimes?

No one can be certain, but he perfectly illustrates society's ambivalence to its most infamous criminals. Nor should we be surprised that he is reported to have been asked to take part in the reality television programme *I'm a Celebrity Get Me Out Of Here* if and when he is released on licence.

12

Not 'Seeking Release'

Victor Miller, Mark Bridger and Rosemary West

Not every whole life prisoner wants freedom. The European Court of Human Rights may believe that they should, but there are at least three killers who have accepted that they will end their days behind bars, and are apparently content to do so.

One of them, fifty-nine-year-old Victor Miller, a gay black man from Wolverhampton, has even specifically requested that he never set foot beyond the prison gate, even though he has already served twenty-seven years for the murder of fourteen-year-old paperboy Stuart Gough in January 1988.

Declining the chance of release could well see him spend half a century in jail for a single murder conviction, though the police suspect he may have committed as many as twenty-eight other assaults on boys and young men. That is on top of the fact that he has already served part of a seven-year term for abducting a thirteen-year-old in 1980. Miller had only just completed this earlier sentence, some of it spent on early release, when he killed Stuart Gough.

A computer operator, Victor Miller was thirty-two and living with a convicted paedophile named Trevor Peacher, some fourteen years older than he was, in the first weeks of 1988. The couple were not getting on and there were persistent rows. Miller, who had a history of attraction to teenage boys, vented his rage by targeting newspaper boys as the object of his particular sexual compulsion. He regarded them as especially vulnerable.

In the first week of January 1988, eighteen-year-old Richard Holden, who was not actually a paperboy, was attacked by a man while riding his bike down a country lane near his home in Wellington, not far from Hereford in Shropshire. A knife was held to his throat and Holden was partially stripped before he managed to fight off his attacker by kicking him in the groin.

Just a few days later, on 17 January 1988, Malcolm Higgins and his wife, who ran the village newsagents in Hagley, Worcestershire – where Miller had once lived – alerted the police to a second attack on a young man. One of their paperboys, Anthony Dingley, told them he had been stopped by an 'Afro-Caribbean' man driving what he later described as a silver Datsun Sunny car.

The following day, Saturday 18 January, another of their paperboys, Stuart Gough, a fourteen-year-old asthmatic, turned up at the Higgins' shop to do his paper round. He was due to do two that day. Stuart loaded his bag and said he would come back to the shop for the second load, but he never returned. Within twenty-four hours a police manhunt had been launched.

It did not take police long to link all three incidents, and after a further interview with Richard Holden, they discovered the car involved was actually a silver Colt Sapporo, not a Datsun. They also discovered that local man Victor Miller owned exactly that sort of car, and that he had a criminal record for attacking boys and young men. The police found tyre marks at the scene where Holden had been attacked which matched the tread on Miller's car tyres, and this immediately made Miller the prime suspect in the Gough missing person's inquiry.

For the previous two years Miller and Trevor Peacher had been sharing a flat in Pennfields, Wolverhampton, and when the police first interviewed the pair about the disappearance of Gough, Peacher gave Miller an alibi for the time when the paperboy disappeared. Without a body there was little the police could do to arrest either Miller or Peacher, or both, no matter what their suspicions.

Over the next few days the police launched a massive manhunt for Gough, using more than 170 officers, underwater divers and a helicopter, but they found nothing. They then decided to go back and re-interview Miller and Peacher, and on 29 January, the police decided to arrest both men on suspicion of abduction and murder, even though they had still not located the boy's body. They did not have to wait long. Two days later, after a prolonged series of interviews with both men, they decided that Peacher was not involved and agreed to release him on bail. It was the turning point. Almost immediately, Miller confessed to the killing of Stuart Gough and told the police he would lead them to where his body was hidden. Peacher was later sentenced to three years' imprisonment for providing Miller with a false alibi.

The following morning, 1 February 1988, Miller took officers to Bromsberrow, near Ledbury, Herefordshire, and led them to a drainage culvert not far from the M50 motorway. Here, they discovered Gough's partially-clothed dead body under a pile of leaves. He had been sexually assaulted and then battered repeatedly with a rock so that his face was all but unrecognisable. He was only finally identified from his dental records.

When Miller appeared before Hereford Magistrates Court he sat in silence in the dock as the formal charges were read out to him, but he did ask that a written statement be read out. It said: 'I fully accept what I have done and I have co-operated fully with the police. I can never make up for taking Stuart from his family. But I would ask that justice will be done, and I will receive the maximum sentence available.'

That remained Miller's stance when he arrived at Birmingham Crown Court on 4 November 1988. He pleaded guilty to Stuart Gough's abduction and murder and was sentenced to life with a minimum term of twenty-five years. The judge expressed his doubt about whether it would ever be safe to release him, and a year and a half later the Home Secretary agreed, extending Miller's sentence to a whole life term.

In the wake of the decision in late 2002 that politicians should no longer have any sentencing powers, which were transferred to the judiciary under the Criminal Justice Act 2003, Miller's minimum term was reinstated at twenty-five years – which meant that he would be at least eligible to be considered for release after February 2013. That was not what he wanted, however.

Miller has persistently indicated to the Prison Service that he does not want to be considered for parole and actively wishes to die in prison, even though that could mean that he could spend a further twenty-five years or more behind bars. His case will be automatically reviewed every five years, and it is, of course, possible that he may change his mind as time passes, but there is little sign of that now.

There is another male prisoner, in a much more recent case, also convicted of only one murder and sentenced to a whole life term, and who appears to have made exactly the same decision as Victor Miller. He is former slaughterhouse worker Mark Bridger, the murderer of five-year-old school-girl April Jones in North Wales in October 2012.

April was last seen alive on Monday 1 October 2012 after

she was witnessed climbing willingly into a vehicle, possibly a Land Rover, near her home in Machynlleth, Powys. In this close-knit rural community in North Wales, her completely unexpected disappearance provoked an immediate reaction. Within a day a full-scale hunt had been launched and on Wednesday 3 October her mother made an appeal for information about her daughter.

The following day the Prime Minister David Cameron issued an appeal for information, saying, 'Clearly having this happen to you, and the fact that she suffers from cerebral palsy, something I know a little about from my own children, only makes this worse. My appeal would be to everyone. If you know anything, if you saw anything, heard anything, have any ideas you can bring forward, talk to the police.' His own son, nine-year-old Ivan, had succumbed to cerebral palsy in 2009.

In the next few days one of the biggest missing persons' searches in British history expanded still further, but without success. In spite of the fact that officers from forty-six police forces and hundreds of members of the public scoured 650 acres near her village, the body of the smiling-faced little girl with delicate blonde hair was never found.

One local resident rapidly attracted the attention of the police, however. He was former lifeguard, fireman, welder and slaughterhouse worker Mark Bridger, aged forty-six, who lived in an isolated cottage on the banks of the fast-flowing River Dovey on the outskirts of the village. A regular at the local pub and an enthusiastic pool player, he was well regarded, and had never aroused any suspicions whatsoever.

But on Friday 5 October, the police officially altered April's disappearance from a missing persons' inquiry to a murder enquiry, and the following day Mark Bridger was charged with child abduction, murder and attempting to pervert the course of justice. He appeared before magistrates at Aberystwyth on 8 October, where he was additionally charged with the unlawful concealment and disposal of a body. Bridger was then remanded in custody and held at Manchester Prison pending an appearance at Caernarfon Crown Court on 10 October by video link. By then April Jones had been gone for just nine days.

Born in Carshalton, London, on 6 November 1965, and christened Mark Leonard Bridger, he was one of the three children of policeman Graham Bridger and his wife Pamela. He grew up in a semi-detached house in the south London suburb of Wallington and went to school in Croydon, leaving with seven CSEs. But Bridger did not turn out to be a stable young man intent on a career. He rapidly became very troubled.

When Bridger was nineteen he was convicted of firearms offences and theft, and finally moved to Wales in his late twenties. There he was convicted of criminal damage, affray and driving without insurance in 1991, and the following year he was convicted again, for driving whilst disqualified and without insurance. Hardly surprisingly he rarely settled anywhere and often moved from job to job, including working in an abattoir, as a mechanic and as a welder.

Bridger also had six children by four women, including two by his wife, whom he married in 1990, but he nevertheless did not seem to present a particular threat to children. However, in 2004 he was convicted of battery and threatening behaviour and in 2007 received a fifth conviction, for assault. The cheerful man in the pub, who seemed to have not a care in the world, clearly suffered from his own demons.

On 14 January 2013, Bridger officially pleaded not guilty to the charge of abducting and murdering April Jones, but nevertheless accepted that he was 'probably responsible' for her death. But when his trial began on Monday 29 April 2013 at Mold Crown Court, before Mr Justice Griffith Williams, Bridger again pleaded not guilty to the murder of April Jones.

At his trial Bridger confessed that he was an alcoholic, and described how he had 'accidentally' crushed the five-year-old to death with his Land Rover, and had then made repeated attempts to resuscitate her. 'There was a little girl under the wheels of the car. She had gone a funny colour. She was only a little thing,' he told the jury, giving evidence on his own behalf.

'I need to say sorry to her family. I can't believe I didn't just call an ambulance or the police. The intention was to head to the hospital. There was no life in her. No pulse. No breathing. No response in her eyes.' But he insisted that he had not dumped her body. 'She is a human being,' he said. 'I wouldn't have done that.'

The jury did not believe a word. On Thursday 30 May 2013, after retiring for less than a day, they found Bridger guilty of abduction, murder and perverting the course of justice. Later that day, the judge delivered his brief two-page, sentencing remarks. They were coruscating.

'For the last four weeks,' Mr Justice Griffith Williams told Bridger, 'the Court has listened to compelling evidence of your guilt, evidence which has also demonstrated that you are a pathological and glib liar.' The judge paused. 'There is no doubt in my mind,' he went on, 'that you are a paedophile who has for some time harboured sexual and morbid fantasies about young girls, storing on your laptop not only images of pre-pubescent and pubescent girls, but foul pornography of the gross sexual abuse of young children.'

Mr Justice Griffith Williams did not know what had prompted Bridger to kill April Jones, but he did allow himself to reflect, 'What prompted you on Monday 1 October to live out one of those fantasies is a matter of speculation but it may have been the combination of the ending of one sexual relationship and your drinking. Whatever, you set out to find a little girl to abuse. I am not sure you targeted April specifically – it was probably fortuitous that she cannot be seen on some of the images, which you stored on your laptop, of her older sister – but you were on the prowl for a young girl.' Pointing out that April would not have been afraid of him because he knew her elder sister and was a familiar face in the locality, he added, 'And so it was that April got into your Land Rover smiling and happy.'

'What followed is known only to you, but this much is certain,' the judge continued, 'you abducted her for a sexual purpose and then murdered her and disposed of her body to hide the evidence of your sexual abuse of her, which probably occurred on the way from the estate to your home because there is some sixty minutes of your time which cannot be accounted for.'

Mr Justice Griffith Williams then made a series of withering remarks about Bridger's insincerity. 'The grief of April's parents cannot be over-stated,' he said. 'They lived with the torment of a missing daughter, praying that she would be found alive and then, following your arrest, with the knowledge that you were providing the police with no assistance at all as to her whereabouts. To add to that torment, they have had to endure the spectacle of your hypocritical sympathy for their loss and of your tears, flowing not because of any regret for your crimes, but because of your enduring self-pity.'

Finally Mr Justice Griffith Williams told Bridger, who sat in the dock at Mold Crown Court utterly unmoved by his conclusions, 'Your offences were aggravated by their pre-meditation and by the destruction of at least part of her body and the concealment of the rest. It is also a relevant consideration that you not only abducted April with a sexual motive but then sexually abused her in some way. I have no doubt there can be only one sentence,' he concluded firmly. 'Life imprisonment with a whole life order.'

Bridger was led down to the cells, still showing no signs of emotion whatever. He was practised at hiding the truth. Indeed Dyfed-Powys Police believe that parts of April Jones's body were burned in a wood-burning stove in Bridger's cottage, while other fragments of the five-year-old's remains were distributed around the wooded local countryside. Certainly his disposal of her body, and refusal to admit exactly what he had done with it, served only to confirm Bridger's lack of empathy or remorse.

Barely five weeks later, on Sunday 7 July 2013, the forty-seven year old was attacked with a makeshift blade by a fellow prisoner as he walked along a gangway at Wakefield Prison in West Yorkshire. His attacker wanted to know what Bridger had done with the body of April Jones, but Bridger refused to tell him – and as a result was cut from the throat up the side of his face to his temple. He was treated in hospital, where he required thirty stitches, but was returned to prison on the same day.

The attack on his father provoked a fierce reaction from Bridger's son Steven Verona, aged twenty-seven, and one of his father's six children by four women. 'Personally I wish whoever slashed him had gone for his throat. It's hard to accept I'm related to someone so inherently evil. I dread telling anyone who my dad is, in case they think I have evil in my blood. But sometimes I am terrified at what I might have inherited from him.' Bridger's son also revealed that he wanted his father 'to get the electric chair, I wanted him to experience the pain April and her family have.'

Six months later, on 16 December 2013, Bridger launched

an appeal against his whole life sentence, which horrified every member of April's family. Coral Jones, her mother, told one reporter, 'It's disgusting. He's in prison where he belongs and should stay there. He's just torturing my family with these legal battles. It's like he's taunting us, like he wants to show he has got the upper hand.'

Then, quite suddenly, on 13 January 2014, Bridger dropped his application for permission to appeal against his whole life term – just eleven days before the formal hearing was due to take place at the Court of Appeal in London. The decision delighted April's grandfather, who told the BBC, 'I don't think he should have been allowed to appeal. He's done an horrific crime and he should spend the rest of his life in prison. That's it as far as I am concerned. He should never be let out.'

Perhaps Bridger's legal team pointed out to him that the Court of Appeal in England and Wales was not likely to uphold the judgement of the European Court on the 'inhumanity' of a whole life term, or, equally possibly, Bridger had come to understand that he was one killer who could never be rehabilitated because of the strength of public opinion against him. His name had become as notorious as that of Ian Brady – who had also always refused to identify the exact whereabouts of one of his and Myra Hindley's victims, fourteen-year-old Keith Bennett.

Bridger may also have sensed that April's mother Coral – like Keith Bennett's mother before her – was certain to campaign relentlessly against his release. She had already called for the return of the death penalty in the wake of his conviction for the murder of her daughter.

'They should bring death row back to the UK,' she said after he withdrew his appeal '. . . but instead of having it for years and years, have it for five years and before the five are up he should . . . have a lethal injection. I'd be there to push the button and make sure he saw me.'

Coral Jones gave one of the most poignant descriptions of the plight of a close relative confronted with the killing of a loved one, even though she accepted that the return of the death penalty was highly unlikely.

'Life should mean life,' she said. 'I don't think they should have an easy life in prison where they have three meals a day. Perhaps years ago they had to earn stuff – today they have human rights. Our rights went when he killed our daughter and we still suffer now . . . He's ruined my life, my husband's, my kids' and everybody else's in my family. The next time he comes out he should be in a box.'

Mrs Jones has also pointed out, 'If they're allowed out you don't know where they've gone and what else they could do . . . My little April was only five, she was small and she had health issues and he did it to her.'

Bridger is already is his late forties and therefore unlikely to spend more than half a century behind bars, unlike Jamie Reynolds, who could spend far longer, or Michael Adebolajo, who could also spend longer. But one thing unites the three men – they each committed just one single murder, no matter how loathsome and depraved.

That is not the case with the one other prisoner who has accepted being condemned to spend the rest of their life behind bars. Rosemary West is one of only two women serving a whole life term of imprisonment – the other is Joanna Dennehy. Now aged sixty-two, West has already served more than twenty years in prison, and shows every sign that she too has accepted that her notoriety makes it all but impossible for her ever to be released.

During the first years of her imprisonment in the late 1990s, West talked to her fellow prisoner Myra Hindley about the prospect. At that point they were being held in the same prison and there is no doubt that they became friends. Hindley was still campaigning for release, a campaign that ultimately failed, but there is little doubt that West sensed the parallels between them. She too believed that she had fallen under the spell of a man she loved, her husband Frederick West, and had been forever tarred by the sadistic brutality of his relentless killing of girls and young women, including their daughter Heather. But unlike Hindley, she was not prepared to admit her guilt.

As the official biographer of Frederick West – I was appointed by the Official Solicitor to the Supreme Court to give financial support to three of the Wests' other children – I watched every single day of Rosemary West's trial at Winchester Crown Court in the autumn of 1995. It was an unforgettable, unnerving experience, with its appalling litany of the killing, dismemberment and burial of nine bodies beneath their home at 25 Cromwell Street, Gloucester, over a period of almost thirty years. Another body, of an eight-year-old girl named Charmaine, was buried beneath the kitchen of the Wests' previous flat at 25 Midland Road, also in Gloucester.

Rosemary West, then a portly woman aged forty-one with dark hair, a fearsome stare and large ivory glasses, sat impassively in the dock throughout some of the most chilling evidence it is possible to imagine, including the details of the torture many of the victims had suffered at the hands of the Wests, which included the removal of fingers and knee-caps – bones that were notably missing when the victims' remains were eventually recovered from beneath the cellar and garden.

At her trial in October and November 1995, West repeatedly sought to paint herself as the victim of her husband, a mere bystander who had no knowledge of, or collaboration with, the killings that took place in their small, cramped semi-detached house just three minutes' walk from the centre of the cathedral city of Gloucester on the River Severn. Indeed, when she came to give evidence in her own defence – answering questions from her defence counsel the late Richard Ferguson QC – she spoke in a low monotone, rather as if she were no more than a parking warden addressing magistrates about a car owner who disputed a fine. There was an arrogant calmness about her demeanour, a sense that she was determined to disguise the true depths of her own emotions and sexual compulsions. For there can be no doubt whatever that Rosemary West was consumed by sex – in all its manifestations.

As her husband Fred's Court-appointed biographer, I was the only author or journalist given access to a string of home-made videotapes that vividly portrayed Rosemary West's sexual appetite and predilections – all of them shot in their home in Cromwell Street by her husband. The image of her apparently open, innocent face in a string of the most sordid acts of sexual exhibitionism is an image that has never left me, and forever colours how I feel about her attempts in Court to pretend to be nothing more than a caring mother, concerned only to bring up her children. Those videotapes were never shown to the jury as they would have been 'prejudicial' to her fair trial, but they convinced me that she was capable of the most chilling, ruthless and wicked deception.

Rosemary West was born Rosemary Pauline Letts on 29 November 1953 in Barnstaple, Devon, to a paranoid schizophrenic father, William Letts, and a profoundly challenged mother, Daisy, who was to undergo prolonged treatment for depression, and who found motherhood daunting. Described by her mother as 'babyish', Rosemary – often known as Rose

– performed poorly at school and was repeatedly sexually abused by her father from an early age. Her parents split up when Rose was fourteen, but then reunited and moved to Bishop's Cleeve, near Cheltenham in Gloucestershire. It was there, at the age of fifteen, that Rose first encountered the man who was to become her one and only husband, Frederick Walter Stephen West, who was twelve years her senior.

Starting out as a babysitter, she rapidly fell under the spell of the perpetually grimy, curly-haired, chattering West, a child of Much Marcle in Herefordshire, not far from Gloucester, and a man whose fascination with sex exceeded even Rosemary's own. Within a matter of weeks of her sixteenth birthday in November 1969, she was pregnant with West's child, and their daughter Heather was born in October 1970. By that time West had killed his first victim, babysitter Ann McFall, and buried her body in a field within sight of his birthplace in Herefordshire. It would remain there undiscovered until after his arrest for murder in March 1994. He may well also have killed fifteen-year-old Mary Bastholm, who disappeared from a bus stop in Gloucester in January 1968, never to be seen again, but West maintained a strict silence when that accusation was put to him by the police after his arrest.

Within two months of the birth of their first child together, Frederick West was sentenced to nine months' imprisonment for dishonesty and theft, and was not officially released from an open prison near Gloucester until June 1971. At around that time, eight-year-old Charmaine, his first wife Rena Costello's daughter by another man, went missing when in the care of Rosemary West. Not long afterwards Rena too disappeared – the bodies of mother and daughter remained undiscovered until May and June 1994.

By the time of Charmaine's death in 1971, Rose West had

progressed from being her husband's apprentice to his willing accomplice. Early in January 1972 the couple married, just four months before the arrival of their second daughter, Mae, and in September they moved into 25 Cromwell Street in Gloucester. Here, their joint appetite for sexual abuse, torture and killing flowered still further in a condition described by psychologists as *folie à deux*, where the two partners in crime encourage each other into further and further atrocities. In the Wests' case, their enthusiasm was also encouraged by Rose's father, Bill Letts, who was still engaged in sexual relations with her, even after her marriage and the birth of her first two children.

Barely a month after arriving in Cromwell Street in late September 1972, the Wests engaged a young woman named Carol Raine, originally from the Forest of Dean not far from Gloucester, as a babysitter for their two daughters and Anne Marie, West's daughter from his first marriage to Rena Costello. Uncomfortable with their uninhibited sexuality, Raine stayed with them for less than a month – but the couple abducted her just a few weeks later on 4 December 1972, beat her and indecently assaulted her in a way that was to become the prototype for their later sexual attacks.

The former babysitter reported the Wests to the police, who did not charge either West with rape, only with occasioning actual bodily harm and indecent assault; a fact that still infuriates her now more than forty years later. Almost sixty, and now called Caroline Roberts, she insisted in 2014 that had the police pursued the couple more aggressively over her case, 'I am certain that it would have saved some of their victims.' In fact, the Wests were fined a total of just £100 between them.

'Fred was always really pervy with me,' Roberts told the *Daily Mirror*, 'talking about sex and such like, but I got on well with Rose. When she turned on me I remember feeling betrayed because the person who was helping Fred was someone I considered a friend.' In a grim irony, during the course of the Wests' joint attack on her, Frederick West threatened to bury her under the patio behind the house in Cromwell Street, where the bodies of three young women were eventually discovered in March 1994.

In the six years after the attack on Carol Raine, Frederick and Rosemary West killed no fewer than eight other young women, regularly keeping them as prisoners in the cellar of their house in Cromwell Street, often for several days, sexually abusing them relentlessly, torturing them in many cases, and then killing them and burying their bodies beneath the cellar's concrete floor. They moved on to the patio in the garden outside when there was no more space left in the cellar.

The young women suffered dreadfully at the Wests' hands, as anyone who sat through Rosemary West's trial will bear witness. The fates of two of their victims haunt me to this day. Birmingham-born Shirley Hubbard was just fifteen when she encountered Frederick West for the first time. A troubled young woman, who had spent long periods in foster homes in the wake of her parents' separation when she was two, Hubbard craved a father figure and had developed an appetite for older men. West realised this and played on it until, on 14 November 1974, he brought her back to Cromwell Street to meet Rose, whom he always portrayed as 'just a loving Mum'.

There was no loving in what happened to Shirley Hubbard when she reached the cellar of Cromwell Street. She, like the other girls before her, was kept prisoner in that 'dark damp cave', but this time the Wests went a little further. They covered the fifteen-year-old's head from chin to scalp in two-inch-wide parcel tape, wound overlapping around her skull eleven or twelve times, and with a loop under her chin. This terrible mask would have made it impossible for Hubbard to see or speak, and would have made it almost impossible to breathe. The Wests' solution was to insert two U-shaped pieces of thin clear plastic tubing, each about eighteen inches long, into both of Hubbard's nostrils through the tape. The tubing meant that they could keep her alive to use her as they wanted. The photographs of the mask – which survived Hubbard's burial under the cellar floor – were some of the most horrifying exhibits at Rosemary West's trial, for they somehow epitomised the utter lack of humanity in a woman who claimed to be 'just an ordinary Mum'.

That same depraved indifference was only too clear thirteen years later when the Wests' eldest daughter Heather disappeared from Cromwell Street, never to be seen again until her body was recovered from underneath the patio that covered the Wests' garden. For a mother to assist in the murder of her own first-born child is as gross an act of barbarity as it is possible to imagine. The reason for Heather's death was almost certainly her threatening to reveal to the authorities exactly what had been going on at Cromwell Street during her childhood, which included the Wests 'breaking in' their female children by sexually abusing them. Heather herself may well have been subjected to persistent attacks – her step-sister Anne Marie certainly was, as she was to explain in her evidence at Rosemary West's trial.

Heather West's death has a particular poignancy for me as it was the very first murder that I heard Frederick West describe in his audiotaped police interviews, every one of which I heard during my research for his biography. Soon after I started the project – and while Rosemary's trial was proceeding – I was ushered into a solicitor's office in central London and shown into a small room with no windows whatsoever. It was known as Room K. The only things in the cramped room were a table and chair in the centre, and on one side a large grey filing cabinet with double doors. I was presented with a cassette tape-recorder to listen to West's police interviews and left alone.

When I opened the filing cabinet I discovered a small brown cardboard box, which I opened to discover that it contained Frederick West's clothes – including the suit that he had worn during his Court appearances, his shirt, socks, underpants and shoes. It was a very macabre moment indeed.

Beside the cardboard box were a jumble of police tapes and more than twenty lever-arch files containing the printed versions of his and Rose's interviews with the police. There was no definitive list, and certainly no catalogue, so I simply chose one at random, put it into the cassette player and pressed 'Play'.

There, in that windowless room, I heard West's sing-song voice, with its Herefordshire burr, describe in detail how he had killed his and Rose's first-born child Heather, and then how he had chopped her body into pieces, disarticulating her legs at the hips, cutting off her head, and pushing the remaining torso into a plastic dustbin, as a prelude to burying her dismembered remains in his garden. All the time, he insisted, in a plaintive voice, that Rose had 'been out shopping' in the High Street and did not know what was going on. It was a lie he was to maintain for the rest of his life.

It was the lie that Rosemary West would hide behind at her trial. She never knew what was going on, she told the jury, did not have any responsibility for it, and could not imagine why anyone would think differently – even though one of the young women she was accused of killing was eighteen-year-old Shirley Robinson, murdered in the summer of 1978. Robinson was not only her husband's lover but also hers, and had been eight-and-a-half months pregnant when she met her death at Cromwell Street, to be buried along with her unborn child under the patio in the garden.

The Wests were finally brought to justice by the diligence and tenacity of Detective Constable Hazel Savage, who began to investigate the disappearance of Heather West in the wake of Frederick West's arrest and eventual charge for three rapes, and one of buggery against one of his surviving daughters, in August 1992. Yet just under a year later, when he faced trial, two of the witnesses refused to give evidence and the judge ordered that not guilty verdicts should be returned. A further eighteen months were to elapse before DC Savage initiated the excavation beneath the patio of 25 Cromwell Street in February 1994 and the first bodies were discovered.

Frederick West was eventually charged with twelve murders, including those of his first wife, Rena, their nanny Ann McFall, his stepdaughter Charmaine, aged eight, his daughter Heather, aged sixteen, and the other eight young women whose remains were found at Cromwell Street. Rosemary West was only charged with ten murders, excluding those of Rena and Ann McFall. But her husband was to escape justice completely when he committed suicide in his cell at Winson Green Prison in Birmingham shortly before 1 p.m. on 1 January 1995.

Rosemary West was left to stand trial alone, and on 21 and 22 November 1995, the jury at Winchester Crown Court unanimously found her guilty on all ten counts of murder, accepting that she must have known what was going on under the roof of their cramped semi-detached house in Cromwell Street, and the fact that her attitude towards Carol Raine revealed her partnership with her husband.

In the late morning of Wednesday 22 November 1995, Mr

Justice Mantell passed sentence on the woman who had become Britain's most prolific female serial killer. Sitting in Court watching Rosemary West as she stood to hear her sentence there was an extraordinary hush as the judge spoke softly to her across the light-wood-panelled courtroom. Telling her that he was sentencing her to life imprisonment, he added a final sentence, 'If attention is paid to what I think, you will never be released.'

Rosemary West left the dock as stony-faced as she had been since the beginning of her trial, although her legal team reported that she cried once she was out of sight. Her determination to see herself as a victim of her late husband's evil actions, rather than his wicked apprentice, did not desert her, no more than it had done throughout their time together. She remained determined to present a controlled face to the world, and one which implied her innocence – no matter that the jury at her trial did not believe her for one moment.

Four months later, on Tuesday 19 March 1996, the Court of Appeal in London upheld the jury's decision and refused Rosemary West the right to appeal against the verdict. I watched as the Lord Chief Justice of the day, Lord Taylor, told her – as she had come to Court in person, as was her legal right – 'The applicant and Fred were in the habit of sexually and sadistically abusing young girls in the cellar of their house for their joint pleasure.'

Lord Taylor concluded, 'The concept of all these murders and burials taking place at the applicant's home and concurrently grave sexual abuse of other young girls being committed by both husband and wife together, without the latter being party to the killings is, in our view, clearly one the jury was entitled to reject. The evidence in its totality was overwhelming.'

It was to be the Lord Chief Justice himself who went on

to recommend that Rosemary West should serve a minimum term of twenty-five years as part of her life sentence, but it was the new Labour Home Secretary, Jack Straw, in July 1997, who subjected her to a whole life term, making her only the second woman in British criminal history, after Myra Hindley, to be condemned to spend the rest of her life in prison.

Over the next four years West considered another appeal, this time to the European Court of Human Rights, as well as seeking a referral to the Criminal Cases Review Commission, but – like Mark Bridger before her – in the end she decided not to proceed. When I went to talk to Leo Goatley, her former solicitor, about it, he had already considered the possibility that she would decide not to proceed with either application. On 1 October 2001, Rosemary West did exactly that. In a statement – the only public statement she has ever made about the case (though many others have been attributed to her) – she apologised to her family and announced that she expected to spend the rest of her life in prison.

In her statement, West added that she hoped for 'reconciliation' with her family in future, but insisted that she was no longer 'seeking release' and acknowledged that she would never be able to have a 'normal life'. But she also steadfastly maintained that she was innocent of the ten killings that she had been convicted of.

Five years later, Rosemary West effectively cut off all relations with her family, and especially her stepdaughter Anne Marie, her own daughter Mae, and her son Stephen. In a letter to Mae written from Bronzefield women's prison near Ashford in Middlesex, she again apologised to each of them, saying that they had never had the chance to 'clear the air so to speak'.

'I was never a parent,' she wrote, 'and could never be now . . . Too much has happened and too much damage has been done. I truly do not have the skills to be a parent and although I am sad and ashamed of this, it is something that has to be accepted.'

Rosemary West has accustomed herself to the fact that she will never again be a free woman, acknowledging the lesson she learnt from Myra Hindley that her very notoriety would make it all but impossible for her ever to be granted parole. There can also be no doubt that her actions have deeply affected her children, with both Anne Marie and Stephen West allegedly attempting suicide.

Stephen also admitted seven counts of having sex with an underage girl of fourteen in 2004 at Worcester Crown Court. He was given a nine-month prison sentence and was acknowledged to be suffering from post-traumatic stress syndrome. Meanwhile, West's second daughter Mae asked in a newspaper interview, 'I just don't know why Mum bothered having us. Why would you just subject more and more children to that?'

Presently serving her whole life sentence in Low Newton high-security prison in Durham, Rosemary West has made the best of her life behind bars, at a cost approaching £60,000 each year to the taxpayer. With her own cell, equipped with television, radio and CD player, as well as toilet facilities, she reportedly enjoys listening to *The Archers* on Radio Four, doing embroidery, cooking and shopping from catalogues. She also buys beauty products and reportedly earns £16 a week as an orderly, having been promoted from being a cleaner, which entails making tea for the prison officers. West is also alleged to have had a series of lesbian affairs during her twenty years in jail.

Apparently content with her life in prison, West has never displayed one moment's contrition or regret for her crimes. Indeed, she still maintains her innocence, and by doing so she renders it all but impossible that any parole hearing in the future could consider her for release – as one of the principal criteria for allowing it is that the prisoner has repented and accepted his or her guilt. West has done the opposite.

Rosemary West has even rejected a letter of forgiveness from the sister of one of her victims, twenty-one-year old Essex University undergraduate Lucy Partington, who disappeared from a bus stop on 27 December 1973, never to be seen again until her remains were discovered under the cellar floor in Cromwell Street. Lucy's sister Marian wrote to West in 2008 to say, 'I do not feel any hostility towards you, just a sadness, a deep sadness, that all this has happened, and that your heart could not feel a truth that I wish you could know.' A few weeks later Marian Partington received a response on behalf of West, pointedly refusing to accept her forgiveness and demanding that she 'cease all correspondence'.

West's belligerent attitude to her sentence, coupled with her desire to make life as comfortable as possible in prison, must bring into question the European Court's conclusion that whole life terms are, by definition, 'inhuman', even though there can be no doubt that to deny any individual their liberty without any possibility of release takes a particular toll. Yet it is a toll that Victor Miller, Mark Bridger and Rosemary West are prepared to accept and live with, as all three see no chance whatever that it will be revoked. In the case of Bridger and West, there is also an acknowledgment that their celebrity merely confirms the impossibility of their freedom.

13

A 'Cushy' Life

Arthur Hutchinson and Ian Huntley

One whole life prisoner who certainly did not accept his punishment, and did everything in his power to appeal against it, including taking his case to the European Court of Human Rights in 2014, was the triple murderer and rapist Arthur Hutchinson, now aged seventy-four. Hutchinson had spent the previous thirty years of his life in prison and was determined not to die behind bars – if he could find a legal process that would help him to avoid it.

Given the inhuman bestiality of Hutchinson's rape and murders, it is hard to see how he had the nerve to launch his string of appeals. In fact, he did not do so until twenty-five years after the killings in October 1984, when he clearly realised that he was never going to be released. But his punishment cannot have been a complete surprise as Hutchinson had been a life-long criminal with a history of violence when he was finally convicted of a murderous spree that resulted in the death of three members of the same family in September 1984.

By that time Hutchinson, who was then aged forty-three, had already spent more than five years in prison for the attempted murder of his brother-in-law, even escaping from a Magistrates' Court in the process. But let us begin at the beginning.

A resourceful, wily man, who later nicknamed himself 'The Fox' – 'because of my cunning ways' – Hutchinson was preoccupied by sex and violence from childhood. Born in Hartlepool, County Durham, on 19 February 1941, he was the illegitimate son of Louise Reardon, wife of a local coal miner. Together she and her husband Cuthbert had four children, but she also had two illegitimate children with the couple's lodger, Arthur Hutchinson, whose name her son took. As his mother put it later, 'I had five girls and they made life hell for Arthur. They called him a bastard, which was true.'

Nevertheless, Hutchinson remained utterly devoted to his mother who, in turn, remained loyal to her son, calling him her 'little angel' until her death in 1985. After his murder convictions she insisted that his crimes were the result of an accident he suffered as a small boy, when he rode his bicycle into a lamppost, leaving him in a coma for three days. The incident certainly left him with a fractured skull, and – some said – a bipolar personality, with a distinct appetite for violence. At the age of seven he stabbed one of his sisters with a pair of scissors.

Hutchinson rapidly became sexually precocious. At the age of eleven, he made his first appearance in Juvenile Court, where he was charged with indecent assault. Nineteen further appearances followed during his teenage years, including four charges of sexual intercourse with girls under the age of sixteen. Then, at the age of eighteen, Hutchinson married a neighbour, Margaret Dover, who was already pregnant with his child. The couple separated after only three years, and at the age of twenty-two he was sent to prison for the first time, after being convicted of unlawful sexual intercourse.

After his release, Hutchinson married for a second time, to a girl called Hannelore, who rapidly came to experience his sexual preoccupations as well as the violent side of his personality. 'Anything could provoke him, sometimes nothing,' she said later. 'He used to boast about his conquests. The day he left me, he beat me up in the street. He knocked me to the ground and put the boot in. I once saw him knock his mother out of a rocking chair, halfway across the room.'

In his thirties, Hutchinson tried to shoot his half-brother, and was imprisoned for five and a half years. That did nothing to change him, however, and by September 1983 – when he was aged forty-two – he was charged with theft, burglary and rape, and remanded in custody. But he had no intention of remaining in jail.

On the morning of 28 September 1983, Hutchinson was brought to Selby Magistrates' Court in North Yorkshire for a hearing on the three charges, but shortly after he arrived he told the two prison officers who had brought him from Armley Prison in Leeds that he needed to use the bathroom and they removed his handcuffs to allow him to do so. It was to prove a catastrophic mistake.

No sooner had they done so than Hutchinson sprinted up the stairs from the ground floor reception area to the courtrooms above. He ran into Court One, jumped over the dock and dived through the window, shattering the glass and cutting himself in the process, only to land on a barbed wire fence, which inflicted severe damage to his knee. Undaunted, Hutchinson worked himself free of the tangled wire and set off to run to freedom.

In a taunting audiotape that Hutchinson later sent to the police, he described his escape from Selby Magistrates' Court. 'I hurled myself through an upper window, crashing into a barbed wire net, ripping my leg to pieces,' he said, explaining that he then ran for four miles, barely stopping before collapsing.

'I stopped in the bushes for hours then I see the helicopter hunt,' he went on. 'So I dragged myself into the gutter, crawled along the gutter and forced myself into bramble bushes and stayed there till it got dark.' Hutchinson then claimed that he spent the next four nights on the run, surviving on dandelions and roots, before going to hospital in Doncaster in search of medical help.

Amazingly, when he arrived at Accident and Emergency no one seemed to question his bloodied and torn trousers. 'I got my treatment,' he said, 'left and walked another three to four miles back into the wilderness. You just have to keep continuing sometimes. I just had to live day by day but I won't give in. I'll never give in.' Hutchinson managed to evade recapture by the police for the following three and a half weeks, and it was while he was on the run that he was to commit the heinous crimes that would mark him out as a man who should spend the rest of his life in prison on a whole life sentence.

On the night of 22 October 1983, Hutchinson was lying in wait outside a prosperous detached house with large grounds in Dore, near Sheffield, more than forty miles from Selby. There had been a wedding that day – local solicitor Basil Laitner, aged fifty-nine, and his doctor wife Avril, fifty-five, had hosted the wedding reception of their eldest daughter Suzanne in their house, with a marquee in their large garden, after the formal ceremony at the United Hebrew Congregation in Sheffield. The wedding reception had started at four in the afternoon, but had come to an end just after eight that evening. The Laitners and their son Richard, aged twenty-eight, then went out to dinner with relatives not far away, leaving their eighteen-year-old daughter Nicola, who had been a bridesmaid, at home because she said she felt tired and wanted to go straight to bed.

Empty champagne bottles were left everywhere in the marquee, as was food left over from the reception. Perhaps it was the food and drink that attracted Hutchinson but, more likely, the ordeal of his weeks on the run had sharpened his appetite for sex and violence. He almost certainly watched the reception from the bushes and became aroused by the fact that the Laitners' daughter Nicola looked exceptionally beautiful as a bridesmaid. There was the added attraction that Hutchinson was also intent on collecting whatever cash and valuables he could find in the house to sustain him on the run. No one will ever know for certain what motivated him that night, for he has never explained it.

Whatever the reason, when the Laitners and their son returned home at about 11.15 on the evening of Saturday 22 October 1983 they were not alone. A filthy and dishevelled Hutchinson had broken into the house through a patio door and was waiting for them – but they did not realise it for some time. Not suspecting that anything was amiss, Avril Laitner retired to her downstairs bedroom, her son Richard, who was starting out on his career as a barrister, went to his bedroom upstairs and his father Basil also went to his own upstairs bedroom.

Given Hutchinson's track record, and sexual appetite, it seems almost certain that his primary target was a sexual conquest – Nicola Laitner, the bridesmaid. Seeing her dress on the outside of a bedroom door, he went in – only to find that it was actually her brother Richard's room. Keen to neutralise the threat to his sexual ambitions of a fit young man, and furious that he had got the wrong room, Hutchinson proceeded to 'speedily despatch' the twenty-eight year old, though not before he had let out two plaintive screams. Hutchinson stabbed Richard Laitner twice in the chest, killing him instantly, and then calmly moved on to Nicola's room. Richard was found later covered in blood, half in and half out of his bed, with his hands clasped to his chest above the fatal wounds.

Richard's screams woke Nicola Laitner, who then realised that there was someone in the room with her when she looked around. It was Hutchinson. But she was so terrified that she was unable to move. Having established she was there and petrified, Hutchinson went back out on to the first-floor landing, where he encountered Basil Laitner who had also been alerted by the screams. From her bedroom Nicola Laitner heard her father arguing with a man whose voice she did not recognise before she heard a 'gasping, choking sound – and then all returned to deathly quiet'. Basil Laitner had been stabbed twice in the throat and then, as he slumped to the ground, once more in the back.

Confident that the two men in the house no longer presented any threat to him, Hutchinson went downstairs to approach Avril Laitner. Nicola heard her mother shout, 'Just take the money and go, leave us alone,' before another series of 'terrible screaming'. Avril Laitner was later found face down on the floor of her bedroom, surrounded by her jewellery and credit cards. She had twenty-six knife wounds, including four stab wounds in her left arm and thirteen in the palm of her left hand as she tried to fend off her killer. She died from a stab wound to the left side of her neck, which severed her jugular.

Now the only person left alive in the house was Nicola Laitner, and she was at Hutchinson's mercy. He retraced his steps back upstairs and went into her darkened room, before flashing a torch in her eyes and saying, 'Put the light on, scream and you're dead.' He was nevertheless clearly aware that the screams may have alerted the Laitners' neighbours, but as time passed and no one came to investigate he relaxed.

Hutchinson marched the terrified teenager out of the room at knifepoint, although also urging her to hide her eyes on the stairs in case she saw 'something horrible' – her father's dead body.

In the hours that followed, Hutchinson subjected the girl to a prolonged sexual assault, raping her in the marquee and twice back in her bedroom. He affected a Scottish accent, presumably to try to conceal his true identity, and told her that he had killed everybody left in the house. Finally, as first light started to reveal the extent of the carnage, he left her tied up in her bedroom. As he left he told her, 'I'm going now. Don't suffocate yourself.'

When a group of workmen arrived to dismantle the marquee that morning, they discovered the bodies of the Laitner family as well as Nicola, whose nightdress was stained with blood from Hutchinson's hands, and whose foot was caked in her father's blood. But she was not in total shock and, crucially, she was able to give the police a detailed description of her attacker. A police sketch artist rapidly produced a portrait that bore a stunning resemblance to the man who had limped away from Selby Magistrates' Court three and a half weeks earlier.

Not that Nicola's attacker was to be found easily. In the days that followed, the police launched a wholehearted search for Hutchinson, identifying him as their suspect after matching a handprint found on a champagne bottle with a print on his criminal file. No fewer than ten police forces throughout the North of England were briefed to search for him. Yet, once again, he managed to escape by criss-crossing the country, at one point staying in a Darlington guest house under the name of 'A. Fox'.

Barely two weeks after the Laitner massacre, Hutchinson was finally arrested on 5 November 1983 in a field on a farm near Hartlepool, County Durham, after being spotted trying to call his mother from a telephone box. He tried and failed to stab himself when he was apprehended, but then told one of the arresting officers, 'I'm not a murderer. I should have stayed down my fox hole, shouldn't I?'

At the Darlington guest house, where Hutchinson had been staying before his arrest, the police found an audiotape that he had made while he was on the run. On it he boasted of having a transistor radio with a tape-recorder which meant he could listen in to police broadcasts. 'I've been able to listen to everything that's been going on – where they've been waiting for me, where they've been looking for me, so I knew exactly which way to head out of the way from them. Like playing cat and mouse, or should I say fox on the trot.'

'I'm making no comment on the triple killings,' Hutchinson went on in his recording. 'Let the police do what they want. I'm saying nowt. They knew I was finished but makes no difference whether they shoot me for this or anything else. If they think I'm dangerous, let them think that. Maybe I am, maybe I'm not. I'm still free and that's the main thing.'

Hutchinson concluded by insisting with a laugh, 'However crackers I might be, I've walked past them several times and they haven't even noticed me. Like I say, I'm a master of disguise.' Significantly, Hutchinson firmly denied having anything to do with the Laitner murders, although he admitted to escaping from the Magistrates' Court. He maintained firmly, 'I did not kill them people.'

Even though the forensic evidence against him was compelling, Hutchinson continued to protest his innocence for months. Scene of crime officers pointed out that he had a rare blood group which matched the blood found on Nicola Laitner's bed sheets, which had leaked from the wound in his knee from Selby. He had also left teeth marks on a piece of cheese from the family's fridge which matched his dental records.

Eventually Hutchinson changed his story, but only slightly, claiming that Nicola had invited him into the house for consensual sex, and that he had nothing whatever to do with the murders. Even knowing his own guilt, his decision to maintain that Nicola had been a willing sexual partner was an act of gratuitous barbarity for, by doing so, and pleading not guilty to the rape, he forced the teenager to relive her ordeal at his hands in open Court.

Hutchinson's trial for three murders and rape finally began before Mr Justice McNeill on 4 September 1984, at Durham Crown Court. But there was controversy from the outset, after the judge decided that reporting restrictions could be lifted, allowing the media to identify Nicola Laitner as the rape victim. The prosecution argued that there was no way she could remain anonymous when it was common knowledge locally – from the initial reports of the massacre – that Hutchinson had committed an act of rape on a further family member who had survived.

The judge also ruled that preserving Nicola's anonymity would mean keeping the names of the three murder victims out of the trial; something he deemed legally difficult as the case had attracted considerable public interest and the Laitners had already been publicly identified as the victims.

In the wake of that decision, no neutral observer could have failed to be moved by Nicola Laitner's ordeal in the witness box. On behalf of Hutchinson, James Stewart QC suggested to her that she had met his client in a local pub on the day before the wedding and organized for him to come to the house after the reception. She denied each and every suggestion. Visibly shaking, she also denied that there had been consensual sex between them, and then broke down in tears, sobbing, 'I want to go home.' After regaining her composure, she continued answering the defence barrister's questions, but steadfastly refused to tie her own hands using the grey spotted tie that Hutchinson had allegedly used to tie her up.

In his closing speech to the jury at the end of the ten-day trial, the prosecution barrister suggested that Hutchinson had 'told a tissue of lies' about the rape, and that he was a 'deliberate and repetitive liar' who had 'no concept of the truth'. It took the jury of six men and six women just four hours to find Hutchinson guilty of all the charges on 14 September 1984.

Mr Justice McNeill, passing sentence, called Hutchinson 'arrogant, manipulative,' with 'a self-centred attitude towards life, and a severe personality disorder, which is not amenable to any form of treatment'. He then sentenced Hutchinson to life imprisonment, with a minimum term of eighteen years. Ten months later his appeal against his conviction failed at the Court of Appeal, where Lord Justice Watkins explained that he had been convicted on the basis of 'devastating evidence' that proved he had committed 'outrageous and almost unbelievably horrid' murders. Not long afterwards the then Home Secretary, Conservative Leon Brittan, decreed that he should be subject to a whole life term of imprisonment, with no prospect of release.

It was not until 2008, twenty-five years after the Laitner killings, that Hutchinson launched a campaign for his freedom, questioning his whole life term and saying it breached his 'human rights'. The Court of Appeal rejected the argument. Reviewing the case in May, Mr Justice Tugendhat ruled that the sixty-six year old should remain in prison for the rest of his life for the crimes. He also refused to allow the appeal to go any further. 'There is no reason at all for departing from the decision of the Home Secretary,' he concluded.

Undeterred, Hutchinson and his legal team pursued an appeal, and in October 2008 returned to the Court of Appeal in London, once again on the grounds that his whole life term was a breach of his human rights, and that – in any event – his conviction was flawed. Once again Hutchinson received short shrift. Three Court of Appeal judges told him that his crimes were so deranged that life must indeed mean life.

Lord Justice Dyson, sitting with Mr Justice Henriques and Mr Justice Openshaw, said there was 'no substance' in Hutchinson's application. 'This was a truly shocking case,' he added. 'In the experience of all three members of this court we can say that none of us is aware of a case of greater gravity or more heinous than this case. In our judgement Mr Justice Tugendhat was plainly correct in saying that this applicant should spend the rest of his life in custody without prospect of release.'

Even then, Hutchinson was not prepared to give up his appeal. He pursued his case to the European Court of Human Rights in Strasbourg. In August 2013 he became the very first British prisoner serving a whole life term to appeal against it in the Strasbourg Court in the wake of their decision in June 2013 questioning the right of the English Courts to pass a whole life term sentence, which it considered inhuman and degrading.

His appeal provoked a furious reaction from the remaining members of the Laitner family. 'Whenever even the name Arthur Hutchinson rears its ugly head,' the Laitner family said in a statement, 'it does nothing but create fear and distress to the victims of this heinous crime. Let the [European Court of] Human Rights judiciary members be thrust into our position for just a day and maybe they would understand this. We are confident that justice will be done and more importantly be seen to be done, so that this matter can finally be put to rest.'

It was a view echoed by the then Secretary of State for Justice, Chris Grayling MP, who commented, 'To be told this breaches human rights is absurd . . . What about the rights of the victims and their families?'

Nevertheless, Hutchinson and his legal team still hoped that the European Court's decision might eventually lead to his release. But that hope was effectively ended by the English Court of Appeal's decision in February 2014, upholding their right to pass a whole life sentence, as there remained some prospects for release in exceptional circumstances. Yet, even then, Hutchinson persisted with his case in Strasbourg. It was not until February 2015, two weeks before his seventy-fourth birthday, that any faint hope he may have had for his release was finally extinguished.

On 3 February 2015, the European Court ruled that his whole life order could not be overturned on the basis that it contradicted his rights under Article Three of the European Convention on Human Rights, which relates to inhuman and degrading treatment. In a stark contradiction of their decision in June 2013, the Strasbourg-based Court also said that it now considered that the United Kingdom *was* in line with European human rights laws. They were taking into account the Court of Appeal's verdict in February 2014 that prisoners do have the opportunity of release – even when serving a whole life term – as the Secretary of State for Justice has the right to release them under very specific circumstances.

The European Court acknowledged the Court of Appeal's decision, when its judges said in their written ruling on 3 February 2015, 'In the circumstances of this case where, following the Grand Chamber's judgement in which it expressed doubts about the clarity of domestic law, the national Court has specifically addressed those doubts and set out an unequivocal statement of the legal position, the Court must accept the national Court's interpretation of domestic law.'

In other words, the fate of a whole life prisoner now lay unequivocally in the hands of the British legal system and the Secretary of State for Justice. That decision also meant that the appeal by Douglas Vinter, Jeremy Bamber and Peter Moore that their whole life terms could be overturned by the European Court fell away. Just as significantly, Arthur Hutchinson, the 'Fox' from Teesside, who has spent almost thirty-two years in jail since the Laitner massacre, is thereby condemned to remain there for the rest of his life.

For his part, Hutchinson has remained unrepentant, indeed boastful of his crimes, hinting to his half-brother in a series of threatening telephone calls that he would find the surviving members of the Laitner family, if he were ever to be released, even though that possibility must now be so remote as to be all but meaningless. That thought will no doubt torment a man who is possessed by a desire to control and manipulate everything and everyone around him. Hutchinson is reported to be still regarded as a danger to his fellow prisoners – so deep is the rage he feels at not being able to dictate his destiny.

As Dan Hodges put it in the *Daily Telegraph*, 'This is not a man who deserves to wake up every morning hopeful that he is a day nearer to his release. He is a man who should know with brutal, unequivocal certainty that the bare walls of his cell will encase him till the days he dies.' Many would agree in Hutchinson's case, so grotesque and heinous were his crimes, but there are others who would question it. Janet Crowe, of the Penal Reform Trust, for example, believes that prisoners need at least the hope of freedom: 'If a prisoner has no hope and they feel they have nothing to lose,' she has said, 'it may make them far more dangerous to work with inside the prison.'

But the case of Arthur Hutchinson throws into sharp relief the case of another multiple murderer– school caretaker Ian Huntley – who was not sentenced to a whole life term of imprisonment, in spite of committing crimes that may have seemed to many every bit as heinous as Hutchinson's. On the surface it is difficult to see why there should be a difference between the two sentences, but Huntley's crimes underline the ambiguity that lies behind the current judicial attitude to whole life terms of imprisonment. To see why that is, we need to look at his case in some detail.

Just after 6.15 on the sunny Sunday early evening of 4 August 2002, two ten-year-old schoolgirls, Holly Wells and Jessica Chapman – both wearing Manchester United football shirts – were walking home from the local shop in the pretty Cambridgeshire village of Soham after buying some sweets. They had both attended a barbecue that day at Holly's house and were in high spirits. On their way home they passed the rented home of twenty-nine-year-old Ian Kevin Huntley, who opened his front door and went out to talk to them. The girls knew him, just as they knew his live-in girlfriend, Maxine Carr, who worked as a teaching assistant at St Andrews primary school, which they both attended.

Telling Holly and Jessica that Maxine Carr was inside the house, and would love to speak to them, Huntley ushered the two ten year olds inside – only for them to discover that Maxine Carr was not actually there. She was in her home town of Grimsby in Lincolnshire visiting her mother. But Huntley did not let them leave, and within a matter of minutes both young girls were dead.

No one can truly say why Huntley killed them on that sunny August day, for he certainly did not appear to have planned the killings. Huntley's mother later suggested he had killed them in a 'fit of jealous rage' in the wake of slamming the phone down on Carr after a bitter argument over the fact that she may have been cheating on him with another man, and that he was stuck at home alone, while she was out 'enjoying herself'. The police also believe that this was Huntley's motive for the killings, as they found no evidence whatever of premeditation.

One thing is certain. Huntley has never explained why he killed Holly and Jessica inside his tidy little house on that day. But the transcript of a telephone call Huntley made from prison to a member of his family, which was published in *The Sun* newspaper in March 2007, revealed some of the details of the killings, though not the motive for them. In the tape Huntley said that Holly had died in the bathroom of the house, possibly from drowning, and that Jessica had died in the living room, probably after being asphyxiated.

In the ninety-minute tape, alleged to have been made in September 2006, Huntley explained that he had been brushing his dog, Sadie, when he had seen Holly and Jessica that Sunday. Holly had a nosebleed, he explained, and Jessica needed the toilet, so he had taken them into the house and upstairs to the bathroom. Huntley then maintained that Holly had 'fallen' into the bath, which was full of water, and Jessica had 'started to cause a bit of commotion'. He also revealed that he had taken Jessica's mobile phone – 'I grabbed it from her and turned it off as she was constantly saying I had pushed Holly.'

'As soon as I got Holly out of the bath,' Huntley was quoted as saying, 'and realised she was dead, Jessica went schiz.' The caretaker took her downstairs to try calm her down, but she tried to leave. 'I don't know what was going through my head, I don't recall thinking, "I've got to kill her to stop her leaving". I think it was my intention just to stop her . . . I guess you could say that she acted, I reacted without even thinking. I grabbed hold of her, realising that I couldn't let her go. At that point, with one hand over her mouth and the other round her neck, she died.

'I feel it's important to reiterate that there was no sexual motive,' Huntley added. 'There was no sexual interference with either girl.' He also insisted that he was not 'evil'.

What is not in doubt, however, is that Huntley had a track record of taking a sexual interest in young girls. In August 1995, for example, when he was twenty-one years old, a joint investigation was launched by police and social services in his home town of Grimsby after a fifteen-year-old girl admitted that she had been having sex with him. But no prosecution took place.

In March 1996 he was investigated again over allegations that he had been having sex with an underage girl, but again he was not charged. Then, in April 1996, Huntley was investigated yet again over allegations of underage sex, but this allegation, too, did not result in a charge. The following month he was investigated over further allegations of having sex with a thirteen-year-old girl, and yet again no prosecution followed.

Two years later, in April 1998, Huntley was arrested on suspicion of raping a woman. He admitted having sex with her but claimed it was consensual. The police decided not to charge him. The following month, May 1998, he was formally charged with rape and remanded in custody after an eighteen-year-old Grimsby woman claimed to have been raped by him on her way home from a nightclub in the town. The charge was dropped after the Crown Prosecution

Service determined that there was no realistic chance of a conviction.

Then, in July 1998, Huntley was investigated once more over allegations that he had indecently assaulted an eleven-year-old girl the previous September, but again he was never charged. He was investigated over allegations of rape on a seventeen-year-old girl in February 1999 but yet again no charges were brought against him.

One final allegation came in July 1999, when a woman was raped and Huntley was interviewed by police about his possible involvement. But an alibi was provided for him by his latest girlfriend, Maxine Carr, and again there was no charge. The woman subsequently said that Huntley was not the rapist. The BBC also revealed in 2012 that North East Lincolnshire Social Services had received four separate complaints of underage sexual relations against Huntley in the late 1990s.

Huntley's marital record was every bit as chequered. In December 1994, then aged nineteen, he met eighteen-year-old Claire Evans, embarked on a whirlwind romance and married her within weeks. The marriage was short lived, however, and she left Huntley within a matter of days, moving in with Huntley's younger brother Wayne. An enraged Huntley refused to grant his wife a divorce until 1999, thereby preventing his brother's marriage to Evans.

In February 1999, at the age of twenty-five, Huntley met twenty-nine-year-old Maxine Carr at a Grimsby nightclub, and they moved in together after just four weeks. The relationship endured despite some turbulent rows, and they moved to Soham in 2001, where Huntley took a job at the Village Centre as the manager of a team of caretakers. In September 2001 he applied for the post of caretaker at Soham Village College, a secondary school; and in November 2001, despite his history of sexual contact with underage girls, he was awarded the position. Carr, meanwhile, became a teaching assistant at the local primary school.

Cambridgeshire police knew none of those facts when they embarked on their investigation into the disappearance of Holly Wells and Jessica Chapman in August 2002. They also did not know that Huntley had hidden the girls' bodies in the boot of his red Ford Fiesta on that Sunday evening – bending their young limbs to do so – while pretending to the world that he had 'no idea' where they had gone, even though, as one television reporter put to him, he could well have been the last person to see them alive.

'Yeah, that's what it seems like,' he said calmly, while insisting that their disappearance was 'absolutely' a mystery. Chillingly, he also told the reporter, 'While there's no news there's still a glimmer of hope, and that's basically what we're all hanging on to.'

For her part, Maxine Carr showed another television reporter the 'thank you' card that Holly Wells had given her on the last day of the summer term at school that year. 'She was just lovely, really lovely,' Carr said, urging Holly and Jessica to 'just come home'.

The grim reality was that at about 8.30 in the morning of Monday 5 August, the day after the murders, Huntley drove the bodies of the two dead girls, still in his boot, to a field at the perimeter of the Royal Air Force base at Lakenheath in Suffolk, about six miles from Soham. There he stripped their clothes from them, leaving them naked, dropped them into a six-foot ditch, poured petrol from a can that he had brought with him over them and then set fire to them both, hoping to destroy any forensic evidence that might incriminate him. Huntley then calmly drove home, taking the girls' clothes with him.

By that time a police search for the two girls was in full swing. Pictures of them were circulated throughout the community in the hopes that someone had seen them. Their parents held an emotional news conference pleading for any information about their whereabouts. Even the Manchester United football star, David Beckham, whose name adorned the back of the two girls' shirts, made a televised appeal for their safe return. Huntley played his part in the search, as did Maxine Carr, who had, by then, returned from Grimsby.

Holly and Jessica's Manchester United shirts were eventually found in a rubbish bin in a storage building at Soham Village College, along with their shoes. It was one of the first breaks in the investigation, but it did not come until Saturday August 16, twelve days after the girls' disappearance. The police arrested Huntley and Carr in the early hours of Sunday 17 August on suspicion of murder. Later that same day a game warden walking through the woods at the edge of RAF Lakenheath came across the girls' partially-burned bodies, which were by then 'severely decomposed' and 'partially skeletonised'. An autopsy revealed that they had both been asphyxiated.

At the outset of the inquiry into Holly and Jessica's disappearance, Carr had provided Huntley with an alibi for the time of the girls' deaths, telling the police that she had got back from Grimsby when the girls arrived. It did not take them long to discover that she was actually in Grimsby at the time of the murders. Nevertheless, both she and Huntley maintained their innocence.

Three days later, on Thursday 20 August, Huntley was charged with two counts of murder and detained under Section 48 of the Mental Health Act at Rampton Secure Hospital in Nottinghamshire, where his mental state was assessed to determine whether he suffered from mental illness and whether he was fit to stand trial. Consultant psychiatrist Dr Christopher Clark carried out the assessment and concluded firmly, 'Although Mr Huntley made clear attempts to appear insane, I have no doubt that the man currently, and at the time of the murders, was both physically and mentally sound and therefore, if he is found guilty, carried out the murders totally aware of his actions.'

On 8 October 2002, a judge agreed with Dr Clark's conclusions and found that Huntley was indeed fit to stand trial. As a result, the school caretaker was moved to Woodhill Prison in Milton Keynes, Buckinghamshire, where he attempted suicide on 9 June 2003 by taking twenty-nine anti-depressant pills which he had saved up in his cell. Within forty-eight hours, however, he was back in prison and transferred again, this time to Belmarsh Prison in south-east London.

Meanwhile, Maxine Carr was charged with perverting the course of justice shortly after her initial arrest on 17 August 2002, and in January 2003 she was formally charged with two counts of assisting an offender. She, like Huntley, was remanded in custody to await trial.

Huntley and Carr's trial opened at the Central Criminal Court in Old Bailey, London, on 5 November 2003, before Mr Justice Moses, but in spite of Huntley's private 'theory' about the case, he pleaded not guilty to the two counts of murder. It was a plea that Richard Latham QC, for the prosecution, belittled throughout his opening remarks to the jury of five men and seven women. Latham explained that he would present the court with overwhelming evidence that Huntley had indeed brutally murdered the girls and tried to cover it up. He also claimed that there was evidence that Carr misled the police to protect Huntley, although it was likely that she was not directly involved in the murders.

Over the ensuing weeks, Latham meticulously built up a picture of Huntley taking precise precautions to cover up his crimes, not only by cleaning out his Ford Fiesta, but also getting four new tyres for it to make sure it could not be identified from tracks that might have been found near the ditch on the edge of RAF Lakenheath. He also suggested that Huntley had lured the two children into his house with the promise that Maxine Carr would be pleased to see them.

After Latham's prolonged destruction of Huntley's story, and three weeks into the trial, there came a moment of high drama. Huntley changed his story, and his plea, admitting that he had been with the girls in his house when they died, but claiming that their deaths were entirely accidental. Huntley's defence counsel, Stephen Coward QC, offered a statement from the school caretaker, who was not in court because he was reportedly ill, claiming that the girls stopped by his house to talk to Ms Carr and during that time Holly had a nosebleed. While getting some toilet paper, Huntley accidentally knocked Holly backwards and into the bathtub, which was half full of water. After that, he had 'accidentally' stifled Jessica when he put his hand over her mouth to stop her screaming.

Maxine Carr also made a confession that week. She told police that it was her idea to claim she was in the house she shared with Mr Huntley on the day Holly Wells and Jessica Chapman disappeared, because she wanted to protect her boyfriend, whom she believed was innocent of murder. Carr also alleged that she lied because she wanted to prevent the 1998 'false' rape allegation against Huntley from being unearthed again.

Almost immediately after these two dramatic twists in the trial, the defence opened its case to the jury, and sought to substantiate Huntley's theory of the deaths. Richard Latham QC ridiculed Huntley in the witness box when he came to give evidence in his own defence. During his cross-examination he accused Huntley of lying and changing his story to fit the facts, calling the nosebleed story 'rubbish' and telling him that he had been 'tempted' by the girls the moment they arrived at his doorstep. Latham also suggested that Huntley deliberately intended to murder the girls, which would account for the fact that he made no attempt to resuscitate them after their deaths. For his part, Huntley angrily stated that he did not do so because he was 'frozen by panic'.

After three days in the witness box, Huntley stepped down, and Carr's defence began. Her counsel, Michael Hubbard QC, told the court that his client had 'no control' over the events on that fateful Sunday. Carr testified that she didn't think Huntley could ever commit murder and said that had she known at the time he was responsible for Holly and Jessica's deaths she would have 'been out of that house like a shot straight to the police or straight to the nearest person I could talk to, to tell them.'

On 12 December the jury retired to consider their verdict – but there was no quick conclusion. Indeed it was not until five days later, on 17 December, that they returned. The jury accepted Carr's explanation that she had never believed that Huntley had murdered Holly and Jessica and that she had only lied to the police to protect Huntley. She was found not guilty of assisting an offender, but the jury accepted her plea of guilty to the charge of perverting the course of justice. She was sentenced to three and a half years in prison.

As for Huntley, the jury retired again and struggled to come to a conclusion, until in the end they found him guilty, but only by a majority of ten to two. Sentencing him to two terms of life imprisonment, Mr Justice Moses said that he had displayed 'merciless cynicism' after killing the two 'best friends'.

'You murdered them both,' the judge went on. 'You are the one person who knows how you murdered them, you are the one person who knows why. There are few worse crimes than your murder of those two young girls.' Mr Justice Moses also castigated Huntley for his pretence of helping to search for them and his offers of sympathy to their parents.

After sentencing, Leslie Chapman, Jessica's father, told reporters, 'The next time I'd like to see him is how we last saw our daughters and that was in a coffin.' Holly's father added that he hoped the Home Office inquiry, which had just been set up by Home Secretary David Blunkett MP, would make sure that 'no other families have to endure what we have over the past sixteen months'.

But Mr Justice Moses had not set a minimum term for Huntley's life sentences as, ironically, he was now caught up in the argument over the decision, encouraged by a judgement of the European Court of Human Rights, about whether the rights of politicians to confer whole life terms on prisoners should be replaced by that power being restricted to the judiciary alone. Ironically, had Huntley been convicted the very next day, 18 December 2003, the judge would have had the power to set his minimum term as that was the day that the new Criminal Justice Act came into force.

Astonishingly, it was to be almost two years before Huntley's minimum term was finally set. On 29 September 2005, Mr Justice Moses announced that Huntley must remain in prison until he had served at least forty years; a minimum term that would mean that he could not even be considered for release until at least 2042, by which time he would be sixty-eight years old. Announcing the decision Mr Justice

Moses said, 'The order I make offers little or no hope of the defendant's eventual release.'

At that point the judge concluded that Huntley's crime were not heinous enough to qualify for a whole life term of imprisonment – a curious decision in that there were two victims, both of whom were children, although there was no explicit evidence of a sexual or sadistic element to the killings. It is difficult, however, to see what other motivation there could have been, given Huntley's sexual history with underage girls that had emerged in the wake of his conviction.

The Lord Chief Justice, Lord Woolf, had come to the conclusion that Huntley should be treated under 'transitional arrangements' as the murders were committed before the guidelines as to what constituted a sufficiently heinous crime for a whole life term were reconsidered in the light of the demands of the new Criminal Justice Act. Had Huntley been convicted five years later, in 2010, there seems little doubt that the trial judge would have given the thirty-one year old a whole life term.

Dr Julian Boon, a forensic psychologist at the University of Leicester, who made an assessment of Huntley's character on the basis of his trial, told the BBC in 2003, 'There is a strong suggestion that we are dealing with a psychopath. It is very difficult to believe that this was not sexually motivated.' Suggesting that Huntley had acted impulsively as he thought he could get away with the murders, Dr Boon added that the way he disposed of the bodies was exceptionally significant.

'Psychopaths treat other people as if they do not have an identity,' he explained. 'Look at what Huntley did with the bodies of the girls, trying to burn them. It was done with callous self-interest. His reaction to their deaths was all about self-preservation. He put his own future before the girls.'

The lack of emotion Huntley demonstrated during his evidence in the witness box was another reason that Dr Boon concluded that he had a psychopathic personality.

The court may not have thought Huntley's crimes sufficiently serious to warrant a whole life term, but his fellow inmates in prison did not agree. One senior prison official, for example, remarked before his forty-year minimum term was announced that his attitude towards the killings was one of 'sarcastic nonchalance', just as he demonstrated no sign of remorse or contrition after his conviction.

His fellow inmates were clearly infuriated by his attitude, and on 14 September 2005, just days before his minimum term was announced, he was scalded with a bucket of boiling water by quadruple-murderer Mark Hobson, who was then aged thirty-six and serving a whole life term himself. Huntley's injuries meant that he could not attend the hearing that confirmed his forty-year minimum term.

A year later, on 5 September 2006, Huntley was found unconscious in his prison cell, where he was thought to have taken an overdose, and spent two days in hospital before being returned to Wakefield Prison. There seems little doubt that Huntley's narcissism meant that he was perpetually anxious to draw attention to himself. His fellow prisoners clearly resented the child killer's posturing and his swaggering self-interest.

On 21 March 2010, Huntley was once again taken to hospital, his throat having been slashed by another inmate, fellow life sentence prisoner and convicted armed robber Damien Fowkes. Huntley received twenty-one stitches but his injuries were not said to be life-threatening and he was returned to Frankland Prison near Durham after three days in hospital – having moved from Wakefield two years earlier. In October 2011, Fowkes pleaded guilty at Hull Crown Court to the attempted murder of Huntley, and received a second life sentence.

Huntley's self-obsession was again underlined in 2012, when his younger brother Wayne, who had married Huntley's first wife Claire, although by this point they were no longer together, published a book called *The Blood We Share*. It outlined how his elder brother 'swaggers around prison' boasting about what a 'cushy' life he had. Huntley reportedly watched Manchester United football games on his own television set, while enjoying pizzas and steaks with some fellow prisoners.

'His notoriety and reputation is all he has to live for,' his brother Wayne insisted in his book, 'so he gets what he can from it. He has a swagger to him.'

'I don't think he will ever tell the truth now,' his brother went on. 'I believe he knows the truth is too awful for him to admit – it would mean even more people in prison would want to kill him . . . Yet he has never uttered a word of contrition to me.'

Maxine Carr was released from prison on 14 May 2004, having served half her three-and-a-half-year sentence – the first sixteen months having been spent on remand – and immediately received police protection. She won an injunction on 24 February 2005, granting her lifelong anonymity on the grounds that her life would otherwise be in danger.

In doing so, Carr became one of four former prisoners to be given entirely new identities, along with the Newcastle-born double child killer Mary Bell, herself a child at the time, and the two children convicted of the murder of toddler James Bulger. Carr was reported to have given birth to a child with her new husband in November 2011. That child, too, is protected by her lifelong anonymity order.

For his part, Huntley brushes aside criticism and concentrates instead on his own comfort and wellbeing. 'I'm currently serving life in Belmarsh Prison,' he tweeted recently, 'it's not so bad though – I have internet access and Sky +. My favourite show is *Robot Wars*. Life is sweet in Belmarsh.'

They are hardly the words of a man despairing of his future, crushed by the reality that he will not even be able to be considered for parole until 2042 – but they are the words of a man who has never once launched an appeal against his conviction or his sentence.

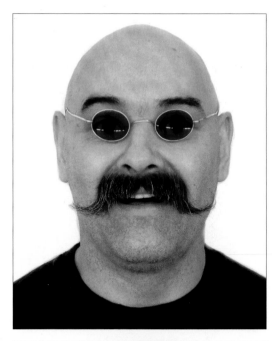

8. *Left* Charles 'Salvador' Bronson: A high-security lifer known as Britain's 'most violent criminal'.

9. *Below* Kenneth Regan: Along with an accomplice, murdered three generations of the same family in a bid to steal their business.

10. *Right* Ian Huntley: A school caretaker sentenced to life for the 'Soham murders' of pupils Holly Wells and Jessica Chapman.

11. *Below* Mark Bridger: Abducted and murdered 5-year-old April Jones in 2012.

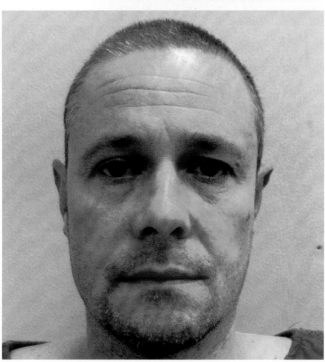

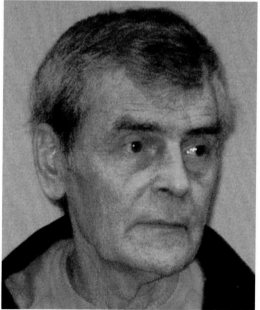

12. *Above* Roy Whiting:
Serving life for the murder
of 8-year-old Sarah Payne
in 2000.

13. *Left* Peter Tobin: A serial
killer and sex offender
serving life for the murder
of three women.

14. *Right* Harry Roberts: The notorious police killer who served 48 years in jail before his release, age 78, in 2014.

15. *Below, left* Dale Cregan: Committed four murders, including of two police officers, as well as three counts of attempted murder.

16. *Below, right* David Bieber: An American fugitive who murdered PC Ian Broadhurst and attempted to murder two other policemen before his capture.

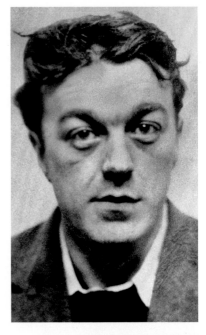

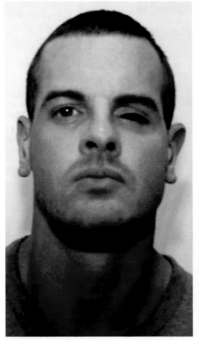

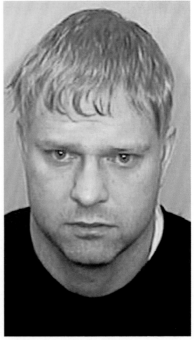

17. Fred & Rose West: The infamous couple who together murdered at least 12 people.

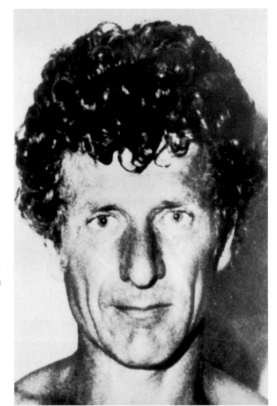

18. *Right* Arthur Hutchinson: Crashed a wedding reception before murdering the bride's mother, father and brother, as well as raping her sister.

19. *Below* Anthony Rice: A sex offender who committed murder after being released from a life sentence.

20 & 21. *Above* David Mulcahy and John Duffy: The 'Railway Killers' who attacked numerous women at train stations, murdering three.

22 *Below* Steven Wright: The 'Ipswich Ripper' who murdered five sex workers.

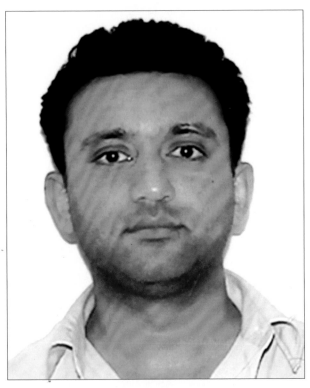

23. *Above* Rahan Arshad: Murdered his wife and their three children after discovering she was having an affair.

24. *Left* Mark Martin: Known as the 'Sneinton Stragler', he was sentenced to life for the murder of three homeless women in Nottingham.

14

Who 'Deserves' Life?

Mark Hobson and Roy Whiting

The crimes of Mark Hobson, the quadruple murderer who scalded Ian Huntley in Wakefield Prison in September 2005 – using that 'invisible licence' to commit crimes in jail that so many killers serving a whole life term seem to feel that they have to harm others – are in many ways every bit as heinous as Huntley's. Yet Hobson has little or no prospect for release while Huntley has at least the prospect that he will return to being a free man under licence at some point after 2042, when he will be aged only sixty-eight.

The disparity between their two sentences again underlines the uncertainty in the use of a whole life term for the 'most heinous of crimes'. No one could deny that by suffocating the two ten-year-old schoolgirls Holly Wells and Jessica Chapman and setting fire to their bodies to disguise the forensic evidence Huntley was committing a crime of the most heinous kind, yet Hobson is serving the ultimate sentence under the law of England and Wales – for committing crimes every bit as gratuitous and unprovoked.

Unlike Huntley, however, Hobson had no track record of brushes with the law before the crimes for which he was given a whole life term of imprisonment. It is worth comparing the lives of the two men to see why one should deserve a whole life term and the other not. Born on 2 September 1969 in Wakefield, West Yorkshire, Hobson was the son of a coal miner and a factory machinist, with two sisters. His childhood has been described as 'happy and stable'. One of his teachers remembered him as 'very well behaved . . . so average and ordinary that he was almost anonymous'.

With a thin, oval face and piercing eyes, his teenage years were equally unremarkable – and certainly showed no sign whatever of the violence that was to emerge so dramatically after his thirtieth birthday. At the age of twenty-two, in 1991, Hobson moved in with his childhood sweetheart Kay and her two children from a previous relationship, and they married in 1993 – after the birth of their own daughter, Alice. At that point Hobson worked at Drax power station and as a landscape gardener. Indeed, his wife described him as the 'perfect husband'. Sadly, that was not to last.

In 1998 Hobson registered as a nightclub doorman and began working at a nightclub in Selby, North Yorkshire. It was the first clear evidence that his life was slowly beginning to spin out of control. On New Year's Day 1999 he walked out on his family without giving a reason. His wife Kay said later, 'There was no one else involved, he just didn't want married life any more . . . I couldn't believe it. He turned to pot and drinking heavily . . . He became like a zombie . . . His life just went completely off the rails.'

The 'ordinary' schoolboy suddenly became a violent criminal. In the four years after leaving his family, Hobson committed a string of ever more serious crimes. In 2002, for example, he stabbed what he called 'a love rival' five times in the chest with a handyman's knife in broad daylight outside an off licence in Selby, watched by a stunned crowd of local shoppers. His victim was left with a punctured lung. Hobson admitted causing grievous bodily harm, but avoided a prison sentence, receiving a community punishment order instead. The leniency of this sentence was to come under close scrutiny in the light of his later behaviour.

By now working as a refuse collector, and in an increasingly wild, untamed state, Hobson had taken to abusing the women in his life, particularly his new girlfriend Claire Sanderson, who was aged twenty-seven. They made an odd couple. She was as heavy a drinker as he was and the pair would often 'take chunks out of each other', according to one friend, as their relationship lurched from row to row. She followed him around 'like a lapdog' and was sometimes nicknamed 'eight ball' because of the bruising to her face from Hobson's regular beatings.

In the first weeks of 2004, Hobson's life began to disintegrate still further. His relationship with Claire grew ever more violent, while his by now ex-wife Kay denied him access to their daughter Alice, as well as to her own son and daughter, because of his irrational and often brutal behaviour. She later described his relationship with Claire as like 'a powder keg ready to ignite'.

'She carried the scars and bruising around the eyes that Mark had inflicted during their drunken rows,' Hobson's ex-wife Kay explained. 'But she obviously dished it out, too. Mark would sometimes visit my home covered in cuts and bruises. One time she left his chest and head littered with bloody bite marks. Mark didn't seem bothered though. He just said, "You know what we're like when we've had a drink."'

In the spring of 2004, Hobson lost his job as a refuse collector, which ignited his final descent into rage against Claire Sanderson and, arguably, against women in general, fuelled by an alcohol addiction that saw him consume twenty or more pints of lager in a day. He confessed to a friend that he had 'chosen the wrong sister' when he started going out with Claire and much preferred her twin sister Diane.

Increasingly irrational, in the first days of July 2004 Hobson began planning to kill Claire and replace her with her twin sister, even to the extent of writing a 'to-do' list outlining how he planned to lure his girlfriend's sister to his flat and a shopping list of items he needed to kill Claire, which included 'big bin liners', tie-wraps, fly spray and air freshener. Against Diane's name he wrote 'use and abuse at will', and went on to list a number of other potential victims including the twin girls' parents and the parents of his ex-wife.

Finally, on the evening of 10 July 2004, he carried out his plan to kill Claire Sanderson. The couple were last seen together when they went to a pub near the flat they shared. When they returned home that evening Hobson hit Claire on the head no fewer than seventeen times with a hammer and then strangled her. He then proceeded to wrap her body in one of the bin bags he had bought for the purpose and put a plastic bag over her head. There was no evidence of a sexual assault, though Hobson had stripped her naked when he put her into the bin bag. He then stored her body in the flat they shared for a week before executing the second part of his plan – to 'use and abuse' her twin sister Diane.

On 17 July 2004 Hobson called Diane Sanderson and told her that her sister was suffering from glandular fever and would welcome a visit. But when Diane arrived that evening she too was beaten with a hammer – although not until after she had been tortured with a disposable razor and scissors. Her left nipple was missing, and the police later believed that Hobson may have eaten it. Like her sister, the beatings with a hammer were not the cause of her death, Diane, too, was strangled, while her head was also covered with a plastic bag. There were ligature marks on her wrists, ankles and neck, indicating that she had been 'hog-tied'. Her pubic hair had been shaved and she had been sexually assaulted; she too was left naked with a plastic bag over her head.

Claire and Diane's mutilated bodies were found the following day by Diane's boyfriend and her father, who had come to Claire's flat in search of her. But by that time Hobson had disappeared, intent on continuing with his plans to attack other people. He did not search out the twin sisters' parents, however. Instead he focused his anger – for no apparent reason – on a pair of entirely innocent old-age pensioners.

On 18 July 2004 Hobson murdered James Britton, an eighty-year-old former Spitfire pilot, and his eighty-two-year-old wife Joan, at their home in the village of Strensall, twenty-five miles north of York. Hobson beat both of them with Mr Britton's walking stick before stabbing them to death in the back, and leaving their bodies to be discovered by their neighbours.

Over the next seven days Hobson became the focus of one of the biggest police manhunts in recent times as Britain's 'most wanted man'. Twelve separate police forces and more than five hundred officers formed the search team. But he was not actually arrested until 25 July 2004 when he was found by police in a field near a petrol station not far from York after a tip-off from a member of the public. He showed no remorse, or concern, for his victims or their families.

Immediately after his arrest Hobson merely told the police, 'I'm a fucking murderer, aren't I?'

In a subsequent interview he explained that he had taken a cocktail of drugs, including cannabis, cocaine, ecstasy and alcohol and could not remember anything about his girlfriend's death or indeed her sister's. He claimed that he had 'lost a day and a half' and had 'come round with a blood-stained hammer' in his hand. Later, while on remand in custody at Wakefield Prison, Hobson told a prison officer that he had 'never felt better in my life' – explaining that he felt as though he was taking part in the reality television programme *Big Brother*.

One friend, who had known him for some time, explained Hobson was prone to sudden and violent swings in mood. 'He would be laughing and joking one moment and then totally different the next,' he said. 'He threatened to kill my son, to stab him, but I can't even remember what it was about. He liked to portray himself as a local hard-man, but he was the kind of guy who would pick on easy targets. The kind of guy who would thump you for spilling his pint.'

When Hobson's trial opened at Leeds Crown Court on 18 April 2005 before Mr Justice Grigson, the defendant admitted all four killings at once. Flanked by two prison officers, he bowed his head and appeared to be close to tears as he muttered 'Guilty' four times as each of the counts of murder was put to him. As the details of his crimes emerged over the following four weeks, so the Sanderson family sat horrified in court, as did the family of James and Joan Britton.

Finally, on 27 May, Mr Justice Grigson told Hobson, 'The enormity of what you have done is beyond words . . . The damage you've done is incalculable. You not only destroyed the lives of your victims, but you devastated the lives of those who loved them.' He went on to say that Hobson clearly had an abusive relationship with Claire Sanderson. 'And when you tired of her, you transferred your attention to her sister, Diane. As Claire stood in your way, you murdered her. In my opinion, that was a premeditated act.'

'You also determined to lure Diane to your home,' Mr Justice Grigson added, 'and kill her there and then to use her for your own sexual gratification . . . You battered Claire with a hammer in as brutal and callous a way as is possible to imagine before placing a plastic bag over her head and, having killed her, you wrapped her body in a bin bag.' On 17 July you succeeded in luring Diane to your home. It is plain at your hands she suffered not only terror and pain but sexual harm before she died.'

Concluding his remarks, the judge sentenced Hobson to life imprisonment with a whole life term.

As the sentence was read out, Claire and Diane's mother, Jacqueline Sanderson, stood up in the public gallery and shouted, 'Rot in hell!' After Hobson was led to the cells, she and her husband George issued a statement which asked, 'How could anyone be such an animal? Claire and Diane did not deserve to die such horrid deaths, both ending up naked, with a plastic bag over Diane's head and Claire inside a black bag.'

Outside the court, Detective Superintendent Javad Ali, who led the police hunt for Hobson, added, 'No one who has heard the detail of these horrific crimes can be surprised at the severity of today's sentence. I believe it is totally right and fitting that Mark Hobson is never released from prison. For me, today brings about a conclusion to the most horrendous case I have had to deal with in my twenty-two years' police service.'

No matter how heinous the crimes, however, Hobson felt he had been singularly mistreated. Not least because he had unwittingly set a precedent – by becoming the first prisoner to be subjected to a whole term after pleading guilty to all the murder charges. Incensed, he announced shortly after his conviction that he would be seeking leave to appeal against his whole life sentence on the grounds that he deserved greater leniency as he had admitted all four murders at the earliest opportunity.

Before the appeal could be heard, however, Hobson had tipped the bucket of boiling water over Ian Huntley on 14 September 2005 and was sentenced to three months in solitary confinement as a result. He was still subject to that punishment when his appeal against the whole life term of imprisonment was concluded on 30 November 2005. In a written judgement, the then Lord Chief Justice, Lord Phillips, said the facts of the murders were so horrific that a whole life order was inevitable, regardless of the guilty plea. He added that Hobson did not deserve any compassion for pleading guilty, as he had not demonstrated any towards his victims.

Mr and Mrs Britton's daughter, Catherine Wilkins, said after the appeal verdict, 'Mark Hobson horrifically and sadistically murdered four people without compunction. He has never shown any remorse or given any explanation for his actions. Admitting his guilt does not change the fact that he is a callous, vicious murderer and his victims suffered horrendously.'

But are Mark Hobson's murders distinctly more heinous than those of Ian Huntley? It is my contention that they are not. It is simply a matter of the 'impression' the murders leave in the mind of the judiciary and the public that distinguishes between the two cases. If society is intent on 'throwing away the key' for the most heinous criminals, I fail to see how it failed to do so for the killer of Holly Wells and Jessica Chapman.

Another case that illustrates the ambiguity and uncertainty at the heart of the argument about whole life terms concerns West Sussex-born Roy Whiting, who killed eight-year-old schoolgirl Sarah Payne in July 2000 when he was forty-one. Although Whiting killed only one child – which remains utterly abhorrent in itself – he did not kill two, as Huntley was to do. Yet Whiting received a whole life term in the wake of his conviction for Sarah's murder in December 2001, only for the Home Secretary of the day, Labour's David Blunkett to argue for a minimum term of fifty years, and then for the Court of Appeal to amend that sentencing decision yet again.

It is worth looking back at Whiting's case, and his criminal career in detail, to understand the prolonged argument over his sentencing. For, once again, it is the question of the 'impression' created by the case that seems to have had the most marked effect on the decision the judiciary arrived at in this high-profile case.

A scruffy, six-foot tall, gangly loner with a front tooth missing, Whiting was born in Horsham, West Sussex, in January 1959, where he was brought up. His parents divorced during the 1970s, and he had a strangely isolated childhood. Originally he had five siblings but three of them died in infancy – only his older brother and younger sister survived. Whiting left school at sixteen with no academic qualifications and struggled to keep a job over the next ten years, at one stage working for the local Co-operative store as a delivery man, at another working as a car mechanic and paint sprayer at a local garage.

With the garage as his base, Whiting developed an interest in 'banger racing', which attracted a considerable following in the 1980s. He even came third in the Smallfield Raceway championship in the late eighties, but in spite of being watched by large crowds, he always maintained a low profile, preferring to blend into the background. Then, in 1986, Whiting married petrol pump attendant Linda Booker, who became pregnant that same year; but their marriage did not last and they separated just before the birth of their son in 1987 and were divorced in 1990.

A man with few friends, who 'liked to keep himself to

himself', Whiting was steadily developing an obsession with young girls. That could have been a result of his own disturbed childhood, or his dislike of marriage and the responsibility of his own child, but there is no doubt that on 4 March 1995 – at the age of thirty-six – he abducted and sexually assaulted an eight-year-old girl on the Langley Green estate at Crawley in West Sussex.

Whiting was arrested a few weeks later after a man who knew him came forward to tell the police that Whiting had recently sold him a red Ford Sierra car, the same make as the vehicle that the eight-year-old had been seen climbing into during her abduction. Three months later, Whiting admitted to the charges of abduction and indecent assault and was sentenced to four years in prison. The maximum sentence he could have received was life imprisonment, but the judge took into account his guilty pleas and offered leniency. That proved to be a mistake. While in jail, Whiting was assessed by a psychiatrist who concluded that he was likely to reoffend once he had been released.

Nevertheless, Whiting was duly released from prison in November 1997, having served two years and five months of his original sentence. He then became one of the first people in Britain to be placed on the newly introduced Sex Offenders' Register. Probably sensing that he would not be welcomed in Crawley, given the abduction, he moved some twenty-five miles away to Littlehampton on the West Sussex coast, where he rented a flat in St Augustine's Road.

Two years later, he moved into another flat in the same road, and it was while he was at this second flat that he became involved in the police search for eight-year-old Sarah Payne, who had disappeared from another part of Littlehampton on the afternoon of Sunday 1 July 2000. Sarah had been playing with her brothers and sisters in a field near her grandparents' home when she decided to make her way home alone. She never arrived; instead she disappeared into thin air.

Immediately suspecting a paedophile abduction, and knowing that Whiting was one of five men on the Sex Offenders' Register in the area, West Sussex police officers visited him on Monday 2 July 2002 to ask if he knew anything about the whereabouts of the small, smiling-faced blonde schoolgirl whose picture by now was flooding the media.

Hardly surprisingly, the former car mechanic denied knowing anything whatever about Sarah Payne's disappearance, and insisted that he had been at a funfair in Hove, several miles away, that evening. Nevertheless the officers were suspicious about his demeanour – not least because of his apparent disregard for the little girl – and arrested him on suspicion of her abduction. Whiting continued to protest his innocence, even though the police found a receipt for petrol he had purchased at Buck Barn Garage near Pulborough the previous evening – which contradicted his alibi of being in Hove at 5.30 pm and then returning to his flat by 9.30 pm on the evening that Sarah disappeared.

Whiting spent two days in police custody, but officers had no concrete evidence with which to charge him, and – after he was released on police bail to go to live with his father in Crawley – an exhaustive search of his flat in St Augustine's Road produced no forensic evidence linking him to Sarah or her disappearance. At this point the police were still conducting a missing persons' investigation rather than a murder enquiry.

It was not until Tuesday 17 July 2000 that Sarah Payne's body was finally discovered in a shallow grave. It was identified within twenty-four hours, and two weeks later, on 31 July 2000 Whiting was rearrested on suspicion of her murder – but still the police lacked the concrete evidence they needed to charge him. In spite of the fact that Sarah's body had been discovered just three miles from the service station where Whiting had bought fuel on the night she disappeared, Whiting was once again released on bail.

A few days after this second release, Whiting moved out of his father's house after a vigilante mob smashed some of the windows with bricks. He went to live in a tent in woodland behind a housing estate in Crawley. Clearly unnerved by the events of the past month, he stole a Vauxhall Nova car and was pursued by police at high speed before crashing into a parked vehicle. Whiting was immediately arrested and, on 27 September 2000, he admitted both taking the car and driving dangerously and was sentenced to twenty-two months' imprisonment.

It was only after the former paint sprayer had begun his sentence that the police decided to examine his white Fiat Ducato van, which provided them with vital forensic evidence, but it was not until 6 February 2001 that Whiting was formally charged with the abduction and murder of Sarah Payne while he was in prison serving his sentence for car theft and dangerous driving.

Whiting's trial began on 14 November 2001 at Lewes Crown Court and the jury heard from a succession of vital witnesses, including Sarah's brother Lee, who had seen a scruffy-looking man with yellowish teeth drive past the field where he and Sarah had been playing on the afternoon that she vanished. A female motorist then told the jury that she had found one of Sarah's shoes in a country lane several miles from where her body was found, and forensic scientists had found fibres from Whiting's van on the shoe. But the most damning piece of forensic evidence of all was a strand of blonde hair on a T-shirt found in Whiting's van. The jury were told that DNA test results meant that the chance of the strand of blonde hair belonging to anyone other than Sarah were one in a billion.

The pathologist who analysed Sarah's body told the court that the eight year old had met a 'violent death' and it was his view that she had been the victim of a 'sexually motivated homicide'. Sarah's naked and decomposed body had been found in a shallow grave six inches deep. The jury were told that it would have taken just six minutes to dig.

On Wednesday 12 December 2001, forty-two-year-old Whiting was found guilty of the abduction and murder of eight-year-old Sarah Payne. The jury of nine men and three women had deliberated for nine hours before reaching a unanimous verdict.

Mr Justice Curtis told Whiting – who stood impassively in the dock before him wearing a grey sweatshirt and jeans, 'It is important in ordinary life that children are allowed to have some freedom by their parents and others to learn self-reliance and enjoy their childhood ... You exploited this for your own abnormal sexual desires.'

In a withering attack, the judge went on, 'You took this little child away in a few moments. I am satisfied you were looking for such a little child on that evening on the South Coast. It is ludicrous to suggest that you needed that van for your job. It was a moving prison for Sarah and anyone else that you might have caught.' That moving prison was found to include a rope, nylon-tie handcuffs and a knife.

'You are indeed an evil man,' Mr Justice Curtis added. 'You are in no way mentally unwell. I have seen you for a month and in my view you are a glib and cunning liar ... You are and you will remain an absolute menace to any girl ... You are every parent's and grandparent's nightmare come true.'

Finally, the judge concluded, 'This is one of the rare cases when I shall recommend to the appropriate authorities that you will be kept in prison for the rest of your life.'

Significantly, however, the judge did not specify a whole life term as that power had not yet been conferred on the judiciary. That would not come for another two years. The judge, as had been the case with Rosemary West, could only suggest to the Lord Chief Justice his view about the seriousness of the convicted prisoner's crimes. Mr Justice Curtis was using exactly the same formula that Mr Justice Mantell had used in Rosemary West's case: 'If attention is paid to what I think, you will never be released.' It is a phrase which I can vividly remember hearing at Winchester Crown Court – a day that still reverberates in my memory.

As Whiting turned in the dock to be led down to the cells, Sarah's grandfather, Terry Payne, shouted, 'I hope you rot!'

It was not until after the verdict, however, that it was revealed publicly that Whiting had been on the Sex Offenders' Register when he killed Sarah Payne. The prosecuting authorities had been concerned that the jury's judgement could have been swayed towards a conviction had they known that fact – which might, in turn, have given Whiting grounds for an appeal as he could have argued that he had not been given the benefit of a 'fair' trial.

The jury were also never told that in his 1995 conviction for the abduction and indecent assault of an eight-year-old girl Whiting had used precisely the same technique as he had later used on Sarah Payne. He had bought a red Ford Sierra and then sold it quickly after the attack. In a carbon copy of his first attack, he did exactly the same thing – only in Sarah's case it had been a white Fiat Ducato van.

After the verdict had been announced, Timothy Langdale QC, for the prosecution, described in some detail Whiting's

1995 attack, and explained that the defendant had thrown the girl into the back of a dirty car, locked the doors and told her to 'shut up' because he had a knife. 'The defendant told the girl to take off her clothes. When she refused, he produced a knife from his pocket and threatened to tie her up.' The girl was undressed and 'subjected to a disgusting sexual assault'.

The possibility that this was exactly what may have happened to Sarah stunned the crowded courtroom, reducing Sarah's parents to tears. What few people there that day knew was that the parents and younger brother of Whiting's first victim were there alongside the Paynes and weeping themselves.

Inevitably, in the wake of the revelation that Whiting was a known child sex offender who had used the same modus operandi in a previous attack, there were significant and repeated calls from the public and the press for the government to allow 'controlled' public access to the Sex Offenders' Register. But the Home Office pointed out the day after his conviction that such a system would be unworkable, as it would run the twin risks of driving paedophiles 'underground' as well as putting them in danger of vigilante attacks.

Nevertheless, the controversy did not die down, and was taken still further with the help of the Sunday newspaper *News of the World*, which had been campaigning on the issue – with the help of Sarah's mother, Sara – since Sarah's disappearance in July 2000. Mrs Payne was anxious to see the introduction in Britain of a similar system to the American 'Megan's Law', which gives parents and the public restricted rights to know about paedophiles living in a particular area.

Megan's Law was named in honour of seven-year-old Megan Kanka, who was raped and murdered by her neighbour Jesse Timmendequas in 1994. After the killer's trial, it was revealed that he was a convicted child rapist. The American Megan's Law shows photographs and addresses of sex offenders, but the proposed Sarah's Law in Britain was never intended to go to such lengths. Nevertheless, it was fiercely debated in the years following Whiting's conviction and a modified scheme in which parents could enquire about a named individual was introduced in four areas in England and Wales in September 2008. In 2010 the Home Office announced that the trial had been successful and the Child Sex Offender Disclosure Scheme was rolled out across England and Wales in 2011.

As a result of the controversy and debate about Sarah's Law, Roy Whiting did not sink into obscurity in prison. His name regularly incited the strongest possible reaction, among the public and prisoners alike, even though he had actually committed only one child murder – though a most heinous one.

Perhaps inevitably, on 4 August 2002, only months after his conviction, Whiting was attacked with a razor by another prisoner while fetching hot water in Wakefield Prison. Convicted murderer Rickie Tregaskis, who was serving a life sentence for the murder of a disabled man in Cornwall, was found guilty of carrying out a slashing attack that left Whiting with a six-inch scar on his right cheek. He was later given a six-year sentence, to be served after the completion of his minimum term. The scar remains on Whiting's cheek today.

Yet Whiting continued to attract controversy, not least over the length of the life sentence he should serve in the wake of the trial judge's recommendation that life should mean life. In fact, the then Lord Chief Justice, Lord Woolf, decided that Whiting's life sentence should attract a minimum term of twenty-eight years before he could be considered for release. It was a remarkably long minimum period at that time – although in the last dozen years 'sentence creep' has seen a minimum term reach forty-five years in the case of Michael Adebowale, one of the killers of Private Lee Rigby.

The Lord Chief Justice's decision provided the background to a series of heated clashes between himself and the Labour Home Secretary, David Blunkett, over the issue of politicians' involvement in the judicial process. For his part, Blunkett was well aware that there was a strong possibility that the House of Lords would rule, following a judgement from the European Court of Human Rights and an appeal from the convicted British murderer Anthony Anderson, that the law should be altered to prevent politicians having any role whatever in the sentencing process.

So, on 24 November 2002, Blunkett ordered that Whiting should serve a minimum of fifty years in prison, thereby making him ineligible even to be considered for parole until at least 2051, when Whiting would be ninety-two. It was a whole life term in all but name – and in line with the recommendation of the trial judge. Yet within forty-eight hours the Law Lords, following the European Court of Human Rights, declared that politicians should play no part in any decision regarding how long a murderer should be kept in prison. It was a decision that meant that Roy Whiting would be the last British murderer to have his term of imprisonment set by a Home Secretary.

It also meant that Blunkett could present himself as a Home Secretary who was 'tough on crime' and as someone in tune with the public attitude to a murderer who had become one of the most reviled men in Britain during the previous two years. Naturally enough, the decision was welcomed by Sarah's mother Sara and her father Michael, who saw it as a vindication of their view that Whiting's life sentence should mean a life spent behind bars. That view was underscored by the continuing campaign for the introduction of 'Sarah's Law', and the Home Secretary's decision increased his popular reputation – not least because Whiting was still being portrayed in the media as a monster who had to be controlled at all costs.

Whiting's legal team were well aware, however, that the new Criminal Justice Act 2003, transferring sentencing powers once and for all from politicians to the judiciary, was passing into law, and so the former car mechanic remained studiously quiet for almost eighteen months after the Blunkett ruling that he should serve a minimum of fifty years for his crime. Indeed, it was not until June 2004, when the new Act was firmly in place, that the media reported that he would be appealing to the High Court for his sentence to be reduced.

It would be six years before that appeal would finally be heard. It was not until Wednesday 9 June 2010 that Whiting's case came before Mr Justice Simon in the Court of Appeal in London. Sarah Payne's killer chose not to be present, but her mother was in the packed courtroom on the first floor of the Royal Courts of Justice in the Strand. Other members of the Payne family were there too, as the single judge entered in front of them. His first words startled everyone.

'I invite everyone present in the Court,' Mr Justice Simon began, 'before we go about our daily business, to pause and for a moment remember Sarah Payne who would now be eighteen if she had not been murdered, and reflect on the grave loss her death has caused to her family and others who loved her.' It was an unprecedented statement in the Court of Appeal, and precisely represented the depth of feeling among the judiciary as well as the public about the significance of the case.

As the judge made his remarks, Sarah's mother linked hands with the man sitting next to her, but the judgement she was about to hear would not entirely please her. Mr Justice Simon explained that the Lord Chief Justice, Lord Woolf, had recommended that Whiting should serve a minimum term of twenty-eight years rather than the fifty years ordered by the former Home Secretary David Blunkett. That term had been accepted by the Crown Prosecution Service, but then he added, 'The applicant [Whiting] submits that the appropriate term was the term of twenty-eight years which was recommended by the Lord Chief Justice . . . It is submitted that in this case a term of fifty years was disproportionate and the minimum term of twenty-eight years recommended should be imposed.'

Mr Justice Simon then explained that he had considered the arguments, and that in his judgement the 'appropriate' minimum term should be set at forty years and that from that 'must be deducted the time spent on remand which is calculated to be 234 days'. But he stressed that Whiting's sentence remained one of life imprisonment and that he would be detained 'unless and until the Parole Board is satisfied that he no longer presents a risk to the public'. The judge then reminded the packed court, 'Even if the Parole Board decides then or at some time in the future to authorise his release, he will be on licence for the rest of his life.'

The Court of Appeal's decision meant that Whiting could now be considered for parole, bearing in mind Mr Justice Simon's provisos, in 2041, when he would be aged eighty-two.

Outside the High Court Sara Payne, now walking with a stick as the result of a stroke, spoke with quiet dignity and conviction, just as she had done throughout the ordeal that had lasted almost exactly a decade. Surrounded by her surviving children, Lee, aged twenty-three, Luke, aged twenty-one, and Charlotte, aged fifteen, Mrs Payne said firmly, 'The family is clearly disappointed that the tariff has been reduced, but he will be well into his eighties before he is eligible, so it's not a terrible, terrible thing, and could have been a lot worse, so we carry on as before.'

'He's in prison now,' she went on, 'he can't hurt any children there. All the time it was fifty years my family and I could relax – there was no way he could be near any children and hurt them. Right now, of course, we are a little bit reeling . . . There is no end to this. This is our life from now on.'

But then Sara Payne allowed herself to reveal how deeply she still felt the pain of her loss and the suffering she felt should have been inflicted on Roy Whiting. 'The man is a danger to children and will remain so as long as he lives and breathes.' When questioned by reporters she also insisted, 'All the time it was fifty years it was a good message. Life meaning life is the only fair sentence. He should die in prison.'

The impact that her daughter's abduction and murder have had on Sara and Michael Payne's lives is impossible to over-estimate. Three years after Whiting's conviction they split up after eighteen years of marriage, while Sara was pregnant with their fourth child. Michael then proceeded to descend into a severe alcoholic depression, angry that he had not been able 'to protect my daughter', while Sara suffered a stroke. Then in 2011 Michael was imprisoned for sixteen months for attacking his brother with a broken glass in the wake of another drinking spree, and on 31 October 2014 he was found dead in an armchair in his flat in Maidstone at the age of just forty-five.

I am convinced that the Court of Appeal's decision to reduce Whiting's term to forty years was affected by the forty year minimum sentence given to Ian Huntley for the Soham murders five years earlier. But, just as in Huntley's case, it raised the question of whether a crime that had attracted such public outcry and opprobrium – involving as both did the murder of a child or children – should attract such apparent leniency. What had started out as what looked like a whole life sentence from the trial judge in 2001 had slowly but steadily been diluted so that Whiting was to be allowed at least the possibility of release, even if as a very elderly man.

There is the possibility, of course, that the Court of Appeal may have felt that they must differentiate carefully between the crimes of Huntley and Whiting, making it clear that the killing of a single person, even a child, does not warrant a whole life sentence. But Huntley killed two children and set fire to their bodies. Why does that not qualify for a whole life term if Michael Adebolajo – who killed only Private Lee Rigby (using grotesque and gratuitous violence) – does warrant one? The contradiction leads to a disturbing lack of clarity in the judicial approach to whole life terms of imprisonment.

Or was there a more cynical reason at work? Is it possible that the public notoriety of both Whiting and Huntley would make the possibility of their release only that – a 'possibility' – as their notoriety and the infamy of their crimes will ensure that they will never actually be able to be freed, just as Myra Hindley had no hope of being freed and Ian Brady was never freed though he had long since passed his minimum term. The assumption that public opinion and the media will ensure that both men remain behind bars for the rest of their natural lives – no matter what their 'tariff' may say – is nothing if not disingenuous. For if that is the case, even the implicit case, I believe there is a compelling argument for reconsidering the sentencing guidelines for all murder – especially for the most heinous crimes – as there is little or no clarity over its interpretation now.

Not that Roy Whiting's period of imprisonment has been pleasant. As mentioned in Chapter 5, in November 2012, double murderer Gary Vinter, a whole life prisoner who at that time was still pursuing his appeal to the European Court, sneaked into Whiting's jail cell in Wakefield Prison and attacked him with a sharpened plastic toilet brush handle, stabbing him in both eyes. Vinter told Newcastle Crown Court on 21 November 2012 that he had done it because Whiting was a 'dirty little nonce'.

In a statement read out in court, Whiting explained, 'I was immediately punched and hit to the right eye and nose area and it made me stagger into the cell wall. I then felt a second punch or blow to the left side. Following the second blow I was aware of a severe pain in my eye and my vision was now blurred in my left eye. I slid down the wall to the floor and I raised my arms to defend myself but felt further kicks and punches.'

Vinter, speaking from Long Lartin Prison in Worcestershire by video link, admitted wounding with intent and was given an indefinite sentence, with a notional minimum of five years. Mr Justice Openshaw explained, 'The defendant derived and continues to derive considerable satisfaction from having committed this offence.' After he was sentenced, Vinter said, 'Thank you very much, judge. It has been a pleasure.'

Roy Whiting's notoriety in prison and beyond is not likely to disappear, and he will continue to be pilloried for his cruel depravity towards Sarah Payne, no matter where he may be. But his case represents a further insight into the ambiguity of the whole life term of imprisonment.

If twenty-two-year-old Jamie Reynolds deserves a whole life term for committing a single murder, why should Roy Whiting not warrant exactly the same treatment? If Michael Adebolajo deserves a whole life term for the single murder of Lee Rigby, why should Ian Huntley not warrant that too? If Adebolajo's associate Michael Adebowale warrants a minimum term of forty-five years, why should Huntley and Whiting be given minimum terms of forty years? It is a confusion I shall return to.

15

Charming Psychopaths

Peter Tobin and Levi Bellfield

There can be little doubt about it – the possibility of a 'whole life' term of imprisonment has almost no deterrent effect on the men and women who choose to commit the most heinous crimes. There is no sense of dread amongst the potential perpetrators, as there was, arguably, for those who faced the prospect of death by hanging before the abolition of the death penalty in England and Wales in 1965. When Labour backbencher Sydney Silverman's private member's bill became law that year it suspended the death penalty for five years and substituted a mandatory life sentence in its place. Four years later, the Labour Home Secretary James Callaghan proposed a resolution in the House of Commons making the suspension permanent on 16 December 1969. So it has remained ever since.

No executions have taken place in this country since that suspension – no matter how dreadful the crime. In contrast, between 1900 and 1949 no fewer than 621 men and eleven women were executed in England and Wales, including ten German agents during World War One, and sixteen during World War Two. The concept that the death penalty might act as some form of deterrent – particularly to discourage the use of firearms during a robbery – has effectively disappeared.

Those who commit the 'worst of the worst' crimes now know only too well that the worst fate that can befall them is a whole life term, which certainly does not seem to have deterred any of the more than fifty men and two women, who are now serving those sentences.

One killer in particular seems to have had a total disregard for the consequences of his monstrous actions. He is the Scottish-born murderer Peter Tobin, now aged sixty-nine, who was certainly not deterred from killing by the possibility of a prison sentence, whole life or otherwise. He has been convicted of three murders but is suspected of committing many more, possibly as many as forty.

A lean, short man with brown eyes and a sharp nose, Tobin served ten years of a fourteen-year sentence in prison for the double rape of two fourteen-year-old girls in 1993, and was released in 2004. His first murder conviction came just three years later, in 2007, when he was sentenced to life with a minimum of twenty-one years for the rape and murder of twenty-three-year-old Polish student Angelika Kluk in Glasgow in 2006.

Some time later, skeletal remains of two further young women – who had originally gone missing in 1991– were discovered in the garden of a house Tobin had lived in at the time in Margate, Kent. Tobin was convicted in December 2008 of the murder of fifteen-year-old Vicky Hamilton, and his minimum sentence was increased to thirty years. Then again, he was convicted in December 2009 of the murder of eighteen-year-old Dinah McNicol, and a whole life term was imposed.

Tobin was born in Johnstone, Renfrewshire, the second of eight children, but was a problem a child, so much so that in 1953, at the age of seven, he was sent to an approved school, and later served time in a young offenders' institution. By the age of twenty-four he had been convicted of burglary and forgery in England and sent to prison for a short period. Then, in 1970, he moved to Brighton, Sussex, with his seventeen-year-old girlfriend Margaret Louise Robertson Mountney, a clerk and typist, whom he married on 6 August that year. They separated after a year and she divorced him in 1971.

Two years later, again in Brighton, Tobin married a local nurse, thirty-year-old Sylvia Jefferies, with whom he had a son and daughter, although his daughter died shortly after her birth. That marriage lasted until 1976, when his wife left with their son, and the couple divorced. Tobin then had a relationship with Cathy Wilson, aged sixteen, who gave birth to his son in December 1987. Tobin married her in Brighton in 1989, when she was seventeen. In 1990, they moved to Bathgate, West Lothian, but she left him later that year.

All three women give similar accounts of falling for a 'charming, well-dressed psychopath' who turned violent and sadistic during their marriages. In May 1991 Tobin moved to Margate, Kent, and then, in 1993, to Havant, Hampshire. By that time, however, he had already killed two teenagers and buried their naked bodies in the garden of his small terraced house at 50 Irvine Drive in Margate.

It was while he was living in Havant that Tobin attacked two fourteen-year-old girls on 4 August 1993. They had asked if they could wait in his house until one of his neighbours returned. He agreed but then held them both at knifepoint and forced them to drink a mixture of strong cider and vodka before sexually assaulting and raping them. Tobin then stabbed one of the two, whilst his young son was watching. Clearly determined to kill them, he turned on the gas and left them to die – but they survived.

Tobin went on the run, using one of the twenty or more aliases that he had come to use over the years, and staying with a religious group in the Midlands. It was only when he returned to Brighton that he was caught by the police. On 18 May 1994, Tobin entered a plea of guilty to the rape charges at Winchester Crown Court and received a fourteen-year prison sentence. He was released in 2004, at the age of fifty-eight, and he returned to his native Renfrewshire in Scotland, and the town of Paisley.

Using the false name of 'Pat McLaughlin' – to avoid the authorities discovering that he was on the Sex Offenders' Register – Tobin started working as a church handyman at St Patrick's Church in Anderston, Glasgow, early in 2006. An arrest warrant had been issued in the previous November after he had moved from Paisley without notifying the police, but that was not discovered until he became a prime suspect in a murder at the church.

Angelika Kluk, a twenty-three-year-old student from Skoczow, near Krakow, was staying at the church's presbytery where she was working as a cleaner to help finance her course at University of Gdańsk. She was last seen alive in Tobin's company on 24 September 2006, and is believed to have been attacked in the garage next to the presbytery. Angelika was beaten, raped and stabbed before her body was concealed in an underground chamber under the floor near the confessional. The forensic evidence later suggested that Tobin had buried her there while she was still alive. The police discovered her body five days later, after she had been reported missing. By that time Tobin had disappeared. He was finally arrested in London where he had been admitted to hospital under a false name, suffering from a fictitious complaint.

Tobin's trial at the High Court of Justiciary in Edinburgh

began on 23 March 2007 before Judge Lord Menzies. He flatly denied raping or murdering Angelika Kluk, claiming instead that she had consented to have sex with him. But Tobin was found guilty of rape and murder, and was sentenced to life imprisonment, to serve a minimum of twenty-one years.

Sentencing him, Lord Menzies described him as 'an evil man'. He told Tobin, 'In the course of my time in the law I have seen many bad men and I have heard evidence about many terrible crimes which have been committed but I have heard no case more tragic, more terrible than this one. The advocate-depute describes what you did to Angelika Kluk as an atrocity and that word aptly describes what you did to this young woman. Any case of rape is serious. Any case of murder is serious. But what you did to Angelika Kluk was inhuman.'

In the wake of Tobin's arrest for the murder of Kluk, Strathclyde Police launched Operation Anagram, led by Detective Superintendent David Swindle, who believed that Tobin might well have been a serial killer with other teenage girls or young women as his victims. It was the Anagram team that first searched Tobin's house in Bathgate, Scotland, and then his house in Margate, Kent where, in June 2007, they discovered the remains of two more young women.

On 12 November 2007 the police confirmed that one of the sets of remains belonged to fifteen-year-old schoolgirl Vicky Hamilton, who had last been seen on 10 February 1991 as she waited for her bus home to Redding, near Falkirk. She had been visiting her older sister in Livingston and was waiting to change buses in Tobin's home town of Bathgate. The last sighting of her had been while she was eating chips on a bench in the town centre. The autopsy of her remains confirmed that she had been drugged, raped and strangled, only for her body to be cut in half and buried wrapped in bin bags.

Tobin was charged with Hamilton's murder and his trial began in November 2008, at the High Court in Dundee, Scotland. Once again, Tobin flatly denied the charge, but the prosecution case was overwhelming. It depended on, in particular, eyewitness testimony of his suspicious behaviour and forensic evidence of the DNA and fingerprints left on a dagger found in his Bathgate house, as well as on Vicky's purse and the sheeting in which her body had been wrapped before being buried in the garden at 50 Irvine Drive.

On 2 December 2008, Tobin was convicted of Vicky Hamilton's abduction and murder. Passing sentence, Judge Lord Emslie told Tobin, 'Yet again you have shown yourself to be unfit to live in a decent society. It is hard for me to convey the loathing and revulsion that ordinary people will feel for what you have done . . . I fix the minimum period which you must spend in custody at thirty years. Had it been open to me I would have made that period run consecutive to the twenty-one year custodial period that you are already serving.'

Tobin returned to Saughton Prison in Edinburgh, but he was to return to court again within a year – for his third murder trial within three years.

Just a week after the police had identified the remains of Vicky Hamilton they revealed that the second set of remains in the garden of 50 Irvine Drive belonged to eighteen-year-old Dinah McNicol, who had also gone missing in 1991, although not from Bathgate but from near Reigate in Surrey on 5 August that year. It is believed that Tobin gave her a lift in his car as she hitchhiked back from a music festival in Hampshire. She was certainly never seen again, although regular withdrawals from her bank account were made over the following months from cash machines along the south coast of England. McNicol's remains confirmed that she too had been drugged, raped and strangled before her body was buried, like Hamilton's, wrapped in bin bags.

On 1 September 2008, before the conclusion of the Hamilton trial, Tobin was accused of the killing of Dinah McNicol, and another murder trial was ordered. It began on 14 December 2009 at Chelmsford Crown Court, and again Tobin pleaded not guilty – but on this occasion his defence team offered no evidence and after deliberating for just thirteen minutes the jury found him guilty of murder.

Sentencing Tobin, Mr Justice Calvert-Smith told him, 'This is the third time you have stood in the dock for murder. On all three occasions the evidence against you was overwhelming. Yet even now you refuse to come to terms with your guilt.' He went on to say that Tobin's refusal to cooperate with police meant that Miss McNicol's family 'knew nothing about the circumstances of her death'. The judge then sentenced him to a whole life term of imprisonment – to be served in a Scottish prison. Tobin stood impassively in the dock as the sentence was passed, not a trace of emotion or remorse on his face.

Had Tobin been tried in Scotland a whole life sentence would not have been given, as in 2001 the Scottish Assembly decided that a minimum term must always be designated when a life sentence is imposed, to bring Scottish law into line with the European Convention on Human Rights. In practice, the Scottish courts have stuck to a principle that no minimum term for a life sentence should be longer than fifty years. But as Tobin had committed the murder of Dinah McNicol in England, and been tried in England, he was subject to English law..

Tobin had a long record of abusing his partners. After his

three convictions for murder, the mother of one of his sons and the last of his three wives, Cathy Wilson, detailed the abuse she suffered at his hands. 'It was totally revolting,' she explained in 2009. 'He was very threatening and capable of extreme violence. I hated him.' Yet, like Bellfield, Tobin's partners often stayed with him in spite of the abuse they suffered. He could be charming at one moment and chillingly violent the next.

The police remain convinced that Tobin killed several other young women during his career, yet, in spite of the continued efforts of Operation Anagram, which has been run down in recent years, they have not been able to prove it conclusively. There is no question that Tobin moved around the country repeatedly, using a vast array of false names, and he himself is alleged to have boasted in prison that he has as many as forty other female victims. One thing is certain, however: the prospect of a whole life sentence did not deter him in the slightest.

That is also clearly true in the case of the only person in Britain to have received not one but two separate whole life terms of imprisonment – one for two murders and an attempted murder in 2003 and 2004, and the other for a single murder, though one of the highest-profile ones in recent history, the killing of Surrey teenager Milly Dowler in March 2002.

On Tuesday 26 February 2008, Levi Bellfield, a former nightclub bouncer and wheel clamper, then aged thirty-nine, was sentenced to a whole life term by Mrs Justice Rafferty at the Central Criminal Court in Old Bailey for the murders of Amelie Delagrange, aged twenty-two, and Marsha McDonnell, aged nineteen, and the attempted murder of eighteen-year-old Kate Sheedy.

Mrs Justice Rafferty told him – though Bellfield was not in

the dock to hear her as he had refused to leave his cell, 'You have reduced three families to unimagined grief. What dreadful feelings went through your head as you attacked and, in two cases, snuffed out a young life is beyond understanding.' She went on, 'Aggravating features are the chronicle of violence directed towards lone, vulnerable young women during the hours of darkness and substantial premeditation and planning.'

Just three years later, on 23 June 2011, the bull-necked, muscle-bound Bellfield was given exactly the same whole life term by Mr Justice Wilkie for the murder of thirteen-year-old Milly Dowler, again at the Central Criminal Court, and once again he was not in the dock to hear the sentence being passed as he had refused to leave his cell.

Mr Justice Wilkie described Bellfield as a 'cruel and pitiless killer' who had subjected the bright-eyed teenager to 'what must have been a terrifying ordeal for no other reason than she was at the wrong place at the wrong time,' and in doing so 'he had robbed her of her promising life, he had robbed her family and friends of the joy of seeing her grow up.' The judge went on, 'He treated her in death with total disrespect, depositing her naked body without even the semblance of a burial, in a wood, far away from home, vulnerable to all the forces of nature, thereby, as he clearly intended, causing her family the appalling anguish for many months of not knowing what had become of her.'

Not only did the prospect of a whole-life term not deter him, I would argue that Bellfield specifically sought to carry out his brutal killings with the aim of becoming one of Britain's most notorious killers.

That conclusion is the result of spending two years studying his case and its implications for a biography I wrote called *The Bus Stop Killer*. Bellfield did not 'kill for company' as the gay former policeman Dennis Nilson did before him; Bellfield killed for power and control over women and the fame it brought him. He killed not for fear of the consequences, but to prove he could get away with it, and he relished the notoriety that came in its wake.

There was a profound degree of callousness in Bellfield's murders. They were cowardly, brutal attacks on defenceless young women, often at night, which he committed at random, while stalking the streets of south-west London looking for his prey – young women with blonde hair. Bellfield killed them by hitting them repeatedly on the head with a blunt instrument, probably a hammer, and doing so from behind so that they did not see him. They were crimes that he could treasure in the darkness of the night, giving him a perverted sense of his own importance, and which would also mean that his name would be on the nation's lips – if only for the period of his trials.

There is a vanity about Bellfield that is impossible to ignore; his is an ego so deeply depraved that it insinuates itself into everything and everyone he meets. The more I studied him the more I became convinced of it. I sat through every day of his trial for the murder of Milly Dowler, and he became ever more like a poisonous toad sitting on the toadstool of the dock, constantly inflating his bull-like neck and vast shoulders, glorying in his reputation for his wicked, ugly crimes: a man who truly deserves to be called evil.

At six feet one inches in height and twenty stone in weight, Bellfield is a vast man, whose hair is close cropped, making it look as though his head is slightly too small for his body. His dark-brown eyes are dead and cold, but somehow there is always a glacial smirk on his face as though he knows a joke that no one else is party to.

Bellfield practised the art of seduction at nightclubs he

worked at in west and south-west London, always on the lookout for a young blonde woman who might fall for his 'Jack-the-lad', west-London patter. But he did not restrict his interest to this. He also drove around the suburbs of west London, searching for teenagers standing at a bus stop, intent on persuading them to join him in his van.

Astonishingly, his boastful, lecherous approach did not put off the young girls he targeted. One reported later, for example, 'Levi made me feel special, a grown up. He was very nice to me.' It was one reason he escaped detection for a decade or more.

One of Bellfield's many vehicles was a white Toyota Previa that he called his 'shagging wagon'. It came complete with blacked-out windows, purple neon lights, a mattress with an orange quilt and – perhaps significantly – several pairs of handcuffs. This giant, pasty-faced man would offer any girl foolish enough to accept his offer of a lift in the wagon a can of Red Bull or a glass of Malibu 'just to get us started', and before they knew it the effects of the date-rape drug GHB would render them defenceless.

Marsha McDonnell was just nineteen years of age when she had the misfortune to encounter Bellfield on one of his forays across the suburbs of west London late at night. Just over five feet five inches in height, and weighing a little over nine stone, she lived with her parents in Hampton. Marsha was working in the Bentall Centre in Kingston in her gap year when Bellfield happened upon her.

Just after midnight on Tuesday 4 February 2003, Marsha was on her way home after seeing a film at a local cinema. Bellfield had spotted her on the Number 111 bus from his car, and watched as she got off at the stop near her parents' house in Priory Road. He then circled around and waited for the teenager to walk towards him. Shortly before 12.20 am he hit her three times on the head from behind with a blunt instrument and ran off, leaving her for dead, barely fifty yards from her own front door. Marsha died forty hours later from her injuries, in spite of the doctors' best efforts.

In the early hours of Friday 28 May 2004, Bellfield attacked again, although this time his victim survived, if only just. Kate Sheedy was exactly his type – a slim, eighteen-year-old schoolgirl with blonde hair, who was five feet four inches tall and weighed just over seven and a half stone.

Kate and her friends had been out celebrating their last official day at school at two local pubs. She was a bright student and with just A level examinations left for her to complete before going up to University later that year, there was no doubt that she was going to do well. Kate left her friends at about midnight to catch the Number H22 bus home to Worton Road, Isleworth, where she lived with her mother and sister. At her stop Kate got off – she was the only passenger to do so – and walked towards her home, but as she did so she noticed a white people carrier with blacked-out windows parked about fifty yards ahead of her on her side of the road with its engine running but without its lights on. She was a streetwise girl, and so decided not to walk past what she later described as this 'dodgy' van and crossed to the other side of the road to avoid it. It was a decision that would change her life.

As Kate crossed the road the people carrier suddenly switched its lights on and started revving its engine. She thought it was about to drive off when, without any warning, it did a U turn and drove straight towards her. She screamed and made an effort to reach the pavement opposite, but was hit before she could get there. It knocked her down and drove over her, then stopped and quite deliberately reversed back over her prostrate body. There was no reason for the attack, it was the work of someone with scant regard for human life.

In spite of severe injuries, Kate was sensible enough to call an ambulance. Her first words to the control centre summed up the attack succinctly. 'He ran over me twice,' she said, her voice cracking under the pain. 'The car stopped and checked me out . . . I thought he was dodgy . . . I thought he was going to take me in his car but . . . when he saw that I knew it was dodgy he just ran over me.'

Kate was taken to the nearby West Middlesex Hospital, where she was diagnosed with a collapsed lung and a broken collarbone. More worryingly, however, she was also found to have serious internal damage to her abdomen and liver and was quickly transferred to the liver intensive care unit at King's College Hospital in London. She was not well enough to be released altogether until 21 June – a full three weeks after the attack. In the months that followed she was to undergo still further treatment. Her injuries left her with a large scar on her lower back, which caused her constant pain, a right collarbone that was so out of alignment that it formed an unsightly lump on her chest, and what one consultant called 'severe and lasting psychological effects'.

One of Bellfield's partners, Jo Collings, later described Bellfield's attitude to the girls at Kate's school. 'Throughout the time I was seeing Levi,' she said, 'he would leer at the schoolgirls from Gumley Convent School. When he would see the girls walking along in their uniform he made comments like, "Dirty little whores, they're begging for it."'

Just four months after the attack on Kate Sheedy, Bellfield struck yet again. Shortly after 10.05 pm on Thursday 19 August 2004, he stalked a twenty-two-year-old French woman named Amelie Delagrange as she got off an R267 double-decker bus from Twickenham, where she had been out with friends. After the bus stopped just outside the Ful-well Bus Garage on the Hampton Road, it was about fifteen minutes' walk to the house she was lodging in. Once again, Amelie was Bellfield's type – five feet four in height, nine stone in weight, with collar-length blonde hair.

As Amelie walked along Hampton Road towards Twick-enham Green, Bellfield silently followed her in his car. By the time Amelie reached the south-western tip of Twicken-ham Green, Bellfield had parked and was waiting for her.

Shortly after 10.15 he followed her on to the dark Green – which she had to cross to reach her home – and hit her over the head several times with a blunt object, leaving her fighting for her life. When the paramedics reached her at 10.31 pm there was little they could do, and she was pro-nounced dead in hospital a little over an hour and a half later.

It was to be another three months before Bellfield was finally arrested and charged with the murders of Marsha McDonnell and Amelie Delagrange, and the attempted mur-der of Kate Sheedy. He was only caught as the result of painstaking police work conducted by Detective Chief Inspector Colin Sutton and his Metropolitan Police double-sized murder squad. Crucially, the police had scrupulously examined video recordings from the buses used by all three young women on the nights of their attacks and had identi-fied a particular car and van in each that they traced back to Bellfield.

Those video recordings, together with the police's track-ing of his own and his victims' mobile phones, eventually put Bellfield in the dock of the Central Criminal Court in Old Bailey – but not for almost three years. After his original arrest in November 2004, he was bailed but not formally charged until March 2006, while the case against him was being prepared. His trial did not begin until 2 October 2007, and was to last almost four months, as Bellfield protested his innocence throughout. Indeed, giving evidence in his own defence, he told the jury, 'No airs and graces. This is me. I'm not trying to fool anyone. I'm not an angel. I'm not claiming to be an angel. But I'm not a killer. No way.'

The jury did not believe him. On 25 February 2008 he was found guilty by a majority verdict of the murder of Marsha McDonnell and the attempted murder of Kate Sheedy. Outside the court Kate told reporters that she could not bear even to speak his name. 'Naming him is making him a person, giving him that luxury and somehow making him more human, which he doesn't deserve. In my mind he has just been this thing, an unknown entity – not a person.'

The following day Bellfield was also found guilty – this time by a unanimous verdict – of killing Amelie Delagrange. Sentencing him for the three offences, Mrs Justice Rafferty explained that he would serve a full life term of imprisonment.

He was so disinterested that he refused to come into the court from his cells to hear her.

On that same day Surrey police announced that they were 'very interested' in questioning Bellfield about the abduction and murder of thirteen-year-old Surrey schoolgirl Amanda Dowler, who was always known as Milly, and had disappeared on her way home from school on the damp, grey Thursday afternoon of 21 March 2002, almost a year before Bellfield's attack on Marsha McDonnell.

Shortly after 4.00 on that afternoon Milly had left her friends at Walton-on-Thames railway station to walk the half a mile or so back to her parents' home in Hersham, not far from Twickenham and Hampton. She was wearing the dark-blue blazer and grey skirt of her school uniform, but had taken off her pullover because the drizzly rain had made it feel a little warm. At about 4.08 pm she passed a bus stop on Station Road, where one of her friends was waiting, but just a few moments later Milly disappeared into thin air. This bright, blonde girl, with a ready smile and who played the saxophone was never to be seen alive again.

Though no one knew it at the time, behind that bus stop on Station Road, Bellfield had rented a flat that he had been staying in with his then partner, Emma Mills and their two children – though the family were actually 'house-sitting' for a friend nearby that week and were not in the flat. In the days and weeks that followed, Surrey Police mounted one of the biggest missing persons' inquiries in their history, but to no avail. There was simply no trace of Milly anywhere – and what closed circuit television pictures there were of the area remain inconclusive, although there was a sighting of a red Daewoo Nexia car leaving the area about twenty minutes after the teenager vanished.

It was not until Wednesday 18 September 2002 – almost six months after Milly's disappearance – that a skull and some small bones were found not far from a little-used pathway in a wooded area on Yateley Heath near Fleet in Hampshire, some twenty-five miles from Walton-on-Thames. The following day the police discovered other bones, which were eventually identified as belonging to Milly Dowler. The missing persons' inquiry turned into a murder hunt – but the Surrey police were still baffled.

It was not until after Bellfield's conviction for the two murders and an attempted murder in February 2008 that he began to emerge as the prime suspect. The fact that he had a flat very near where she disappeared, that he had 'gone missing all day' on the very day that she vanished, that he had climbed out of bed in the middle of the night to go back to the flat and had cleared out the entire bedroom when he and his partner went back there the following day, all pointed to the fact that Bellfield could have been Milly's killer. In September 2009, Surrey Police presented their evidence to the Crown Prosecution Service, but it was not until 30 March 2010 that Bellfield was finally charged with the murder of Milly Dowler – at which point, of course, he was in Wakefield Prison, two years into his whole life term.

Just before noon on Friday 6 May 2011, Levi Bellfield got to his feet in the armoured-glass-fronted dock of Court Eight of the Central Criminal Court in Old Bailey to face the charge that he had murdered Milly Dowler nine years earlier. The judge was Mr Justice Wilkie, and I sat there in court as he replied to the formal question, 'How do you plead?' in the softest possible voice, 'Not guilty'. He looked for all the world as though butter would not melt in his mouth, so respectful was his attitude, so gentle was his manner. But that concealed the very much more dangerous man beneath. Wearing a grey suit, white shirt and quiet striped tie he could hardly have looked less belligerent.

Throughout the seven weeks of his trial for the murder, Bellfield took elaborate pains to present himself to the jury as a gentle man who could not possibly have committed such a depraved murder. But the moment the jury left the court he would revert to type, swearing loudly at his counsel for not obeying his orders, complaining about his poor treatment by the prison service, trying to intimidate the witnesses – particularly the young women who had lived with him – from giving their evidence against him without looking him in the eye.

As DCI Colin Sutton of the Metropolitan Police said of him, 'When we started dealing with him he came across as very jokey, like he's your best mate. But he's a cunning individual, violent. He can switch from being nice to being nasty, instantly.' Bellfield also sensed how to take his personal revenge on his accusers. In the case of Milly Dowler that revenge was played out in the windowless courtroom eight at the Old Bailey.

Bellfield's defence counsel, Jeffrey Samuels QC, cross-examined Milly's parents, Bob and Sally Dowler, in great detail about intimate family details – and even suggested that she may have committed suicide. It was a desperate ordeal to watch as the Dowlers suffered a humiliation in court that almost rivalled the terrible loss of their daughter – and one that had been orchestrated by the twenty-stone man sitting in the dock looking utterly unmoved across the court from them.

The ploy failed, not least because Bellfield refused to give evidence in his own defence. He had done so at his earlier murder trial and had been savaged by the prosecuting counsel, Brian Altman QC, who was now prosecuting him for the second time. In his closing remarks to the jury in this second trial Altman drew the jury's particular attention to Bellfield's decision not to take to the witness stand and give evidence on oath.

It took the jury less than two days to convict him.. Yet not once had this devious, violent man expressed even one word of remorse for any of his appalling crimes: nor had he ever described what really happened in the small flat he owned at 24 Collingwood Place, just behind the bus stop on Station Road in Walton-on-Thames on that March afternoon in 2002.

Outside the court, Sally Dowler said bitterly, 'We have felt that our family who have already suffered so much has been on trial as much as Mr Bellfield. I hope while he is in prison, he is treated with the same brutality he dealt out to his victims and that his life is a living hell.' There is no doubt that she was expressing the opinions felt by millions of people who had seen the details of the trial reported day after day in the media.

Like the late Moors Murderer Ian Brady, Bellfield now stands confirmed as one of the most ruthless serial killers in British legal history. He has become infamous, because of the terrible nature of his crimes. When I was writing my biography of him, which was published after the Dowler trial was completed, Bellfield asked me from the dock one day to 'make sure it is a fair and accurate account' – they were the words of a man who wanted to be remembered.

What makes Levi Bellfield particularly significant for me is that he proves beyond most reasonable doubt that the possibility of a whole life term of imprisonment is of no deterrent when it comes to a psychopathic personality like his. Indeed I doubt strongly that it has any deterrent value to anyone intent on murder. Throughout his two trials, Bellfield (or Yusuf Rahim as he is now called, since his conversion to Islam three months after his return to Wakefield, following his second whole-life sentence) continually protested his innocence, no matter how convincing the evidence against him may have been, remaining trapped in a world in which he can portray himself on one hand as an eternal victim, wronged by society, while on the other he can bask in the notoriety that his disgusting crimes bring him. In either event, the idea of spending his life behind bars was no deterrent at all.

16

Killing for Profit and Pleasure

John Childs, Paul Glen, Kenneth Regan and William Horncy

There is another group of men serving whole life sentences who also clearly disregarded the deterrent effect of spending the rest of their life behind bars – killers who murder for money.

These men may be psychopaths, or suffering from overwhelming personality disorders, but they are nonetheless cold-blooded killers who are prepared to take a life for a price, regardless of the consequences. Their personalities may mean they enjoy the killing, but their other motive is financial greed. Some of this group might be called 'hit men' – in that they offered themselves as killers for hire – while others are armed robbers who are prepared to use lethal force in pursuit of personal profit. What unites both groups, however, is their utter lack of conscience or remorse over what they do and its consequences.

Let us begin by examining what I believe is the most ruthless group of all – men who kill to order.

The most prolific contract killer in British police history is John Childs, also known as Bruce Childs, who is now aged seventy-six and has spent the past thirty-seven years behind bars for a series of six contract killings carried out between November 1974 and October 1979. One of Childs' victims was a ten-year-old boy, and none of his victims' bodies have ever been found; neither have the murder weapons.

Yet this is a man whom friends and neighbours described as 'very fond' of his family and who seemed to many of them a 'perfectly nice person'. Indeed, one visitor who went to see him after his imprisonment memorably described him as having a 'ready smile and a warm handshake'.

Spare in stature, with watery blue eyes and pale skin, Childs was born in the East End of London in 1939 and brought up in Bow during the war. As a teenager he joined one of the local gangs in the mid-1950s, before joining the Army as an engineer. He was discharged after nine months for committing a burglary – but his brief military career gave him a lifelong interest in both weapons and books about war.

On his return to civilian life, Childs sustained himself as a petty criminal during the 1960s, and was jailed at one point for stealing a series of motorcycles. But what set Childs apart from his fellow minor criminals was his utter lack of conscience. This made him an attractive accomplice to one of the East End hard men of the day, Harry Mackenney, always known as 'Big H' because of his six-foot-five inch stature, and his associate, Essex-based businessman Terry Pinfold.

The three men embarked on a string of armed robberies in the 1970s, which eventually resulted in Childs' arrest in September 1978 for his part in a £500,000 security van robbery in Hertfordshire. After his arrest, Childs confessed that they had not only been in the business of armed robbery, but also of murder – alleging that they had actually killed six people in the previous four years.

Their victims, according to Childs, were haulage contractor George Brett and his ten-year-old son Terry, nursing-home owner Fred Sherwood, roofing contractor

Ronald Andrews, ex-prisoner Robert Brown and teddy-bear manufacturer Terry Eve.

Childs told the police that he had been hired to kill all six by Mackenney and Pinfold and that his price per 'hit' had usually been £2,000. He also insisted that the bodies would never be found, later suggesting that he had put them through a meat grinder in his living room before burning the remains in the fireplace of his flat in Bow.

After his confession Childs was charged with all six murders, as all the victims he had named were registered as missing persons, and on 4 December 1979 he pleaded guilty to all six counts of murder. At the Central Criminal Court Mr Justice Lawson then sentenced him to six terms of life imprisonment – but the crimes were not revealed in detail. That would not happen until almost a year later when Childs would give evidence against his 'employers' Mackenney and Pinfold in their trial for murder. In the period between his first trial and the second, Childs was kept in solitary confinement for his own protection.

The ugly details of Childs' brutal crimes were eventually revealed to the jury by prosecution counsel at the second trial in November 1980. Ironically, even though Pinfold was in prison at the time for his part in an armed robbery, Childs told the court that he was in fear for his own life and for the lives of his wife Tina and their two daughters for giving evidence against both men, but that he was determined to do so regardless of the possibly lethal consequences. In fact Childs' evidence was to become one of the most bare-faced acts of perjury ever seen at the Central Criminal Court in Old Bailey – but the jury did not know that at the time.

Looking absolutely calm, Childs proceeded to go into the most graphic, sordid detail about each of the six killings, while minimising his own role in each and every one of them. On the first murder, of thirty-five-year-old Terence Eve, for example, he described how it was Mackenney who had hit him persistently with a length of hose that had two heavy nuts attached to it, before strangling him. The next morning he and Mackenney had taken the body to Childs's flat in Bow and used an axe, saw and knives to cut it up, because the industrial mincing machine they had bought for the purpose of destroying the body was not up to the task. Childs then spent almost twenty-four hours burning the remains in the grate of his living room fireplace.

After the murder, Childs told the jury, he and Mackenney set up as contract killers for hire, using Pinfold as their agent. Their first target was to be haulage contractor George Brett, and they were paid £1,800 to do the job. The two men lured Brett – who had his ten-year-old son Terry with him for company – to a church hall on the pretext that they had some work for him. When Brett got there, Childs explained that Mackenney killed both the father and son with shots to the head from an Army sten gun. Once again the bodies were taken back to Childs' flat and the same procedure was followed – with the ashes emptied into a nearby canal.

Their fourth victim was ex-wrestler Robert Brown, who had escaped from Chelmsford Prison and was on the run. He had been witness to a part of their killing of Terence Eve and so was doomed. Once again, Childs claimed that Mackenney shot him in the back of the head – though this time he survived, which resulted in the two men hacking at him with axes. That too failed and Childs told the jury that he had taken a 'short sword stick and stabbed him in the belly, running the blade up into his heart'.

The next target for the two was Fred Sherwood, who

owed a colleague of Mackenney's a large sum of money. This time Childs hit him over the head with a hammer and Mackenney shot him.

Their last victim was not for money, but for an entirely different reason. Mackenney had been having an affair with the wife of a friend of his named Ronald Andrews, and had decided to murder him and move in with his wife, as she had a 'nice house' and was comfortably off. Childs was given £400 to help with the murder. Posing as a private detective, Childs lured Andrews to his flat, where Mackenney shot him in the head with a revolver fitted with a silencer.

After Childs had finished giving his evidence, however, Mackenney's defence counsel, Michael Mansfield QC, called two witnesses who both suggested that Childs had told them individually that Mackenney was innocent, and that he was naming him because he wanted to 'do Mr Mackenney down'. In his closing speech for the defence, Mansfield suggested to the jury that the case against his client 'rests almost entirely upon the word of one man, Childs, a man who is maniacally obsessed in thoughts and actions by violence.'

In spite of that claim, the jury convicted Mackenney of the murders of George Brett and his son, and of Frederick Sherwood, as well as Ronald Andrews, but he was not convicted of the killings of either Terence Eve or escaped wrestler Robert Brown. Pinfold, meanwhile, was found guilty of the murder of Terence Eve. On 28 November 1980, Mr Justice May sentenced Pinfold to life imprisonment, and then turned to Mackenney, whom he also sentenced to life imprisonment but with the recommendation that he should serve at least twenty-five years.

From the dock, 'Big H' shouted, 'I think you are a hypocrite. Bring this farce to a close . . . I killed nobody.'

The Court of Appeal did not believe him. Pinfold and

Mackenney unsuccessfully appealed against their convictions in 1981 and were denied leave to appeal again in 1987. Pinfold served more than twenty-one years in prison before being released on licence in September 2001. But it was not until after an investigation by the Criminal Cases Review Commission that it was finally acknowledged that Childs had lied through his teeth at their trial two decades earlier. Pinfold and Mackenney were hardly saints, but they had been convicted almost entirely on the basis of Childs' evidence, which was fatally flawed.

It was not until 30 October 2003 that the Court of Appeal finally heard the truth about Childs. The Lord Chief Justice, Lord Woolf, sitting with Mr Justice Aikens and Mr Justice Davis, heard from a string of witnesses that Childs suffered from 'personality disorders' – although attempts to introduce that information had been blocked at the original trial. Edward Fitzgerald QC, acting for Mackenney, called evidence to show that Childs was a 'skilled fabricator' and a 'highly intelligent psychopath' who would 'say anything, at any time, when it suited him'. He even questioned Childs' claim about disposing of the bodies in the grate of his flat.

This new evidence convinced the Court of Appeal that there had been a miscarriage of justice and on 15 December 2003 – almost a quarter of a century after Pinfold and Mackenney were convicted – the pair were released. Lord Woolf commented that the court was 'unable to say where the truth lies as to these terrible murders', but concluded that Childs' evidence was 'not capable of belief'. He explained that the new evidence presented to the court proved that Childs' evidence against Pinfold and Mackenney was unreliable because he was a 'pathological liar'.

Outside the High Court in London, 'Big H' Mackenney said, 'I'm shattered at the moment; I'm very relieved. It's been a long time coming – it's twenty-three years too late. The case should never have gone to court in the first place. It was a fiasco.' For his part, Pinfold contented himself with saying, 'Childs gave his story, and looking at the evidence, he was proved a liar.'

Throughout his time in prison Childs has changed his story, but since 1986 he has consistently maintained that he lied about Pinfold and Mackenney. In July 1986, for example, he even swore an affidavit admitting that Pinfold was 'only convicted because of my perjured evidence' – though he declined to clear Mackenney.

In 1998, Childs also told the *Daily Mirror* that he had also committed five other murders – though that has never been corroborated. He told the *Mirror* reporter, Jeff Edwards, 'I know I'm going to die in jail. There's a few things I'd like to get off my mind before I go . . . a few skeletons still in my cupboard.' Those were the other five murders, and whether they are part of his fantasy life or reality is impossible to tell. What is indisputable, however, is that Childs will indeed end his life behind prison bars. The life sentence he received in 1979 was converted into a whole life term by the Home Secretary after 1983, although that has never been officially confirmed; there seems little prospect of his being released.

Childs boasted about his murders in a series of letters to a 'penfriend', thirty-one-year-old Sandra Watson, whom he was introduced to through the Prison Reform Trust. Watson explained in 1998, 'The things he told me have shocked and sickened me. They are so terrible. He shows no remorse for what he did. He's proud of it and would do it again tomorrow if he was released from prison.' Childs described to Watson in grim detail how he had killed his victims, and discussed the best ways to sever a head and limbs.

Childs also told Watson, a divorced mother of three

children, about his part in a bank robbery in 1979, a crime for which he has never been charged, and once again took a positive delight in his violent role. 'Because a couple of guards wanted to be heroes,' Childs wrote, 'and a customer wanted to have a go, I was forced to pistol-whip the customer senseless and shot the two guards at point blank range with my Webley revolver. Any idiot who fails to obey me when I say "Get on the floor or die!" in my opinion deserves to die. It's as simple as that.'

Childs then told Watson that hours later he made passionate love to his wife Tina on a bed awash with banknotes.

'I will kill anyone for money,' Childs gleefully told Watson. 'All I wanted to do was to get rich and I don't give a damn. I will kill for money, revenge, honour!'

Not every contract killer is quite as intelligent or manipulative as Childs, however. One man who most certainly was not is the baby-faced builder Paul Glen, now aged forty-two, who was convicted of two murders and made the subject of a whole life term. Hired as a hit man, the naïve Glen managed to kill the wrong man – murdering builder Robert Bogle, who was a black man in his mid-twenties, instead of Bogle's housemate Vincent Smart, who was white and in his early thirties. It might almost be laughable had not an entirely innocent young man lost his life for no other reason than his killer was an incompetent bungler.

Born in Blackpool, Lancashire, in 1972, Glen committed his first murder when he was just seventeen, killing a gay Blackpool guest house owner called Ivor Usher on 21 February 1989. Originally he and an accomplice had intended to steal the £5,000 that they believed their bachelor victim had stored in his safe, but when it came to the robbery itself Glen seemed to lose all sense of control and bludgeoned Usher to death while he was tied to a chair.

Later that year he was convicted of murder and sentenced to life imprisonment, but was released in 2002 after serving just thirteen years. Like many other men before him and after him, his release on licence after a life sentence did nothing whatever to persuade him not to kill again. Indeed I have discovered that at least eighteen men who have been released from life sentences for murder have gone on to kill again while on licence.

Nevertheless, it was Glen's reputation from the earlier murder as a man who was prepared to kill without hesitation that saw him get a contract to kill again for money just two years after his release. A wealthy local businessman in Lancashire wanted to frighten fellow businessman Vincent Smart because he believed Smart and his three sons had been bullying him. He was recommended to speak to Glen, who was at this point offering his services as a local thug, and who certainly had the credentials to do the frightening. As a result, in return for a fee of just £300, Glen was hired to put the 'frighteners' on Smart – the only trouble was that Glen could not manage to restrain himself. He only really knew how to kill.

Shortly before eight in the evening of 8 June 2004, builder Robert Bogle was cooking supper for his girlfriend in the house they shared with Vincent Smart in the village of Farcet in Cambridgeshire when a man wearing a hooded top, an overcoat and black gloves walked into the kitchen. Without hesitation the hooded man raised a foot-long kitchen knife he was carrying and started to stab Bogle repeatedly, even though the builder tried to fight back. By the time he was finished the intruder had stabbed Bogle ten times, striking his hands, arms, right cheek and, ultimately, his heart. Bogle's girlfriend, meanwhile, was hiding behind the sofa in the living room, traumatised by what was happening in front of her.

Displaying considerable courage and determination, the desperately injured Bogle managed to drag himself through the house and out into the street in search of help. He attracted the attention of three teenage girls and he asked them to call an ambulance, but he did not stop there. He tried to attract the attention of people at a nearby shop before collapsing in the street. His attacker walked calmly away down an alleyway beside the houses, still wearing the overcoat and black gloves. Glen had not bothered to ask the name of his victim – had he done so he would have realised at once that he was not his intended target, Vincent Smart, Bogle's housemate.

Forensic evidence, including DNA, put Glen at the scene of the crime, and mobile phone records confirmed he had been in the area, just as they confirmed that he had returned to Blackpool immediately after the murder. In an attempt to conceal the truth, the Lancastrian claimed to the police that the murder of Bogle had actually been committed by a man named 'Steve' whose name and address he did not know.

That suggestion was ridiculed by the prosecution counsel when Glen came before Norwich Crown Court in June 2005. Rex Tedd QC told the jury in no uncertain terms that there was no 'Steve' and the killing had been committed by a 'professional killer, who had travelled to the area where his identity and appearance were completely unknown. That man on the mission was Mr Paul Glen.' The jury agreed and, after a five-week trial, convicted Glen of Bogle's murder.

Sentencing Glen, the judge, Sir John Blofeld said, 'As a result of your actions a young man, who had a future before him and a devoted family, lost his life in circumstances which were terrible.' The judge added that it was 'immaterial' to discuss a release date as Glen would be subject to a whole life sentence and would never again be free.

'Do I not get a chance to say anything?' Glen shouted from the dock in response, but the judge did not reply and Glen was ushered out of the dock and down into the cells by the prison staff accompanying him. But he did not let his case rest or die. In September 2006, Glen's legal team asked for leave to appeal against his whole life term, but their application was rejected, not only because he had committed a second murder, but also because he had done so for profit – albeit only £300.

Just a few weeks later, at the end of January 2007, Glen took the extraordinary step of getting married in the chapel at Whitemoor high security prison in March, Cambridgeshire. His bride was forty-one-year-old Paula Kelly from Liverpool, who had been corresponding with him in prison, and the ceremony was conducted by a Catholic priest. A matter of weeks later Glen launched an escape attempt with two fellow prisoners. Prison officers thwarted the plan, and the three prisoners were placed in solitary confinement.

Glen's marriage raises an interesting issue about the whole life term. Does it effectively rule out any possibility that the convicted prisoner can ever experience anything resembling an 'ordinary' life at any time? To those who believe the principal purpose of the sentence is to 'lock them up and throw away the key', then it surely does. But what about the possibility of redemption? Might not marriage – however remote it may be because of the couple's physical separation – help that process?

I am not arguing for one moment that Glen is anything other than a psychopathic personality with a clear penchant for the most brutal and sustained violence – nor am I suggesting that he does not deserve the most stringent punishment. I am simply pointing out that if the sole purpose of a whole life sentence is punishment, then society and the judiciary should admit that once and for all. As a former Lord Chief Justice, Lord Bingham, once explained, the law is required to be accessible, intelligible, clear and predictable. If it is not, then it should be revised. I do not believe that clarity exists when it comes to whole life sentences – with some arguing it is simply the ultimate punishment, others that it may allow the possibility of redemption and change.

In the annals of murder for money, however, there can be few more despicable killers than 'gang boss' Kenneth Regan – often known as 'Captain Cash' – and his equally depraved accomplice William Horncy. Between them, they were responsible for a set of the most dreadful killings, and both received whole life terms in 2005 for their part in the atrocities. Both men are in their early sixties now, and have little or no prospect of release – and the reason is clear enough: the public would be at risk, just as they would be from John Childs, if they were to end their time behind bars at any point in the near future. In the longer term, however, that may not be the case.

An ordinary-enough looking man, though with broad shoulders and an intimidating manner, Kenneth Regan gradually became one of the most successful drug dealers, money launderers and passport smugglers in Britain during the 1990s. At one point he was smuggling forty million pounds' worth of cannabis into the country in a single shipment, and quickly used the front of an insurance firm to launder the huge fortune that he was making. Regan relished the gangster lifestyle, taking enormous pleasure in carrying vast amounts of cash in the boots of his Mercedes cars, which led to his nickname of Captain Cash. But in June 1998 his criminal enterprises came to a sudden halt as armed police officers pounced during a heroin deal in north London. Regan tried to escape, without success, and the officers found twenty-five kilogrammes of the drug in the boot of his car.

Facing a jail sentence of at least twenty years, the wily Regan offered the police his 'co-operation' and turned into a 'supergrass'. He proceeded to help with their enquiries into four major investigations involving drugs, smuggling and murder, and his information brought fifteen convictions and five trials. At Regan's eventual trial the judge explained, '. . . you will never again be trusted by your former colleagues, so you can't go back and the enmity of those will make your future life precarious.' The judge then added, 'Those who turn against former associates should receive a very great reduction in their sentence.'

Regan was given an eight-year sentence, but was released in 2002, after serving fewer than four years. He could hardly return to his former haunts and associates, however, even though he was desperate to regain his wealth and celebrity. So he came up with a plan that he was convinced would place him back at the very top of the criminal underworld – he decided he would take over CIBA Freight, a company owned by millionaire Asian businessman Amarjit Chohan, aged forty-five – but he would not buy it, he would steal it.

To help him execute the plan, Regan recruited two of his former accomplices from his drug smuggling and passport days, William Horncy, then aged fifty-three, and Peter Rees, aged forty. The final – though utterly innocent and unwitting – member of the team Regan put together was divorcee Belinda Brewin, aged forty-three, an ex-public relations executive and former best friend of Paula Yates, the late wife of rock singer Bob Geldof, who was to become the spokesperson for CIBA Freight once Regan had control of it. But Brewin had another advantage – she had fifty acres of land near Tiverton in Devon, which would be the perfect place to bury a body or bodies.

Regan began telephoning Chohan in February of 2003,

claiming that he had Dutch backers who wanted to buy his firm. Chohan had something of a chequered reputation, having served a brief prison sentence for tax evasion, and was reported to be desperate to sell his business. That made him the perfect target for Regan's plan to return to his glory days as a drug smuggler and money launderer. To help him to do so, he engaged Chohan in a series of lengthy negotiations – while all the time planning to force him to sell him the company by threatening him with his death and the death of his family.

Regan, who at this point was living with his elderly father near Salisbury in Wiltshire, finally confirmed to Chohan that he had indeed secured a Dutch company which was prepared to buy CIBA Freight for three million pounds, and invited him to a meeting near Stonehenge in Wiltshire on Thursday 13 February 2003 to meet the prospective buyer. In fact there was no buyer – that part in the proceedings was to be played by Regan's former accomplice, Peter Rees.

After attending the Stonehenge meeting on that February day in 2003, Chohan was never seen alive again. In reality, he had been kidnapped by Regan, Horncy and Rees and taken back to Regan's father's house where he was tortured until he signed a series of papers effectively handing over his firm to Regan.

Regan's plan was to kill Chohan and make it look as though he had fled the country in fear of the tax authorities. The only difficulty was that Chohan would have been unlikely to leave his home in Hounslow in Middlesex without taking his family with him – and for Regan that meant only one thing. They too would have to die. After Chohan's disappearance on Thursday, his wife Nancy, who was twenty-five, rapidly became concerned when her husband did not return the following day – especially when he did not answer his mobile phone.

On Saturday 15 February 2003, Regan and Horncy left Rees guarding Chohan in Salisbury and set off for London in a hired van, determined to kill the remaining members of the Chohan family. The two men tricked Mrs Chohan into letting them into the family home and then set about killing every member of the family. Neither man displayed the slightest sign of mercy as they butchered Nancy Chohan and her two infant sons, eighteen-month-old toddler Devinder and his eight-week-old baby brother Ravinder, as well as her mother Charanjit Kaur, aged fifty-two, who was visiting the family from India.

The two killers then loaded the four bodies into Regan's van and drove them to his father's home in Salisbury. That night Chohan was forced to leave telephone messages for his employees telling them that he had sold the business to Regan and that he and his family had left for India. After he had done so, the three conspirators killed him as well.

On the morning of Monday 17 February 2003, Regan arrived at the offices of CIBA Freight complete with a letter from Amarjit Chohan – written, of course, under the most extreme duress – saying that he had been exporting illegal drugs, before adding, 'Some people are after me and I have to escape. I fear for the safety of my family.' The staff accepted the story and Regan installed himself as the new boss.

Two days later Regan returned to his elderly father's house in Salisbury, piled the five bodies of the Chohan family into the hired van and drove them to Belinda Brewin's home in Devon, where he, Horncy and Rees proceeded to bury them. Brewin was not there at the time, but when she came back the men explained they were sorting out a 'drainage problem' for her as a gift. Shortly afterwards, Regan disposed of Mr Chohan's car – in which he had come to the original meeting at Stonehenge a week earlier – to remove all trace of him.

Regan's plan to take over CIBA Freight and go back into the drug smuggling business might have worked, but for the fact that Nancy Chohan had been very close to her brother Onkar Verma, who lived in New Zealand. Sister and brother were so close that they spoke to each other on the telephone almost every day – and so when Regan told Mrs Chohan's brother that she and the entire family had left the country he simply did not believe it. Nancy Chohan would at least have told him, he believed, and he started pestering the police to investigate what had happened to his sister.

Onkar Verma was so concerned about his sister and the family that three weeks after her disappearance he flew to London to urge the police to find them. He also pestered them to search the family house in Hounslow, which was deserted, but looked as though it had been left in a great hurry. There were half-eaten plates of food on the table and the washing machine was full.

The police then discovered that the family's bank accounts had not been touched since their disappearance and launched a full-scale inquiry. Officers arrived at the CIBA Freight offices and interviewed Regan and the staff, and they quickly became suspicious about the letters signed by Mr Chohan explaining the reasons for his leaving the country so abruptly. On the surface Regan looked calm, but beneath that veneer he was in a panic. He returned to Brewin's house in Devon, dug up the bodies of the five members of the Chohan family and put them in another hired van. On Easter Sunday, 20 April 2003, he bought a boat and, helped once again by Horncy, dumped all five bodies in the sea off Dorset.

Just two days later a father and his son canoeing off Bournemouth Pier found a body in the water, which was quickly identified as belonging to Amarjit Chohan. Even more extraordinarily, the police also found that Chohan had managed to leave them a letter, folded up many times and secreted in his shoe, that gave the address of Kenneth Regan and his father. Sensing something may have been amiss in his negotiations with Regan about his company, Chohan had written it the day before his fateful meeting at Stonehenge.

On 15 July 2003, Nancy Chohan's decomposed body was found in fishermen's nets off Poole in Dorset, while her mother's body, even more severely decomposed, was found on a beach on the Isle of Wight several weeks later, on 7 September 2003. Tragically, the bodies of her two sons, toddler Devinder and his eight-week-old baby brother Ravinder, were never to be recovered.

By that point Regan, Horncy and Rees were all in police custody, and fourteen months later, on 8 November 2004, all three appeared at the Central Criminal Court in Old Bailey to face charges of murder and false imprisonment. All three denied any involvement in the killings and pleaded not guilty. What followed was one of the longest criminal trials in recent history, lasting no less than eight months, at an estimated cost of ten million pounds.

Prosecuting counsel, Richard Horwell QC, painstakingly laid out the evidence for the jury, pointing out that Chohan had been drugged and, quite possibly, strangled, while his wife's skull had been smashed, probably with a hammer, although her mother's body was too badly decomposed to offer any concrete evidence of how she met her death. He also explained blood evidence that had been found on the garden wall of Regan's house, in the trench that had been dug in Devon and on the speedboat that he had bought, all linking him to the family.

Mr Horwell then added, 'Regan was penniless. He had no

legal right or interest in CIBA; there were no backers ... Regan's motive and intentions are obvious: he was desperate for a return to the days of "Captain Cash" – banknotes in the boot of the Mercedes and the luxury home. There was only one way he could realise such an ambition and that was through drugs ... CIBA was the perfect vehicle.'

In spite of that argument the jury took twelve days to reach a verdict. It was not until Friday 1 July 2005 that they returned to find Regan and Horncy guilty of all five murders. Rees, meanwhile, was found guilty of murdering Chohan.

On the following Tuesday 5 July 2005, the judge, Sir Stephen Mitchell, addressed Regan and Horncy directly.

'Your crimes are uniquely terrible,' he told them. 'The cold-blooded murder of an eight-week-old baby, an eighteen-month-old toddler, not to mention the murders of their mother, father and grandmother, provide a chilling insight into the utterly perverted standards by which you have lived your lives.' Sir Stephen then added, 'Your characters are as despicable as your crimes. Each of you is a practised, resourceful and manipulative liar. For these crimes you two highly dangerous men must now pay the heaviest sentence.' He then sentenced both men to whole life terms of imprisonment.

Neither Regan nor Horncy displayed the slightest emotion as the judge passed sentence – just as they never admitted their guilt. To this day, both men protest their innocence, and have never revealed what happened to the bodies of the two innocent children.

Rees was also found guilty of false imprisonment and helping to kill Chohan, but the judge accepted that he was not the planner of the crimes, although his responsibility for the murder was of the 'utmost gravity'. He was given a sentence of life imprisonment with a minimum term of twenty-three years.

Outside the court, a family friend of the Chohan's read out a statement on behalf of Onkar Verma, the man who had persuaded the police to take an interest in the family's disappearance two years earlier. It said simply, 'The last two years have been a living nightmare. The deliberate, premeditated slaughter of my innocent family is akin to me being given a life sentence – a life with no laughter, no happiness and no joy.'

Predictably, given their persistent claims of innocence, Regan and Horncy appealed against their convictions, and the appeal was heard on Friday 16 May 2014. Regan maintained that they had been forced to dispose of the bodies by the militant Islamic terrorist organization Al-Qaeda – who had threatened to kill them if they did not do so. But Lady Justice Rafferty, sitting with Mr Justice Holroyde and Mrs Justice Andrews, dismissed their appeal without hesitation.

In her judgement Lady Justice Rafferty said, 'Regan's contention that he did not give evidence because he was threatened by Al-Qaeda is not an arguable ground for appealing.' She also told both men, 'The evidence against you was formidable and the case was very fairly and comprehensively summed up.'

There is little chance that either man will launch a further appeal, and both are almost certain to spend the rest of their lives in prison – keeping the secret of what happened to the Chohan children to themselves. There can be little doubt that they would present a danger to the public were they to be released. But did the possibility of a whole life term of imprisonment deter either man? The answer must surely be no.

17

Partners in Crime but Not in Sentence

John Duffy, David Mulcahy and Steve Wright

Two men who were partners in a devastating series of rapes and murders in north London during the early 1980s are now both serving life sentences of imprisonment. Yet, ironically, only one of the two was sentenced to a whole life term – by the Home Secretary of the day – while the other is serving life with a minimum term of thirty years, which means he could be eligible for parole in 2031 when he will still only be in his early seventies.

The two men represent yet further examples of the conflicting standards that seem to be at work in the sentencing of offenders who commit crimes of the utmost gravity. For both men were found guilty of exactly the same crimes – although they were sentenced eleven years apart.

Known originally as the 'Railway Rapists' and then as the 'Railway Killers', John Duffy and David Mulcahy were born within a few months of each other in north-west London in 1959. At the age of eleven they arrived at the same secondary school, Haverstock Hill Comprehensive in Hampstead, at exactly the same time. Both misfits with few friends, Mulcahy was the taller of the two, with a round white face, high forehead and boyish expression, while Duffy was far shorter, with an ugly, menacing grin and a mop of curly ginger hair which he kept hidden under his parka jacket's hood for fear of being ridiculed. Duffy would never stand more than five feet four inches in height, which led his friend Mulcahy to call him 'the midget'. As Duffy grew he would also develop severe acne, which pockmarked his face and increased his feeling of being an outsider still further.

In spite of their physical dissimilarities, however, the two boys struck up an almost telepathic bond that was to remain with them for more than thirty years and see them commit a series of attacks on women. Neither achieved anything academically at school, but they did develop an uncanny joint instinct that encouraged them to break the law. At one point Mulcahy had been suspended from school for killing a hedgehog with a plank of wood and stamping on it, while his friend Duffy looked on and smirked. There was no doubt in either boy's mind that Mulcahy was the dominant partner in the relationship.

As the boys turned into teenagers they also developed a passion for martial arts and started to practise 'kung fu' head locks and grips as well as survival skills together on Hampstead Heath, not far from their homes in Chalk Farm and Brondesbury. They then graduated to wearing Halloween masks and jumping out from hiding places behind bushes on the Heath to terrify courting couples and homosexuals who sought the privacy of the extensive wooded areas on the Heath to meet. The more terrified the people they revealed themselves to, the greater the excitement and pleasure Mulcahy and Duffy took from their behaviour.

In 1976, just after they left school, the pair were convicted of causing actual bodily harm when they shot four passers-by on the Heath with a powerful air rifle – apparently 'for fun'. Far from frightening them into a law-abiding way of life, the brush with the law only served to encourage the pair still further, and shortly afterwards the manipulative Mulcahy suggested to Duffy that they should rape a woman together. It was to be the first of a relentless series of crimes that terrified women in north London for more than a decade.

As Guy Toyn, a reporter for CourtNewsUK.com was to put it later, 'Their "wicked bond" was cemented by deep feelings of sexual inadequacy – Duffy's irrational hatred of women sprang from a low sperm count which prevented him from fathering children. Throughout his life Mulcahy had been troubled by difficulties in maintaining an erection which would drive him to escalating sexual depravity and violence in an attempt to arouse himself.'

What is not in doubt, however, is that Mulcahy chose their first target – a woman whose house he was helping to decorate. He told Duffy he thought she 'needed teaching a lesson' and that they were going to break in and rape her. But their scheme did not go according to plan. The two men broke into the house and laid in wait, but the lady in question did not return to her home that night. Not long afterwards the two broke into a house in Notting Hill, west London and laid in wait in the bedroom for a woman that Mulcahy had suggested was 'stuck up'. Again their plan failed, the two young men eventually escaping through a window when the lady in question returned home with a male friend that evening.

Neither failure deterred them, however, as they became more and more brazen in their determination to commit a rape. By now they had equipped themselves with a 'rapist's kit' of balaclava helmets, knives and tape to gag and blindfold their victims. The Michael Jackson cassette tape *Thriller* would become another essential part of the kit, with the two men singing along to it as they drove around north London hunting for victims.

On 24 October 1982, Mulcahy and Duffy raped their first

known victim, a twenty-one-year-old woman who was walking home from a party in west London carrying a teddy bear she had been given by a friend. Wearing balaclavas to prevent her identifying them, the two grabbed her by the neck, put sticking plaster over her mouth and said, 'Don't worry, all we want is your teddy bear.' It was a cruel joke, for they dragged her into the front garden of a nearby house where she was stripped, blindfolded and raped. The victim recalled, 'I put my hands up and the taller man said, "Don't worry, it is a knife."'

'We were both very excited,' Duffy was to admit later, 'and said we should do it again.' In the following years they were to do so many times, leaving a string of victims aged between fifteen and thirty-one. 'We used to call it "hunting",' Duffy was to explain. 'We were playing games with the police and generally making it fun.'

On 27 March 1983, they targeted a twenty-nine-year-old French woman who was working as a restaurant manager and walking home near Finchley Road railway station in West Hampstead. The two launched their attack, but the woman bit Mulcahy's hand very hard, despite being kicked and punched as she lay on the pavement curled up into a ball, and the two let her go.

It was almost a year before they struck again. On 20 January 1984, they attacked a thirty-two-year-old American social worker on Barnes Common, in west London. Mulcahy and Duffy, who were in the area decorating Duffy's parent's home at the time, stripped and raped her. The victim was to explain later that Mulcahy told Duffy to 'gouge out my eyes, slice off my ears and slice off my nipples . . . I believed I was going to be murdered, disembowelled, tortured.'

Four months later, on 3 June 1984, a twenty-three year old became their fourth victim. They grabbed her in the waiting room of West Hampstead railway station and put a knife to her throat before marching her to a dark spot under a railway bridge not far away. She said later, 'They had a knife and said they would cut me if I didn't do as I was told. All I could say was, "Please don't hurt me."' The two men merely laughed.

By this time both men were married and living outwardly respectable lives. They were both working for Westminster City Council, Duffy as a carpenter and Mulcahy as a plumber. Mulcahy had married Sandra Carr, an Anglo-Indian, in 1978, while Duffy had married nursery nurse Margaret Byrne in 1980. Mulcahy continued to have difficulty in maintaining an erection unless the sex was apparently against his wife's will.

In July 1984 the pair tried to drag a twenty-two-year-old woman into the back garden of a house in Highgate, north London, but the owners switched on the garden lights, forcing them to leave her untouched. But on 15 July 1984, they dragged two Danish au pair girls into bushes on Hampstead Heath, stripped and raped them.

It was six months before Mulcahy and Duffy were to strike again. On 26 January 1985 they raped a German au pair girl in Brent Cross, north-west London, and five days later returned to Hampstead Heath and grabbed a sixteen-year-old girl but did not go through with the rape. There quickly followed another attack – on a twenty-three year old in South Hampstead – but she managed to escape, as did another prospective victim on 2 February 1985. Undeterred, the very next evening, the two men stalked a solicitor's clerk on Hampstead Heath, whom they blindfolded and raped on a bench. Their desire to rape was escalating, while Mulcahy was becoming ever more sadistic as the attacks continued.

The two men had developed an almost telepathic understanding. Their victims talked about an uncanny, almost psychic relationship that had now lasted fifteen years. One was to explain, 'They didn't tell each other anything. It was two bodies but one brain,' while another added, 'The two men seemed to be able to communicate without words – by nodding their heads.'

The rapidly escalating number of rapes across London saw the police launch Operation Hart in an attempt to bring the culprits to justice – and it quickly became the largest police operation since the hunt for the 'Yorkshire Ripper', Peter Sutcliffe, five years earlier. Conscious of the mistakes in that enquiry, however, the police also decided to invite forensic psychologist Professor David Canter to participate, bringing to bear a technique that he was pioneering – a 'geographical profile' of where the rapists attacked as a means of narrowing down the search area and the pool of suspects. Professor Canter, who quickly established himself as one of the first criminal profilers in Britain, sought to demonstrate that the rapists usually operated in a geographical 'comfort zone' which would include where they lived and worked.

Certainly, Mulcahy and Duffy attracted police attention as 1985 progressed. They were arrested in the autumn of that year when they were stopped in Mulcahy's car with stolen building materials. A black balaclava was found by the police in the car but the pair escaped with fines after Mulcahy told the officers that he used the mask when he was working as a plasterer on dusty ceilings. It was an opportunity lost to stop the pair's attacks – and one which would ultimately cost the lives of three innocent young women: for by the end of the year the two men had progressed from rape to murder.

On the evening of Sunday 29 December 1985, nineteen-year-old Alison Day was the only person to get off a train at Hackney Wick railway station and had the supreme misfortune to encounter the two men – once again on the hunt for a victim. She was on her way to meet her boyfriend at his printing firm nearby. But the teenager never arrived. Mulcahy and Duffy snatched her as she left the station and dragged her to snow-covered playing fields nearby.

After they had both raped her, Alison tried to escape and either fell or was pushed by Mulcahy into the freezing water of a local canal that led to the River Lea. Duffy later claimed he pulled her out, but that Mulcahy had become so sexually aroused by the incident that he raped her again, before tearing off a piece of her blouse to use to throttle her. Mulcahy later told his accomplice that he had killed Alison because she might recognise them. But Duffy insisted, 'David actually enjoyed it, saying it gave him power – the decision over life and death. I remember him going on, "It is God-like – having the decision over life and death."'

Alison's sheepskin coat was weighed down with stones in its pockets and her by-now dead body was hurled back into the canal. She was found seventeen days later, her hands tied behind her back and gagged. What had begun as a sexual adventure for Duffy had turned into murder with Mulcahy's specific and sadistic contribution. There could be no separating the two men now as their spree developed ever more quickly across north London. What was there to lose now? They had already killed. What difference would one or two more bodies make? There was no death penalty to fear – only the possibility of life imprisonment. Rape seemed small beer after murder.

Just over three months later, on April 17, 1986, Mulcahy and Duffy struck again, but this time they abandoned their regular haunts in north-west London and set off for the leafier fields of Surrey – perhaps aware that remaining so close to their homes so consistently might finally have begun to attract the attention of the police. This time the two set a trap by stretching a length of thin fishing line across a path in fields between Effingham and East Horsley in Surrey in the hope of catching someone unawares, who would then fall over helpless in front of them. The plan worked and the fishing line knocked fifteen-year-old Dutch schoolgirl Maartje Tamboezer off her bicycle. She was then marched across the fields and raped by Duffy – only for matters to take an even darker turn. Mulcahy suddenly lost his temper.

'He was becoming very aggressive – hyper, shouting at the girl,' Duffy recalled later. 'He then raised his fists and hit the girl. She crumpled to the floor. She was struck on the head, at the side. It was a swinging blow. I noticed he had a rock in his hand, or a stone. She just crumpled up and fell on the floor. I believed she was unconscious.'

Mulcahy ripped off the teenager's belt and looped it around her throat, telling Duffy, 'I did the last one, you'll do this one.' Mulcahy then passed his friend the belt. 'It had a piece of stick through it which was twisted and he gave it to me in my hand,' Duffy explained. 'I actually started twisting it while David turned away. I think I just got caught up in it. It is very difficult to explain. I just continued twisting until she was dead.'

Their depravity did not even end there, however. Mulcahy broke Maartje's neck after she was dead and then set fire to parts of her body, specifically targeting her genitalia in a desperate effort to destroy any forensic evidence that would link the two men to her rape. There could hardly have been a more profound desecration of the poor girl's innocent and defenceless body as it lay in a Surrey field on that spring day in 1986. Their actions deeply affected the police officers working on the investigation, who responded by increasing still further their efforts to track down the killers.

That did nothing to deter Mulcahy and Duffy, however, who were by now trapped in their own spiral of self-destruction. Barely a month later they struck again, even more boldly, as they returned to their hunting ground north of London – and back at a railway station. Just as they had done with Alison Day the previous April, the pair ambushed a young woman as she got off a train shortly before 10 pm – although this time it was at Brookman's Park station in Hertfordshire on 18 May 1986. She was television secretary Anne Lock, aged twenty-nine, who had only just returned from her honeymoon in the Seychelles.

The terrified young woman was frogmarched to a nearby field with a knife at her throat where Duffy raped her, but then Mulcahy threw him the car keys and told him to collect their car. When Duffy reappeared with the car it was clear something dramatic had taken place. Duffy was to say later, 'David said he had taken care of it. He was very evasive, like he was playing mind games. He was saying, "She won't identify us now." He was very excitable, buzzing. He was even saying, "Keep your eyes open for another one."' The decomposed body of Anne Lock was found two months later in undergrowth just a mile from her home. She had been suffocated with her own sock.

By this time Duffy had come to the attention of the police, although not as a specific prime suspect in the rapes and murders. In August 1986 – after the three murders – he was arrested after beating up his wife at home and was put into the computer system run by Operation Hart to find the killers. Duffy was found to have a rare blood group, a group that had been found at several of the crime scenes. After that connection had been made, Duffy was arrested on suspicion of rape, and was identified by two of the rape victims – not least because of his severely pockmarked face and his piercing blue eyes. But at this stage there was no firm evidence against him – that would come later.

Mulcahy was questioned, but no evidence was ever found

linking him to the rapes or the murders, although the police were certain that Duffy often operated with an accomplice and that Mulcahy was the most likely candidate for the role. For his part, Duffy remained studiously silent about his friend's role in the rapes – still subscribing to the agreement that they had reached as schoolboys that they would never 'grass each other up'. There was also the signal fact that – by this point – Duffy was terrified of the relentlessly sadistic Mulcahy and feared saying anything critical about him.

No action was taken against Duffy by the police immediately, however, and he started to operate as a lone rapist. On Tuesday 21 October 1986, a fourteen-year-old schoolgirl was raped on the outskirts of Watford, and during the assault her blindfold slipped and she was able to describe a short, pock-marked man with a dog he called Bruce. This, together with Professor David Canter's 'criminal profile' of the likely attacker – which matched Duffy in thirteen elements out of seventeen he had created – convinced the Operation Hart detectives that he was indeed their prime suspect. The police team put Duffy under surveillance and on Sunday 23 November 1986 he was arrested.

The detectives who searched Duffy's home found hard-core pornography, martial arts videos and magazines, and several martial arts weapons – while he was also found to have a dog named Bruce. It was during a search of his mother's home, however, that they got their most significant breakthrough. Hidden under the stairs was a ball of a very specific string called Somyarn, which forensic experts were able to match with that used to bind the murder victims. Fibres found on Duffy's clothes also matched those recovered from the body of Alison Day.

For his part, Duffy refused to admit anything whatever, and remained impassive as he was charged with rape and murder. It was a stance that he retained fourteen months later at his trial in February 1988. He claimed he was suffering from 'hysterical amnesia' and was unable to remember any of the events surrounding the offences he was charged with between 1982 and 1986. But the evidence was overwhelming on five counts of rape as well as the murders of Alison Day and Maartje Tamboezer. The trial judge, Mr Justice Farquharson, directed that there was insufficient evidence to convict him of the murder of television secretary Anne Lock.

After being found guilty by the jury, Mr Justice Farquharson proceeded to sentence Duffy to seven life sentences with a recommendation that he serve a minimum of thirty years. 'You are obviously little more than a predatory animal,' the judge told him. 'The horrific nature of your crimes means thirty years is not necessarily the total you will serve. It may well be more.' In fact, the Conservative Home Secretary, Douglas Hurd, was to increase the sentence to a whole life term not long afterwards.

In a richly ironic statement, David Mulcahy told the *Daily Mail* after Duffy's sentencing, 'I don't believe John was capable of doing all these things. He's always been a mummy's boy.' Placing himself firmly above any suspicion of involvement in the rapes, he also announced that he was planning to sue the police for wrongful arrest and for damaging his reputation. That was precisely how Mulcahy was to present himself to the world for the next decade – as a happily married father of four whose name had been besmirched by his childhood friendship with the convicted rapist and murderer John Duffy.

It was not until 6 August 1996 that Mulcahy's façade began to fracture. Another rapist emerged on Hampstead Heath that evening when a sixty-six-year-old woman was attacked.

That sparked a chain of events which would lead to Mulcahy joining his schoolfriend Duffy behind bars. The police launched an investigation into the rape, and by chance two officers noticed similarities between this attack and the ones carried out by Duffy a decade earlier; for example, knives and balaclava helmets were involved again.

At one point the police even suspected that Duffy might have committed the rape while on day release from prison, but when they discovered that was not the case they began to re-examine the forensic evidence from the original cases, not least because investigative techniques had taken significant steps forward in the years since Duffy's original attacks.

Mulcahy's name appeared again. Samples taken from the clothes of one of the au pairs he and Duffy had raped on Hampstead Heath showed there was only a one in a billion chance that he was not the attacker. Then it was found that a piece of tape used to bind the woman attacked on Highgate West Hill had not been tested for fingerprints before it was consigned to a storeroom at Euston station. Four experts confirmed the fingerprint they found on the tape belonged to David Mulcahy.

Meanwhile, the police also discovered that Duffy was now being interviewed by prison psychologist Jenny Cutler, who told them he had given the name of his accomplice as David Mulcahy. Duffy had told her during a long series of sessions at Whitemoor Prison in Cambridgeshire that he 'wanted to get things off my chest'.

'I've been in custody for many years,' Duffy told her, 'and have had a hard time coming to terms with what I'm in for – rapes and murders. I feel a lot of guilt for what I've done and want to make a clean slate.' The police immediately reopened the original railway murders case and spent weeks re-interviewing Duffy, as well as taking him back to the crime scenes. During the debriefing he confessed to twenty-five sex attacks, as well as to the murder of Anne Lock.

In the early hours of Saturday 6 February 1999 – eleven years after Duffy had finally been given seven life sentences for five rapes and two murders – Mulcahy was arrested and charged with seven rapes and five charges of plotting to rape, as well as three counts of murder. His trial began in early October 2000 and between the end of January and beginning of February 2001 Duffy spent no fewer than fourteen days in the witness box giving evidence against his old schoolfriend.

Nevertheless, throughout his evidence in court, Duffy did not try and shift the blame to Mulcahy entirely. He admitted his own part in the crimes. 'I feel a lot of guilt,' he explained. 'I have raped and killed young ladies. I accept that. I am not trying to shift the blame. I did what I did.'

Significantly, throughout his imprisonment and up to that point, Duffy had never lodged any kind of appeal against his sentence or conviction. 'I know I will die in prison,' he told the jury at Mulcahy's trial, adding that he was not 'looking for anything in this' but just wanted 'to get on with my life in the system – to make a fresh start.'

Duffy's counsel told the court, 'Having committed these crimes there is nothing more in his power that he could have done to make amends.'

That assertion infuriated Mulcahy – who persistently condemned his childhood friend from the dock throughout his evidence against him. Mulcahy claimed that he had been framed by the police and that Duffy had been paid £20,000 to give false evidence against him. He steadfastly maintained his innocence during the rest of the trial, forcing six of his rape victims to relive their horrifying ordeals in court, but on 1 February 2001 the jury of six men and six women unanimously found him guilty of all the charges. They had taken five days to reach their verdict.

On the following day, the Recorder of London, the most senior judge at the Central Criminal Court, sentenced him. On 2 February 2001, Judge Michael Hyam told Mulcahy that the killings were 'acts of desolating wickedness in which you descended to the depths of depravity in carrying them out.' The judge went on to add, 'These were sadistic killings and out of the two of you I have no doubt it was you who derived gratification from the act of killing.'

The Recorder then sentenced Mulcahy to three life terms for the murders and twenty-four years for seven rapes and five planned rapes. The Recorder also recommended that he should serve a minimum of thirty years before even being considered for release. Mulcahy demonstrated no emotion whatever as the sentences were passed down.

Judge Michael Hyam went on to sentence John Duffy to a further twelve years' imprisonment for the seventeen additional charges of rape that he had admitted to during his police interrogations about Mulcahy's role in the rapes and killings. The extra sentence did appear to affect Duffy and since then he has seemed to accept that he will remain in prison for the rest of his natural life.

The same has certainly not been the case for his old schoolfriend. In the years since his conviction Mulcahy has repeatedly and consistently claimed to be innocent. He has offered no other explanation of the crimes – beyond the fact they were committed by Duffy.

Mulcahy has also encouraged his friends to launch a website which, like Jeremy Bamber's, insists he has been falsely imprisoned. The website is headed by a quotation from the French writer Andre Gide: 'Believe in the ones who are searching for the truth and doubt about those, who say they have found it.' It then goes on to add: 'This nightmare is not a story of a famous writer, it is the true story of a man, our friend, who is still incarcerated in HMP Full Sutton, who is still praying and who still believes that sometime soon a retrial will prove his INNOCENCE.'

Under the heading 'The Facts', the site proceeds to explain that Duffy's true accomplice in the rapes and murders is still at large and 'enjoying living in freedom', and then outlines the reasons that Duffy falsely implicated Mulcahy in the crimes.

'John Duffy was convicted in 1986 for a series of rapes and murders and assault on his ex-wife and her boyfriend,' it explains. 'Duffy and Mr David Mulcahy went to school together. Mr David Mulcahy gave a statement to the police that resulted in Duffy being questioned for the rapes and murders that Duffy would later be sentenced for. Duffy's defence during questioning, and later at trial, would be that he was suffering from hysterical amnesia (proven to be false) for the entire offending period.'

The site then insists, 'After making a deal with the police, Duffy wrongfully gave evidence against Mr David Mulcahy. The only evidence against Mr David Mulcahy was the statement of a murderer and rapist. There is no scientific evidence either to support or refute the allegation that Mr Mulcahy was involved in these cases.'

After maintaining that Duffy wanted revenge on Mulcahy for his statements to the police about his attack on his wife, the site concludes with an exposition of why Mulcahy is innocent, which focuses on nine key facts which revolve around Duffy's collaboration with the police and prison authorities, but also covers some of the DNA analysis linking Mulcahy to the rapes.

'No smoke without fire!' the site concludes. 'Good saying and I used to use it a lot before, but I know smoke can also be used as a smoke screen . . . I don't expect to be believed on face value. All that I ask is that you look at the evidence and come to your own conclusion. If having done that, you see that I am innocent, check your memory; see if you know anything about Duffy . . . The guilty belong in jail, not the innocent. Do you know anyone who would be willing to look at this case to aid my appeal? Please get in touch. You could be the person who rights a massive wrong.'

Mulcahy's protestations of his innocence are likely to have exactly the same impact on his life behind bars as they have had on Jeremy Bamber's. The possibility of release from a life sentence with a fixed minimum term is predicated on the prisoner in question accepting his own guilt and standing by that recognition. To refuse to do so increases the likelihood of never being released – and so it becomes entirely possible that Mulcahy will, like Duffy, end his natural life behind bars even though, were he to admit his guilt, there would be at least the possibility that he would be eligible for release in his early seventies.

But there is another serial killer of recent years serving a whole life term who is equally convinced he is innocent, though he does not have a website to argue his case for him. He is forklift truck driver and former merchant seaman Steve Wright, now aged fifty-seven, who murdered and dumped five prostitutes during a killing spree in Ipswich, Suffolk between 30 October and 10 December 2006. He was given the maximum sentence the law in Britain allows on his conviction in February 2008. The details of Wright's killings have been widely reported, so I do not propose to go back over them in great detail, but his reaction to his sentence and his crimes throws further light on what convicted prisoners serving whole life terms feel about their crimes.

Like Mulcahy and Duffy, Wright had a lifelong obsession

with sex – although in his case with prostitutes rather than identifying young women as targets for rape. All three saw women as objects that inspired a simmering rage – even though all three were married, and two had children. Indeed, all three presented themselves to the outside world as normal-enough men, even though behind closed doors they could be both violent and abusive towards the women in their lives. Interestingly, all three were also almost the same age, born in the late 1950s, with an attitude to sex that owed more to the pre-war era than to the world of the swinging sixties where attitudes to sex became increasingly relaxed.

Steven Gerald James Wright was born on 24 April 1958 in the Norfolk village of Erpingham, the second of four children of a military policeman and a veterinary nurse. He had an elder brother, David, and two younger sisters. While Wright's father was on military service, the family lived in both Malta and Singapore, but Wright's mother left the family home in 1964 when Wright was six – his father divorced her and both later remarried. Wright and his siblings went to live with their father, who had a son and daughter with his second wife, Valerie.

At the age of sixteen, Wright left school and quickly joined the Merchant Navy, becoming a chef on ferries sailing from Felixstowe, Suffolk. At the age of twenty he married Angela O'Donovan, with whom he had a son, Michael, but they later divorced. Wright went on to become a steward on the Cunard liner *QE2*, then a lorry driver, a barman and – prior to his arrest – a forklift truck driver.

Wright's second marriage came in August 1987 when he married thirty-two-year-old Diane Cassell, but the couple split up within a year while he was a pub landlord in Norwich. He then formed a relationship with Sarah Whiteley between 1989 and 1993 and they had a daughter together, born in 1992. It was during this time that Wright managed a public house in south London, a job he was to lose as a result of his gambling and heavy drinking. He was convicted of stealing £80 in 2001 to pay off his gambling debts. By then his drinking and gambling had escalated out of control and he twice tried to commit suicide, once by carbon monoxide poisoning in his car, and then by an overdose of pills. He was a man living on the edge.

One constant in Wright's life, however, besides his heavy drinking and gambling, was his use of prostitutes. In 2001 Wright met Pamela Wright – their shared surname is mere coincidence – in Felixstowe and they moved to a house in Ipswich together in 2004. She was apparently aware of his habitual interest in sex with sex workers, and while the couple were in Ipswich Wright admitted to her that he went to massage and sauna parlours that were actually brothels. During this period he is reported to have had sex with three prostitutes who were to become his victims in the final weeks of 2006.

What tipped Wright over the edge into killing the women he chose as sexual partners has never been clearly established – he himself has offered no explanation. He has remained studiously silent on the whole question of his motivation for killing from the time of his arrest until his conviction. After his arrest on suspicion of murder, he refused to answer any of the questions put to him by the police – replying throughout with just two words, 'No comment'.

Intriguingly, Wright's victims – although all sex workers in the Ipswich area, three of them known to him – were not sexually assaulted as part of their murder, although all of their bodies were stripped naked before they were dumped in the surrounding area. Each had, however, been strangled – the most intimate method of murder, implying as it does an extraordinarily close connection between murderer and victim. No evidence has ever been produced to suggest that the act of strangulation during the killings might have brought Wright some form of sexual arousal, but it must, at least, be a possibility. But there is no evidence that he was impotent or incapable of an erection during his relationships with prostitutes over many years.

Whatever the motivation, there is no doubt that Wright was responsible for the deaths of five sex workers in December 2006, whose bodies were discovered in a ten-day period between 2 and 12 December. The killings had taken place over a six-and-a-half week period, beginning on 30 October 2006.

The first body to be found was that of twenty-five-year-old Gemma Adams, whose body was discovered in the water of Belstead Brook at Thorpe's Hill, near Hintlesham, Suffolk. Six days later, on 8 December, the body of nineteen-year-old Tania Nicol, a friend of Adams, who had been missing since 30 October, was discovered in water at Copdock Mill just outside Ipswich. There was no evidence of sexual assault on either body, although both were found naked.

On 10 December, a third victim was found in an area of woodland by the A14 near Nacton, Suffolk. She was identified as twenty-four-year-old Anneli Alderton, a mother of one child. According to a police statement, she had been asphyxiated and was around three months pregnant when she died. She too was found naked, but had not been sexually assaulted. Her body had been posed, however, in what was later described as a 'cruciform' position.

Two days later, on 12 December, the police announced that the bodies of two more women had been found. On 14 December, they confirmed that one was twenty-four-year-old Paula Clennell, a mother of three, who had disappeared on 10

December. According to the police, she died from 'compression of the throat'. The next day the police confirmed that the other body found was that of twenty-nine-year-old Annette Nicholls, a mother of one child, who disappeared on 5 December. Her body, too, was posed in a 'cruciform' position. The bodies of Clennell and Nicholls were also found in Nacton, close to where Alderton had been found.

Suffolk Police launched a major investigation after the discovery of the second body, and quickly established a link between the killings. Officers from thirty other forces participated in the investigation and the police rapidly seized upon Wright as a prime suspect. At 5 am in the morning of 19 December, just a week after the discovery of the final two bodies, Wright was arrested. Just two days later, on 22 December 2006, he was charged with all five murders.

On 16 January 2008, Wright appeared at Ipswich Crown Court charged with all five murders and the prosecution opened their case against him. In particular they revealed that Anneli Alderton and Annette Nicholls had been deliberately posed in the 'cruciform' position, that DNA evidence linked Wright to three of the victims and fibre evidence connected him to all five victims.

For their part, the defence argued that Wright was a frequenter of prostitutes, and had had 'full sex' with all of the victims, except Tania Nichol. He had picked up with the intention of sexual relations, before apparently changing his mind and dropping her off back in the red light district of Ipswich.

On 21 February 2008, after eight hours of deliberation, the jury returned a unanimous verdict. They found Wright, who was then aged forty-nine, guilty on all five counts of murder. Mr Justice Gross passed sentence the following morning. Wright sat motionless in the dock, staring straight ahead, as the judge told him he had targeted vulnerable women. 'Drugs and prostitution meant they were at risk,' he told him. 'But neither drugs nor prostitution killed them. You did. You killed them, stripped them and left them,' Mr Justice Gross went on. 'Why you did it may never be known.' The judge then pointed out that Wright had carried out a 'targeted campaign of murder' and drew his attention to the 'macabre' way in which he had arranged two of the women's bodies in a 'cruciform' position. There had been a 'substantial degree of premeditation and planning' in the murders, the judge went on, which meant, 'It is right you should spend your whole life in prison.'

When Wright was led down to the cells he made no eye contact with anyone in the courtroom; neither did he make any comment whatever.

In the wake of the verdict, some of the victims' families expressed their satisfaction with Wright's whole life term, but others most certainly did not.

The families of Tania Nicol and Paula Clennell, in particular, expressed disapproval. 'Today, as this case has come to an end, we would like to say justice has been done,' they said in a statement outside the court, 'but we're afraid that where five young lives have been cruelly ended, the person responsible will be kept warm, nourished and protected. In no way has justice been done.'

They went on to demand a return to hanging. 'I wish we still had the death penalty,' their statement went on, 'as this is what he truly deserves . . . These crimes deserve the ultimate punishment and that can only mean one thing. Where a daughter and the other victims were given no human rights by this monster, he will be guarded by the establishment at great cost to the taxpayers of this country and emotionally to the bereaved families.'

Yet within a matter of weeks, Wright had launched an appeal against his conviction. In a letter to the Court of Appeal he claimed that the trial should not have been held in Ipswich, that his defence team did not represent him effectively enough, and that much of the evidence against him did not add up. Wright also accused the police of not adequately investigating other potential suspects.

'The prosecution alleged I had drugged all five women and then strangled them and yet there wasn't a shred of evidence found on myself, home or car relating to drugs,' Wright said. 'All five women were stripped naked of clothing/jewellery/phones/bags and no evidence was found in my house or car.'

Wright's appeal was heard four months later, in July 2008, when Lord Justice Hughes, sitting alone, concluded that Wright had no 'arguable' grounds for the appeal. By this time Wright had dispensed with his previous legal team, and was representing himself. The judge did not criticise the former forklift truck driver for doing so – indeed he said that his arguments had been 'moderately and carefully expressed and coherently formulated'. Nevertheless, Lord Justice Hughes dismissed his claim that the jury was unduly influenced by the press and concluded that it was 'quite clear' that 'the defendant was fairly treated'.

Wright refused to accept the judgement and two weeks later on 15 July he asked for a further appeal before three judges.

By that time he – like David Mulcahy and Jeremy Bamber before him – had claimed publicly that he was innocent of the crimes. In a letter, sent from Long Lartin Prison in Worcestershire, to his local newspaper, the *East Anglian Daily Times,* Wright claimed that he did not have a 'violent bone in his body' and felt 'deep sorrow and heartfelt pain' for the families of the five murdered women.

'People should believe I am innocent,' he wrote, 'because I have gone through my whole life trying to be fair and considerate to other people as I possibly could . . . to take a life I would have thought would be the ultimate form of aggression. I just know in my heart that one day my innocence will be proved and I will be able to go home to try and rebuild my life, whatever that home will be.'

The former merchant seaman added, 'What I would say to the people of Suffolk is, "Be on your guard because the real killer is still out there."' He also explained that he had been distressed and embarrassed that his sexual habits had been revealed in court, but insisted they did not mean he was the killer. 'All their evidence proved was that I had contact with said girls, but not one shred of evidence showed that I killed them.'

The letter infuriated the families of the victims. Rosemary Nicholls, the mother of Annette, was particularly angry. 'I think it is a load of rubbish and it is him trying to get the sympathy of the people of Suffolk and beyond,' she explained. 'We sat in court and listened to all the evidence against him and I cannot possibly see how he is innocent. He did not look in court as though he felt any sorrow at all. There was no remorse. He is a disgusting object. He should do the decent thing and tell us what he did to our daughters and where everything happened.'

Meanwhile, Paula Clennell's father Brian added, 'It has turned my stomach. He can do what he wants. He has hobbies and a TV and the gym and meals every day. They live the life of Riley. I say let him rot in hell.'

In February 2009, a few months after his letter, and the

strong reaction to it from the families, Wright withdrew his second appeal, and – although he indicated in 2012 that there was a possibility that he would launch a third with the support of his brother David and partner Pam Wright – as yet no further official action has been taken.

Indeed, as time has passed, more evidence has emerged of Wright's violent tendencies. In a television documentary in 2014, for example, Wright's second ex-wife, Diane Cole, explained just how quickly his mood could change. 'When I first met Steve in 1985,' she said, 'he would inundate me with flowers and presents, and he was quite a charmer really. But he had a very possessive streak though, very possessive, which I didn't like.'

In particular, she remembered a time when she and Wright had been working on a cruise ship together. 'I walked back to the ship with the shop manager and when I got to the cabin it had been written on the door "Slag. Whore". I opened the door and he said, "You liked him that much, there's your grass skirts." And he had cut all my work skirts . . . Then he went at us with a knife, whether it was meant to hit me I don't know as it hit the door. He was so strong, he used to call himself "The Mean Machine".'

No matter the face he presented to the outside world, Wright's true personality has begun to emerge. There must be a possibility that he could attack prostitutes again were he to be released on licence.

18

Lifers Who Kill Again

Glyn Dix, Anthony Rice and David Tiley

At the start of this book about the men and women subjected to whole life terms of imprisonment I asked two simple questions – does life mean life? And its corollary – should life mean life?

The answer is, as we have seen, both ambiguous and confused. The truth is that life means life sometimes, often depending upon the publicity associated with the crime committed, and it does not at other times, sometimes when there is less celebrity associated with the murder.

A whole life term is the ultimate penalty available under English law – although it is no longer used in Scotland. Once a prisoner has been sentenced to spend the rest of his or her life behind bars, and any appeals process has been exhausted, then the law suggests that is where they should stay.

Yet there are times when an appeal can downgrade a whole life sentence to life with a minimum term, which allows for at least the possibility of release, while there are other occasions in which a life sentence without a whole life term attached to it can mean that a prisoner can be released to kill again. That is what I would like to deal with here.

The trouble with allowing a prisoner serving a life sentence without a whole life term the possibility of regaining his or her freedom, albeit under licence, is that the Parole Board, who are charged with making the decision to release on licence, marches to a significantly different drum than the judiciary.

In the Court of Appeal, for example, the details of the original crime are always included in the written judgement handed down when the appeal is considered – which means that everyone involved is fully aware of the true nature of the murder that led to the sentence.

Yet, when considering a prisoner with a life sentence for release, the Parole Board does *not* take significant interest in the original crime. It concerns itself far more with how the offender has responded during his or her period in prison – whether, for example, there has been an acceptance of guilt, whether there has been evidence of rehabilitation, and whether he or she has displayed an attitude that suggests that they would no longer pose a threat to the population at large were they to be released on licence.

It is a well-intentioned position, but sadly one which can go spectacularly wrong – and one case illustrates that beyond all reasonable doubt. It concerns the schizophrenic Glyn Dix, who is now aged sixty and living in Ashworth Special Hospital on Merseyside alongside the much more celebrated killer Ian Brady.

Dix's case illustrates just how frail the concept of a life sentence can be – for he killed brutally and without a hint of remorse not once but twice – the second time twenty-four years after the first – and he did so after his release from a life sentence for the first murder.

His case reveals just how poorly equipped the parole system can be to deal with the most disturbed and violent offenders – who may take great pains to appear to have been transformed by their sentence but who, in dreadful reality, have not. No matter how rehabilitated they may seem to the Parole Board when they come before it for consideration for release, beneath the surface they have been skilful and manipulative enough to conceal the dreadful danger to society they can still present once they have been released.

But let us look at the case of Glyn Dix carefully. In the early evening of 2 October 1979, thirty-two-year-old Pia Overbury, a mother of two, left the cake shop in the county town of Gloucester where she worked and set off for a friend's party. She was never seen alive again. Three weeks later her body was found in an isolated copse of trees near the village of Hartbury, a few miles north-east of the town. She had been tied to a tree, raped and shot in the head – for no apparent reason. She had no enemies, no dark secrets in her past, no furious lover, no unhappy spouse. Pia had fallen victim to that rarest of all murderers – a 'random' killer.

The police investigation into the murder led officers to a twenty-six-year-old hospital porter named Glyn Dix, who came from the area, and who was finally charged with Overbury's murder. At his trial at Bristol Crown Court in July 1980, the jury heard his extraordinary version of events – that Pia had offered him £2,000 that evening to kill her husband and that they had gone to the isolated wood to discuss it. Dix then claimed that she had begged him to kill her as she could not go on living with her husband, and he had carried out her wishes.

On the third day of the trial, however, Dix changed his plea to guilty. He confessed to the court that he had forced the terrified young woman into the woods, tied her to the tree and then raped her before shooting her in the head and leaving her body in what resembled a shallow grave. Dix insisted he had been inspired to do so by what he called 'the change of the seasons', which suggested that there might have been some sort of link to the dark arts of black magic, at least in his mind.

Dix was duly sentenced to life imprisonment, although with no fixed minimum term. He served no fewer than nineteen years behind bars, a large portion of those years at Ashworth high-security psychiatric hospital. Over the years Dix demonstrated signs of redemption and rehabilitation, and he was eventually transferred to the relatively relaxed Gloucester Prison as part of his preparations for his eventual release.

While Dix was in Gloucester Prison, one of his cell-mates was a twenty-one-year-old man named Adam Langford, and the two men became friends. In fact, after Langford's release the young man kept in touch with Dix as his release became more and more likely. Langford's fifty-year-old mother Hazel often drove her son to meetings with Dix in prison, and the two got along well. So well that Hazel Langford and Dix started a relationship by post while he was still in Gloucester Prison. His letters were reported to be 'warm, witty and charming' – and so, not long after he was released on licence in September 1999, the couple married at Redditch Register Office.

Significantly, Dix's announcement of his intention to marry Hazel Langford may have played its part in securing his release from prison on licence. His attachment to her, and their apparent happiness together, must at least have had some impact on the Parole Board's decision to release him. Yet the terrible truth – in the light of what was to come – must have been that he was using her for his own far darker and malign purposes.

On the surface, however, everything seemed normal enough between the couple over the next five years. Dix moved into Hazel Langford's home in Redditch, and the family reported that they appeared happy. But slowly and steadily something much more threatening began to emerge. Dix's self-control steadily ebbed away, so much so that the slightest disagreement between the couple could see his temper erupt within seconds. They could be enormously close at one moment, and yet at each other's throats the next.

One sunny afternoon, on Saturday 19 June 2004, Dix finally lost control completely. He had an argument with his wife about what to watch on television and he attacked her viciously, so viciously that when her son Adam came home at about 3.30 pm, Dix was to be found standing over her naked body with a kitchen knife in his hand. He had stabbed Hazel Langford to death and chopped her body into no fewer than sixteen separate pieces, cutting off her head, arms and legs with a hacksaw, and had then used a total of fifteen different instruments, including scissors and other knives, to mutilate her body. He had also cut out her heart, liver and kidneys.

Dix had also painted a mural on the wall of the living room depicting an almost naked woman on her knees and a hooded attacker with a knife in his hand standing over her. As his stepson entered the room, Dix grinned at him and said, 'We had a little argument.'

By that time Dix had put all his clothes in the washing machine to clean them of blood, and had washed the knife in his hand. Utterly terrified, Adam Langford ran across the road to the home of his sister Rachel, who then went back to her mother's house with him, where they encountered Dix together. When the police arrived not long afterwards Dix told them calmly, 'That's my wife Hazel, and I love her. We had a little argument and it went too far.'

Adam Langford blamed himself for his mother's death, saying, 'My mum gave him everything. He took her life and ruined mine ... If I'd never gone to jail I'd never have met this animal and Mum would be alive today. I knew he was in for murder, but couldn't find out anything about his past.'

Dix made no excuse for the killing or the terrible mutilation of his wife, but neither did he deny killing her. He was subsequently diagnosed as suffering from severe schizopsychotic affective disorder, a condition made worse if he refused to take the medication required to control it, and on the day of the killing he had clearly not taken any. Dix was remanded to Ashworth Hospital and, on 16 December 2005, pleaded guilty at Birmingham Crown Court to Hazel Langford's murder.

It transpired that Dix and his wife had been naked after making love when the argument over what to watch had broken out. The prosecution quoted from a statement that Dix made to the police after his arrest which said, 'Hazel had said, "Right, that's it!" and she got hold of a knife and I got hold of a knife and as we started facing each other, I stabbed her. She was going on and on, and I felt under pressure. I felt my anger rise, I said I had had enough of her.'

He also told the police that he had heard her voice in his head after the killing telling him to chop her body into pieces because 'she liked the place to be clean.'

In his defence, Dix's counsel told the court, 'Mr Dix wants to ... acknowledge the gravest regret and deepest remorse for what occurred ... He is bitterly, bitterly regretful and remorseful for what he did that day.'

The remorse fell on deaf ears. Passing sentence, Mr Justice Butterfield told Dix, 'You stabbed her to death and dismembered her body. It was brutal, horrific and abhorrent. You took the life of a woman who did much to help you and showed you much kindness. You have also deeply hurt the family, who welcomed you with open arms.' The judge then went on, 'Your counsel has sensibly decided that I should not apply a set period and you will be detained on a whole life order. You will be detained either in a specialist hospital or a prison until you die. You are an extremely dangerous man.'

The impact of Dix's killing on the members of the Langford family was dramatic. Hazel's brother John Denver said outside the court, 'We have all lost a sister, mother, grandmother and a very dear friend. No words can describe the devastation this family feels about a man who gave a persona of a quiet, loving, caring person. We were all taken in by the deceit.'

Deeply upset, Hazel's daughter Rachel, added, 'I wish they could bring back hanging. But that would be too quick for him – he should be buried alive.'

Another daughter, Jodie, called for life to mean life, and bitterly criticised the authorities for releasing Dix from his first life sentence. 'It's ridiculous that people get let out early after committing such terrible crimes . . . if there were different laws in place I'm sure my mum would still be here with us now. I think it's absolutely disgusting that criminals are let out early. When someone is given life it should mean life.'

The family firmly condemned the decision to let Dix out of prison in 1999. 'Someone decided to let this man out to kill again,' one niece explained; while the daughter of Pia Overbury, Dix's first victim in 1979, told a television documentary in 2014, 'He's a natural born killer, that's what he is, and a risk to society. I get very angry about it sometimes now.'

Yet Glyn Dix was not, and is not, an isolated case. My research for this book suggests that there are at least eighteen men who have been released from prison on licence after being given an initial life sentence – and have gone on to kill again.

As the former Attorney General Dominic Grieve QC has put it, 'People will be rightly shocked at this level of reoffending by people who have received life sentences. The whole point of the life licence for released murderers is to keep them under supervision and prevent reoffending.' But he then went on to argue, 'If prisons and the Parole Board were not so over-stretched there would be better rehabilitation and greater supervision before people are released.'

But would a whole life sentence really have been justified for the killing of Pia Overbury in 1980? I doubt it. If the offender is clever enough, and patient enough, he can groom the prison authorities into thinking that he is a reformed character and therefore no longer a danger to the public. After all, in March 2009 the Labour Justice Minister David Hanson announced, 'Only a very small minority, just over six per cent, of mandatory life sentenced prisoners who were released between January 1, 2003 and February 17, 2009, were recalled and found guilty of a further offence.'

Those figures nevertheless include serial sex attacker Anthony Rice, then aged forty-eight, who murdered mother-of-one Naomi Bryant, aged forty, in August 2005. This was just nine months after he walked out of jail in November 2004 after serving a life sentence with a minimum term of ten years for rape and indecent assault in 1989. He was freed in spite of having no fewer than twenty-two previous sexual convictions spanning a period of thirty-four years, including rape and violent assaults on women and children.

Discussing Rice's case while he was in custody, one psychologist estimated there was a seventy-two per cent chance that he would commit more crimes. Yet his parole hearing was 'so distracted' by protecting Rice's human rights that it failed to appreciate the threat he posed to society – according to an official inquiry into the events.

Rice strangled and stabbed Naomi Bryant to death just days after they had met in Winchester, where he was living at a hostel. She was found under her bed by her fourteen-year-old daughter Hannah.

The official enquiry later confirmed that Rice was too dangerous to have been released into the community. In May 2006, the Chief Inspector of Probation at the time, Andrew Bridges, found that there had been 'substantial mistakes and misjudgements' by the probation, parole and prison services in his supervision after his release, and that he should never have been released in the first place.

In its assessment before Rice's release, for example, the Parole Board had concluded that he presented only a 'minimal risk'. They pointed out that a decision in 2001 to move him to an open prison created a 'momentum towards release'. But the enquiry found that the Board's final decision to free him 'gave insufficient weight to the underlying nature of his risk of harm to others'.

Underlining how poor the supervision of Rice was during his period of release on licence is the fact that, four months before Naomi Bryant's murder, he slipped out of the hostel he was living in one night and assaulted a woman with a brick in Southampton. The enquiry noted, 'Rice later reported that he expected the police to call . . . but when they did not, he started to feel that he could do anything and get away with it.'

Every bit as tellingly, the enquiry also concluded that the Board had received 'over optimistic' reports of Rice's progress under treatment and did not have a full picture of his previous crimes. That is the point in the Dix and Rice cases – the Parole Board's lack of knowledge of, or interest in, the crimes for which the prisoners they were considering for release were found guilty in the first place.

As Professor Andrew Coyle, a former prison governor

and leading academic in this area, put it to me, 'The Parole Board tend only to look at an individual's change while he is a prisoner, and the acceptability of his or her release – they do not consider the original crimes.'

The deaths of Hazel Langford and Naomi Bryant certainly suggest that the Board should look into the nature of the original crimes committed by the prisoners before them – and do so with very considerable care indeed. Both women might still be alive had that been the case.

Probably the most horrifying case of all concerning a prisoner who killed while on licence after his release – although not from a life sentence – concerns another rapist. In 1995, thirty-five-year-old David Tiley was convicted of two counts of rape and one of buggery and sentenced to serve six years in prison. He had broken into a woman's home and attacked her while her children were asleep in the next door bedroom, brutally beating her around the face with his fists.

Yet when Tiley was released in 2001 the official judgement on him was that there was a 'low to medium' risk of his harming members of the public again. It was to prove a tragic misjudgement. In the six years after Tiley's release he was returned to prison no fewer than three times for failing to inform the police of his whereabouts – thereby breaching his licence. In the same period he also violently and sexually assaulted a string of former girlfriends, but not all of those attacks were reported to the authorities, and no official action was taken.

The truth is that the six-foot-tall, broad-shouldered and heavily tattooed Tiley, whose criminal record stretched back two decades, knew exactly how to work the parole and release supervision system to his advantage. He groomed the police and the Probation Service into assuming that he no longer posed any kind of sexual or violent threat to anyone. He did so by striking up a relationship with a forty-nine-year-old mother of five sons called Susan Hale, who suffered from cerebellar ataxia – a rare degenerative brain disorder which brought her difficulties in walking.

The couple met in an amusement arcade in Southampton in the summer of 2006 – which Mrs Hale was visiting on her mobility scooter. An active, outgoing woman, in spite of her disability, she worked part-time in a charity shop in the city and prided herself on not giving in to her poor balance and need for support. Tiley clearly saw an opportunity and seized it. Early in August 2006 he moved in with her, but did not tell the police. When his failure to do so was discovered, it led to another breach of his licence which saw him sent back to prison for five months. But when he was released again early in 2007, Tiley duly moved back in with Mrs Hale.

To be fair to Hampshire Police, who were in charge of supervising Tiley, no sooner had he settled into Mrs Hale's flat in Southampton than an officer went to visit the couple together. He went to ensure that Mrs Hale knew about her new companion's criminal background, and later reported that she 'implied' she was aware of his past and was 'happy' to continue the relationship. No one will ever know whether Susan Hale made that commitment willingly, or under coercion from Tiley; suffice to say that it was taken at face value by the officer visiting her, however naïve that may have been, and the matter was left. Within a matter of weeks Susan Hale was dead.

In the evening of Wednesday 7 March 2007, the diminutive, kindly Mrs Hale, who was known for her sense of humour, made the mistake of teasing her new lover – to whom she was by now she was engaged to marry – about his criminal past. In an instant, Tiley exploded with rage and hit her viciously on the head with a hammer that he grabbed from a tool box in the kitchen. Now clearly bent on sexual violence, he tied his terrified fiancée up with dressing gown cords, binding her ankles and wrists before dragging her into an upstairs bedroom. There he committed a serious sexual assault with a table lamp before stabbing her twice in the head and twice in the chest with a six-inch kitchen knife. Tiley did nothing to save her; instead he stayed with her, plainly intent on watching the life drain out of her body. Pathologists were to say later that she died 'rapidly, but not immediately'.

Demonstrating no remorse, Tiley wrapped his dead fiancée in a duvet from the bed and turned on a fan in the bedroom to lower the temperature and conceal any subsequent smell from her decomposing body. After doing so, he sprayed deodorant around the room. Mrs Hale's decaying corpse was to remain in that bedroom for the next eight days, while Tiley went about his normal business of visiting betting shops and amusement arcades on Southampton seafront, cooking himself meals in the kitchen and sleeping on the sofa in the front room, regardless of the ever-increasing smell. When family or friends called or sent text messages to her mobile phone, he would reply and tell them that she was not well, but that he was looking after her.

Eight days later, on the morning of Thursday 15 March 2007, Mrs Hale's regular carer, Sarah Merritt, aged thirty-nine and a mother of two children, who was responsible for looking after the forty-nine year old's general health and well-being, arrived to give her a scheduled bath. Tiley opened the door and let her in, but when she asked where Mrs Hale was he told her she was dead and produced a knife. Tiley proceeded to tie Sarah Merritt's wrists and ankles, take her bank card from her purse and demand to know the PIN so that he could remove money with it. Desperate, Merritt told him, and Tiley left her gagged and bound while he went out to withdraw £150 from her account.

When Tiley returned he removed the gag from her mouth and 'had a conversation' with her while he smoked two cigarettes. Sarah Merritt may have thought that he was going to spare her life, but she was wrong. When she began to sob with fear Tiley became angry again, tore off her clothes and raped her before stabbing her twice in the neck with the same kitchen knife that he had used to kill Susan Hale. Tiley left her body in the hall of the flat, but, realising that she would be traced, left himself – going on the run to nearby Dorset – but not before he had scrawled the word 'GOTCHA' in Mrs Merritt's blood inside the front door.

Just two days later, on Saturday 17 March 2006, police received information that Tiley had been seen in Swanage, about fifty-five miles along the coast from Southampton, and he was arrested at 2 pm on the seafront. He had removed another £100 using Sarah Merritt's bank card before taking a train to Weymouth. On 14 June he appeared at Winchester Crown Court, where, faced with overwhelming evidence against him, Tiley pleaded guilty.

Sitting in the dock, displaying no emotion, Tiley listened to a heart-rending victim's impact statement read to the court by Sarah Merritt's husband Peter.

'What is this world coming to,' he asked, 'when a kind, loving and caring person such as Sarah loses her life doing the job that she did, and being killed in such a wicked way while caring for others? I cannot get the thoughts out of my mind of how scared and so very afraid she must have been that day and that I could do nothing to help her in her hour of need. I am going to have to live with that for the rest of my life. Sarah didn't do anything to deserve such an end to her life.'

On behalf of Susan Hale, one of her five sons, David Chopra, told the court that the horrific details of what had happened to his mother and her carer had shocked the family 'to the core'.

But those were not the only statements read to Winchester Crown Court on that June day in 2007.

Tiley himself instructed his defence counsel, Lisa Matthews, to read a note that he had written and which he wanted the relatives of both victims to hear. 'I want to express to you all my regret,' his statement read. 'No words that I can say will replace Susan and Sarah. I am so sorry for what I have done. I deeply regret what has happened. But no amount of justice would compensate for what I have done. I hope that when I am sentenced you will be able to find some closure and get on with your lives. I am totally to blame for what has happened.'

Lisa Matthews then added, underlining that Tiley's statement was not a plea for mitigation of his sentence, 'There is nothing I can say that is going to change the outcome of the sentence. He knows that and everyone in court knows that. He knows that life is going to mean life.'

And so it did. Mr Justice Irwin was coldly dismissive as he addressed the prisoner in the dock. 'David Tiley,' he began, 'I will speak to you about what you have done, but your case is such I'm quite unsure if you will ever grasp the enormity of your own acts.'

The judge went on to explain that the police knew he was living with Susan Hale in Southampton. 'As we have heard, she was disabled with cerebellar ataxia, making her vulnerable and needing care. You applied to the Department of Work and Pensions to become her registered carer. Instead of caring for her, you killed her. Mrs Sarah Merritt was a dedicated community carer, who did look after Susan Hale. You raped her and you killed her.

'The brutality and evil defies adequate description,' Mr Justice Irwin went on. 'The pain and grief of the victims' families left in the wake of the deaths is profound ... One's heart goes out to them; nothing can repair the damage done to them.'

The judge concluded by sentencing Tiley to two life terms. 'These offences are quite exceptionally serious,' he said firmly, 'and the only appropriate sentence should be a whole life order. The only proper punishment for you is that you must never be released.'

In particular, Mr Justice Irwin used the word 'punishment' in his sentencing remarks. There was no question of Tiley 'paying his debt to society' or being 'given an opportunity to consider his actions', implying there was at least the possibility of eventual redemption and rehabilitation. The whole life sentence was a matter of punishment, pure and simple – and in that respect was only an inch away from the death penalty, had that still been a possibility under the law. Mr Justice Irwin concluded bluntly that he saw no alternative to locking Tiley up for the rest of his life – with every possibility that he would spend the final thirty to forty years of his life behind prison bars.

Yet the failure of the authorities, including the police, to supervise Tiley during his release cannot be ignored for its contribution to the deaths of both Susan Hale and Sarah Merritt. Defending the action of the force after the end of Tiley's trial, the Assistant Chief Constable of Hampshire, Simon Cole, said that Tiley had been the 'subject of visits in accordance with national standards'. He went on, 'Short of twenty-four-hour surveillance or locking up an offender for life, there can be no guarantees, and it is just not possible for agencies involved to do that. The professionals involved in monitoring this man did their best working within the system.'

If 'their best' was visiting Susan Hale and Tiley when they were together (*not* separately) and asking her if she was aware of his criminal past – and accepting an 'implied' response that she was – is 'working within the system', then it would be fair to say that the system leaves a great deal to be desired. Yet it later turned out that Tiley was one of 300 violent or sex offenders being monitored in the Southampton area early in 2007 – by a team that had originally consisted of just two officers but had been expanded.

It also transpired that there had been a lack of 'communication' between the many agencies involved in Tiley's case, which meant that details of Tiley's breaches of his licence – and his three returns to prison in the wake of his 2001 release – had not been shared 'effectively' between them. It is a sign, if any were needed, that the profound demands on the professional agencies charged with the monitoring and supervision of the most violent criminals to protect the public often go unsupported and virtually ignored – until a very public case reminds society of what is expected of them.

In fact, some argue that the whole life sentence is a safeguard against having to rely on the supervision of prisoners (and particularly murderers) in society, as it places the worst of the worst offenders within the prison system so that they can be monitored, although that does not – as we have seen – always prevent them from killing again within the prison walls.

Like the fifty or more other prisoners serving whole life terms, Tiley may have hoped that the decision of the European Court of Human Rights in July 2013 – that the sentence was 'inhuman and degrading' – would lead to every whole life term being reconsidered by the Court of Appeal in England and Wales. But, as we have seen, those hopes were firmly squashed by the Court's decision in February 2014 that they were entitled to sentence prisoners to whole life terms, as there were 'exceptional' circumstances that would allow the Secretary of State for Justice to release a prisoner serving a whole life term. That ruling was accepted by the European Court in 2015, and thereby dashed any hope that Tiley and others may have nurtured that their terms would eventually be reviewed and replaced by a fixed minimum sentence.

It is hard to feel sympathy for Tiley, whose two murders could hardly have been more depraved, just as it is all but impossible to feel sympathy for the other men serving whole life terms for murders of the utmost callousness.

These three cases prove that a life sentence for murder or rape offers no guarantee that the offender will not kill again upon his release. Each one demonstrates the weakness of the Parole Board and the Probation Service which tragically failed to protect the public from these three violent men. They were each freed to commit the most terrible crimes and yet the system that released them remains in place today.

It is difficult to ignore the conclusion drawn privately by some in the judiciary that the only effective way to protect the public when it comes to the most heinous crimes is to rely more and more upon the whole life sentence, as that apparently protects the public – if not the perpetrator's fellow prisoners.

19

They Deserve Nothing Less – Or Do They?

Rahan Arshad and Mark Martin

Families of murder victims often feel very strongly that the killer of their loved one should spend the rest of his or her life behind bars, so heinous were their crimes, and it is difficult to disagree with them. Two men in particular epitomise the revulsion society feels for murderers whose crimes set them so far apart from the morals of a civilised society that it is difficult to see any other punishment as appropriate – they deserve to go to prison for the rest of their natural lives.

These two men are a private hire/minicab driver called Rahan Arshad and a 'homeless drifter' from Nottingham named Mark Martin, both of whom killed more than one person and did so without hesitation, conscience or remorse, in the most dreadful ways imaginable.

Let us begin with Arshad. At some point during the late evening of Friday 28 July 2006, this thirty-six-year-old Pakistani, who worked as a driver for a firm in Didsbury, Manchester, killed his wife Uzma, aged thirty-two, and their three children, Henna, aged six, Abbas, aged eight, and eleven-year-old Adam.

He killed his wife first, beating her to death in the bedroom he shared with her using a £1.99 'Funsport' rounders bat that he had bought for the purpose just the day before. He hit her no fewer than twenty-three times. Then, quite calmly, he ushered their three children downstairs into the family playroom and beat them to death using the same rounders bat. He then covered all four bodies with duvets, left the house, and then the country.

The four victims, who all had very severe head injuries, were not discovered at the family's home in Cheadle Hulme, Manchester, for almost a month – not, in fact, until Sunday, 20 August 2006. The stench of decaying human flesh had finally alerted the neighbours that something was wrong.

As one of the first police officers on the scene said later, 'The bodies were so badly decomposed that the floor was soup because the bodies had basically melted. The forensic team who worked on this deserve a medal – they could hardly step anywhere.' Uzma and her three children could only be formally identified by their dental records, so bad was their condition.

Arshad had planned the attack with some care, telling friends that he was taking the family to Dubai for a holiday – thereby making sure no one would be suspicious when their house appeared deserted. In the meantime, however, he bought himself a single ticket to Thailand.

He actually left the country on Saturday 29 July, the day after the killings, abandoning his wife's BMW car at London's Heathrow airport before boarding a flight to Bangkok and travelling on to the holiday destination of Phuket. The last-known sighting of his children was the day before, on the final day of term at their school, Cavendish Road Primary.

Shortly after the discovery of the bodies the police tracked Arshad down in Thailand – with the help of the Thai police – and he agreed to help the British police with their investigation, possibly fearing that conditions in a Thai prison might be distinctly harsher than those in England. On 30 August 2006, he was arrested by officers from Greater Manchester Police in Thailand and flown back to England the following day.

There was no other suspect for the killings, and it rapidly emerged that Arshad had been consumed by jealousy as a result of his wife Uzma's affair with a neighbour's husband. It transpired that his and his wife's marriage had been 'arranged'. They were first cousins who had never met, and only knew of each other through their families.

It also became clear that after their marriage Arshad had rapidly become infuriated by his wife's acceptance of western style and dress, including wearing tight jeans and tops. He insisted privately that by doing so she was 'disrespecting him', an attitude only made more acute by his subsequent discovery of her affair.

'It wasn't right for a mother and someone who came from Pakistan to change the way she dressed all of a sudden. It wasn't right at all,' he said later. His wife certainly knew about her husband's feelings – even confessing to a friend, 'Count the days before he kills me,' – although she did nothing practical to protect herself or her children; and she certainly did not leave the family home.

On his return to Manchester from Thailand, Arshad freely confessed to murdering his entire family, telling the police, 'My beautiful kids. I don't regret killing that bitch but my kids. Killing my kids.'

Arshad later retracted that confession, however, claiming that it was his wife who killed the children and that he killed her as a result. His claim meant that there had to be a full trial for the four murders. It began on 27 February 2007 at Manchester Crown Court before Mr Justice David Clarke with

Arshad pleading guilty to just one charge of manslaughter – that of his wife – and not guilty to the murder charges.

When the prosecution opened their case against him, outlining the details of the injuries to Uzma and her three children, one female member of the jury broke down and wept.

For his part, Arshad gave evidence in his own defence, telling the jury that he adored his wife – 'she was beautiful,' – but also depicting her as a bad-tempered, materialistic spendthrift who continually put him down and thought herself to be his superior. He maintained that he struggled to keep afloat financially and was forced to work longer and longer hours to sustain her and the family. He also denied the prosecution's claims that he abused her – insisting instead that actually she had hit him.

As for killing her, Arshad told the court that he had 'blanked out' after confronting his wife about killing their children and his next recollection had been waking up naked in the bath holding the rounders bat. 'I don't feel any responsibility,' he insisted. 'What happened is nothing to do with me.'

The jury declined to believe him, not least because of the extensive forensic evidence linking him to the crimes, including the fact that when he flew back to Heathrow his Nike trainers still bore some of Uzma's blood, while some of his daughter Henna's was on a T-shirt in his suitcase. It took the jury just two hours to find him guilty unanimously of all four counts of murder on 13 March 2007.

Uzma's brother, Rahat Ali, shouted, 'Yes!' as the foreman of the jury announced their decision, and a statement from him and the rest of Uzma's family was then read out in court. 'No one can heal the grief we have suffered,' it began. 'Uzma was my best friend, our beloved sister and beautiful daughter. My mother can't understand how he could destroy them . . . None of us could understand how a father could do such a thing to his own children and his wife.'

Passing sentence, Mr Justice David Clarke told Arshad bluntly, 'You beat your wife to death in her bedroom and then coldly and deliberately you brought your sleepy children downstairs to meet their deaths. You left the scene and fled the country. It was over three weeks before the bodies were discovered. There is no suggestion of mental illness on your part . . . Life imprisonment in your case means life. You killed your entire family in circumstances of great brutality.'

For his part Arshad displayed no emotion whatever – beyond shutting his eyes as the judge pronounced sentence. Four members of the jury, by contrast, were in tears.

Outside the court, Uzma's brother Rahat applauded the judge saying, 'I am glad this man will never get out of prison. The judge made a brilliant decision. A person like this should never be freed.'

As for the reasons for the murders, Detective Superintendent Martin Bottomley of Greater Manchester Police explained, 'We will never really get to the bottom of it. There are a number of theories but I don't think we will know until he tells us.'

That was unlikely to happen, DS Bottomley went on, because Arshad had declined to say a single word to the police after his initial confession. 'When he came off the plane Arshad came across as someone who wanted to tell us everything,' the superintendent said. 'He showed remorse. He was upset. He arrived at Cheadle police station eight hours later and he has not spoken to us since. The first time we saw him open his mouth was at the trial.'

Arshad has not made any comment of any kind on his crime since his conviction, and it seems highly unlikely that he will do so now, for it would appear – according to those close to the case – that he feels 'totally justified in what he did', seeing it as an 'honour killing' acceptable to his religion and community.

The possibility that Arshad might find himself in prison for the rest of his life appears to have made no difference whatever to his actions, and – perhaps significantly – he has also declined to launch any kind of appeal against his sentence or conviction. There can be little doubt that he deserves to spend at the very least a large proportion of the rest of his life behind prison bars.

The same must surely be true of homeless man Mark Martin, who memorably remarked to a fellow prisoner when he was on remand for the killing of three young women in Nottingham between December 2004 and January 2005, 'If you've killed one, you might as well have killed twenty-one. I'm going to be the city's first serial killer.'

As a child, round-faced Martin, who was born in Nottingham in 1981, was fascinated by serial killers, including the Moors Murderer Ian Brady and the 'Black Panther', Donald Neilson. He even boasted to his best friend at school, Gareth Moyes, how the two of them were going to be the next Kray twins, a pair of brutal gangsters. By then Martin had developed an unhealthy appetite for extreme violence.

'I saw him once try to smother a baby because it was crying,' Moyes was to admit later. 'I just shouted at him, "What are you doing?"' Before long, the two teenagers were smoking cannabis and taking amphetamines together, which provoked Martin's aggressive nature still further. Moyes remembered that his friend would hit and swear at young girls they met together.

By the end of October 2004 Martin's already dysfunctional life as a husband, father and ex-homeless man was beginning to disintegrate. He even telephoned the police on

1 November to tell the operator, 'I want to hurt somebody. I'm going to end up killing someone . . . I was locked up last night for trying to strangle my ex-wife.' It turned out that she had told Martin that she no longer trusted him with their son because of his violent temper.

Martin's response was to return to living on the streets of Nottingham, where he was known as 'Reds' because of a distinctive birthmark on his cheek. But he was also known for bullying and intimidating other homeless people while living rough, often stealing what few possessions they had and boasting that he would be famous. The method he chose to achieve his ambition was murder.

On 29 December 2004, an eighteen-year-old homeless girl called Katie Baxter became Martin's first victim. She was last seen alive at her sister Charlene's house that evening, where she had been attending a family party, although she had concealed that fact that she was living rough from her relatives. Two days later, a second young woman, Zoe Pennick, aged twenty-six, also disappeared. She too had been living rough in Nottingham for some time, even though she had a seven-year-old son (who was looked after by her father). Both women had fallen into Martin's vicious clutches.

Yet it was not until Friday 11 February 2005 that the bodies of Baxter and Pennick were found – inside a derelict warehouse in the city which was a favourite shelter for the homeless community, and where Martin had set himself up in a makeshift tent amongst the rubble.

The local police had heard a series of rumours that there might be 'bodies' buried there, and at 11 am on 11 February 2005 a sniffer dog discovered Baxter's decomposed body under a 'carefully placed' mixture of bricks and debris. Five days later, while searching for forensic evidence in an effort to find Baxter's killer, the police also discovered Pennick's decomposed body, less than two metres away from Katie's, and also buried under rubble. Both women had been beaten and strangled.

Police quickly linked the two young women's deaths to that of a third, Ellen Frith, a twenty-five-year-old mother of two, whose partly burned body had been found in a burning 'squat' in the city centre on 24 January 2005. She too had been beaten and strangled.

It did not take long for the police to identify Martin as a prime suspect. As one officer put it later, 'He was a bully with a short fuse and there was barely a homeless person in Nottingham who did not have a bad experience to tell about him. Nearly everyone we spoke to pointed the finger at him.'

Martin had not been acting alone, however. He had called on the help of two other homeless men during the killings. One was John Ashley, aged thirty-four, known locally as 'Cockney John', who played a part in the killing of Baxter and Pennick, while the other was Dean Carr, aged thirty, who was involved in the murder of Frith.

Martin and Ashley were both charged with the murders of Baxter and Pennick and remanded in custody to await their trial, while Carr was charged with the murder of Frith and also remanded.

While he was in prison, Martin began to brag about the killings – telling a cell-mate named Scott Sinclair the precise and grisly details of how exactly he had murdered his victims. After he did so, Sinclair told the prison authorities and the police about Martin's boasts, and his statement to the police left no doubt about Martin's capacity for extreme violence towards women, nor about his scant regard for human life. He had killed them, he told Sinclair, for no reason other than that one had 'scratched his face' and the other had left a hypodermic needle in his bed.

When they appeared at Nottingham Crown Court on 16 January 2006, however, Martin and his two accomplices denied the murder charges.

Opening the case for the prosecution, barrister Peter Kelson QC told the jury that Martin 'seemed to be glorying in his notoriety . . . You will hear evidence that he was relishing the prospect of being known as Nottingham's first serial killer.

'He seems to have a fascination with violence towards women,' the prosecutor went on, 'with the crimes he committed and with the suffering his victims endured.'

Pressing home the point, Kelson explained that both Martin and Ashley – who had once been Katie Baxter's boyfriend – had made comments to friends about the killings even before the bodies were found.

One prosecution witness, who had also spent time in jail with Martin while he was on remand, explained from the witness box that he once asked Martin how many women he had killed and was told, 'Oh five,' and that Martin boasted that he had fed the other two victims to pigs at a farm in Leicester – a claim that has never been substantiated. He added that Martin was upset that he did not have photographs of the two other bodies to prove he had done it.

Another witness from Martin's time in prison on remand, who had been terrified by his grim boasts and was persuaded to give evidence against him anonymously, gave the court some of the details of Martin's account of his killing of Baxter and Pennick.

The witness explained that Martin had reacted badly when Katie scratched him. 'He said he picked her up and took her to the factory (the disused warehouse) because she fancied him. They were chatting and went into his tent. Then he just snapped and strangled her. He dragged her out of the tent, into the factory and buried her with debris.'

The anonymous witness also explained that Martin had persuaded Pennick to go with him to pick up 2,000 cigarettes that he wanted her to sell for him. Once there, he grabbed her by the throat and strangled her. He then laid her body next to Katie's and buried her in a similar way. 'He said he'd sorted her out and "smashed her legs like biscuits" . . . He said it was hard and she didn't want to die. He was punching her, kicking her. In the end he stood on her throat.' The witness also revealed that Martin had vomited on one of the two girls because she had soiled herself while being strangled, but that he had the presence of mind to remove her top in case he had left DNA traces from the vomit.

It was compelling evidence, made all the more so by the testimony of Martin's former cell-mate Scott Sinclair. But Martin himself declined to give evidence on his own behalf. Nevertheless, it took the jury a week to reach a conclusion. It was not until Thursday 23 February that they returned unanimous verdicts of guilty on all three defendants.

The following day, Mr Justice Butterfield passed sentence. Starting with Martin – who was standing impassively in the dock before him – he said grimly, 'These murders were committed by you because you positively enjoy killing. You took the totally innocent lives of these women for your own perverted gratification. You have devastated the lived of those who loved them and have not shown a moment of remorse. You have revelled in the macabre details of each senseless, brutal, callous killing. The facts of the offences are so horrific and the seriousness of your offending so exceptionally high, you are to be kept in prison for the rest of your life.'

'Cockney John' Ashley was then sentenced to life with a minimum of twenty-five years for his part in the murders of Baxter and Pennick, while Dean Carr was also sentenced to life with a minimum of fourteen years for his role in the killing of Frith.

Outside the court, Baxter's father Stephen told reporters, 'Katie was a lovely, happy girl with her whole life ahead of her . . . She associated with people from the homeless community and although she often stayed in those circles, it was no reason for her to be murdered. She did not deserve to die.'

Pennick's father Kevin added, 'The pain of losing my little girl in such a brutal way will always remain with me. Zoe was not homeless. She had a home to go to but chose to associate with other people who led the homeless lifestyle.'

Perhaps predictably, Martin declined to appeal against either his sentence or his conviction, preferring to glory in the notoriety that his killings brought him, and relishing in his new nickname of 'The Sneighton Strangler'. After all, this was the man who had written to his schoolfriend Gareth Moyes from Wakefield Prison before his trial, saying cheerfully, 'I can't believe I'm in jail for murder and three of them as well. Ha ha ha, oh dear, ha. Yeah, it's a mess boy, hey pal, but I'll get over it. I was all over the news.'

It is hard to see what other sentence could possibly have been passed on Arshad or Martin. The full weight of the law as it stands today surely demands that they spend the majority of the rest of their lives behind bars – and yet there remains a lingering doubt in my mind about whether the whole life sentences they both received do not, in some way at least, contradict the basic tenets of a civilised society.

Professor Dirk van Zyl Smit of Nottingham University, an expert on penal law and life imprisonment, pointed out in 2014, 'A commitment that we will never consider the release of some offenders serving life sentences, except perhaps when they are at death's door, means that we write them off permanently. It means that we deny that with the passage of time they may change for the better; or that we may change our assessment of their crimes.'

'Worse still,' Professor Van Zyl Smit concluded, 'we are denying some fellow humans all hope. In that sense we are putting them in the same position as those awaiting execution on death row.'

It is a powerful argument for, as the case of Jamie Reynolds illustrates for all to see, society, in the shape of its judiciary, can effectively condemn a young man in his early twenties to what could amount to sixty, or even seventy, years in prison. Naturally enough, Reynolds' young female victim's family, including her police detective father, are determined that he should pay the maximum possible price for the horrifyingly ugly murder of their daughter Georgia – an entirely reasonable emotion that is shared by almost every other family that loses a loved one to a brutal killing.

Yet there is a sense in which that desire for revenge against a murderer has surely to be tempered by a sense that every prisoner, no matter how heinous the crime, at least deserves the prospect of redemption – however remote. Over a very long period behind prison bars he or she may be capable of rehabilitation and change; and to deny them even the possibility of release is to deny their humanity.

As Professor Van Zyl Smit argued powerfully in *The Guardian* in 2014, 'The United Kingdom is one of the staunchest opponents of capital punishment. Yet it appears to have no moral objection to an irreducible life sentence, which in many ways is simply a delayed death penalty. This must change, not because the European Court of Human Rights says that it should, but because failing to act now is morally untenable.'

There can be little argument that a whole life sentence in its present form is indeed a 'delayed death penalty', and as such deserves to be questioned far more rigorously than has been the case in this country in the fifty-one years since the effective abolition of the death penalty. Indeed, whole life sentences have become an increasingly familiar part of the sentencing process as those five decades have passed – with 'sentence creep' meaning that they are awarded far more regularly than they once were. The political slogan 'Tough on Crime' has effectively translated into more and more whole life sentences.

Yet that disregards a vital tenet of human morality – hope.

As Judge Ann Power-Forde, the Republic of Ireland's representative on the European Court of Human Rights, once memorably put it, 'Hope is an important and constitutive aspect of the human person. Those who commit the most abhorrent and egregious of acts and who inflict untold suffering upon others, nevertheless retain their fundamental humanity and carry within themselves the capacity to change.'

The fifty-two-year-old judge, who has a doctorate in Jurisprudence and Legal Philosophy from Oxford, went on to add, 'Long and deserved though their prison sentences may be, they retain the right to hope that, some day, they may have atoned for the wrongs which they have committed . . . To deny them the experience of hope would be to deny a fundamental aspect of their humanity and, to do that, would be degrading.'

Against that moral background it becomes ever more difficult to defend the whole life sentence in England and Wales in its present form, with no possibility – or likelihood – of a review of the sentence. Most European countries allow for a sentence review of some kind after twenty or twenty-five years. The International Criminal Court at The Hague even allows a review after twenty-five years for offenders sentenced to life imprisonment for mass genocide. A review would be no guarantee of release, nor would it prevent an offender judged still a risk to society being forced to remain behind bars.

With suggestions of a fixed term sentence of one hundred years being bandied about by British politicians – which makes the torture of a whole life term even more excruciating – surely it is right that society in this country should reconsider its attitude to the whole life sentence.

To quote Professor Van Zyl Smit again, 'Instead of suggesting even longer minimum periods . . . the Government should be honest with the public. It should stress that considering someone for release is not the same as releasing them . . . Above all, it should make clear that even the worst offender has the right to hope, for with hope, a person can change.'

Professor Van Zyl Smit advocates an 'impartial Parole Board' as one means of supervising this change, a suggestion I find difficult to accept given the Board's manifest failings in letting so many prisoners serving what are technically life sentences out to kill again. Nevertheless, I would agree that a review by an impartial body after twenty-five years of a prisoner serving his or her sentence, with further reviews every five years after that, would at least begin the process of destroying the 'delayed death penalty' aspect of whole life sentences.

Even the widely admired former Lord Chief Justice, Lord Judge, has been cautious about using whole life sentence ever more widely, as seems to be becoming the practice.

'The whole life order, the product of primary legislation,' Lord Judge has said, 'is reserved for the few exceptionally serious offences in which, after reflecting on all the features of aggravation and mitigation, the judge is satisfied that the element of just punishment and retribution requires the imposition of a whole life order. If that conclusion is justified, the whole life order is justified, but only then.'

In other words, do not rush to give a whole life term without considering the consequences very carefully indeed. Yet an extraordinarily experienced politician, the former Conservative Home Secretary Kenneth Clarke MP, realises that the demand for the most draconian penalty of all – 'locking a prisoner up and throwing away the key' – will always have a visceral appeal, not least to the families of the victims. 'There will always be a small number of prisoners whose crimes are so appalling that judges rule that they should never become eligible for parole,' Clarke has said.

Yet the ugly truth is, as Frances Crook, chief executive of the Howard League for Penal Reform, has pointed out, 'We have sentence inflation. It's because politicians in the last two decades have sunk to a level of punitive competitiveness. But there's no evidence that it offers better public protection. We have more lifers than all the other countries in the Council of Europe together.'

It has been estimated that there are more than 13,000 prisoners in England and Wales who are subject to life or 'indeterminate' sentences – which means that they have to satisfy the Parole Board before they can be released. That is approaching one sixth of the entire prison population, a staggering number of prisoners, and quite unlike any other country in Europe.

I find the suggestion that there should be longer and longer minimum terms for prisoners exceptionally difficult to justify or support, not least because England and Wales are almost alone in Europe when it comes to handing out a whole life sentence. Spain, Portugal and Norway, for example, do not have any kind of life sentence within their penal system. Every other European country, with the exception of Holland, has fixed minimum terms for prisoners sentenced to life.

Even Anders Breivik, the thirty-six-year-old killer of no fewer than sixty-nine young people at a summer camp on the island of Utoya in the summer of 2011 (as well as eight people in a bomb blast in Oslo on the same day) was only sentenced to twenty-one years in prison, in a form of 'preventive detention' that requires a minimum of ten years' incarceration and the possibility of an extension of that imprisonment for as long as he is deemed a danger to society. That is the maximum penalty in Norway; although that is not to say that he will be released after serving the twenty-one years, as he may well still be seen as a risk to the public.

Russia rarely uses an indeterminate whole life sentence for the most heinous crimes, and when it does use one it is restricted to men between the age of eighteen and sixty-five. The maximum sentence most often imposed is twenty-five years, although the period of imprisonment is exceptionally harsh, involving long periods of solitary confinement, sometimes in darkness.

The United States still has the death penalty in some states, as it does a sentence of 'life without parole' (although not usually now for offenders under the age of twenty-one at sentencing).

A number of European countries have abolished all forms of indefinite imprisonment, including Serbia and Croatia, while Spain sets the maximum sentence at forty years. Bosnia and Herzegovina sets the maximum sentence at forty-five years, while Portugal sets the maximum sentence at thirty years.

Three African countries, the Democratic Republic of Congo, Mozambique and Cape Verde, have abolished indefinite life imprisonment; the maximum sentence is thirty years in Mozambique and the Democratic Republic of Congo, and twenty-five years in Cape Verde. In Asia, the former Portuguese colony of Macau has outlawed indeterminate sentences, replacing them with a maximum of thirty years.

In South and Central America, Honduras, Nicaragua, El Salvador, Costa Rica, Venezuela, Colombia, Uruguay, Bolivia, Ecuador and the Dominican Republic have all abolished indefinite life imprisonment, but each has set a maximum sentence. It is seventy-five years in El Salvador, sixty in Colombia, fifty in Costa Rica and Panama, forty in Honduras, thirty-five in Ecuador, thirty in Nicaragua, Bolivia, Uruguay and Venezuela, and twenty-five in Paraguay. Brazil has a maximum sentence of thirty years under statutory law, but capital punishment and life imprisonment during wartime (for military crimes such as treason, desertion and mutiny) are allowed under the Constitution.

It surely must be time for Britain to follow this lead. Scotland has effectively done so since 2001, preferring determinate maximum sentences – with a usual limit of fifty years. Half a century behind bars seems to me the very most that any human being should be condemned to – unless there are profound reasons why he or she presents a continuing risk to the public's safety. That would not mean an inevitable release after fifty years, but it would make release more likely, and would remove forever the 'delayed death penalty' element in a whole life term.

In October 2010, Simon Hattenstone wrote a compelling article in *The Guardian* detailing some of the letters he had received from whole life prisoners, and one letter in particular underlines the point about hope being an essential part of the human personality. It gives a remarkable insight into what a whole life sentence feels like to the man or woman imprisoned, and how it can be coped with.

'The question of a whole life term is very difficult to put into words,' the prisoner wrote. 'It can be simple or complicated, it all depends on the way each individual approaches the sentence. Obviously a sentence such as a whole life takes away all hope of ever being released. So the first thing you do is accept this fact, which strange to say everyone does. It must be part of the human condition to accept disastrous events.'

The man in question was an armed robber who shot a diamond jeweller in the back and accidentally shot his accomplice at the same time. But he left his accomplice to die rather than call an ambulance or take him to hospital, and then buried him in a railway embankment. He was given a life sentence in 1991 with a recommendation that he should never be released. In 2008 that sentence was squashed and replaced with a minimum term of twenty-five years, with an expected release date in 2017, when the prisoner concerned would be eighty-eight.

'Put it this way,' the prisoner wrote, 'every day all round the world people are told by their doctors, you have cancer (for example) and you have six months to live. Once the initial shock wears off, they accept their fate and carry on doing the best they can. Rehabilitation is largely a waste of time. What's the point when you're never going out? Those who do courses do them for purely personal reasons, maybe due to a desire to try and understand how and why they came to be in this position.'

Rehabilitation may be 'a waste of time', but redemption is not, and it is the compelling reason why the concept of an endless whole life sentence disturbs me, and should, I believe, disturb British society. It is a 'delayed death penalty' and seems to me to have no place in a civilised society. Were it to be replaced by a fixed term of fifty years, which would at least hold out the possibility of release, and acknowledge that an individual – no matter how heinous his or her crime

– can change over the period of half a century, would seem to me to a far more accurate reflection of what should be society's ambition.

Another whole life prisoner underlines the danger of leaving whole life prisoners to become institutionalised over decades behind bars, so disillusioned by the experience that they become nihilistic, devoid of all hope.

'The past is the past,' the whole lifer wrote. 'Nothing good can come out of dwelling too much on things like that. Guilt is a product of obsessive thought, it develops into self-pity, and self-pity serves no purpose in prison other than causing depression, to self-harm and commit suicide. A person can accept their crime and acknowledge the effect it's had on the victim's family, and resolve not to do that act again without guilt interfering to complicate matters internally. If I could bring the person back I killed by dying, I wouldn't hesitate. But I can't, so I never think about what can't be changed.'

Even more dramatically, he concluded, 'What keeps me going is knowing I'll be dead soon enough anyway of natural causes. The average male only lives until he's 60-65. The way I see it, I'm closer to death than birth.'

Is the aim of a whole life sentence to force the prisoner to look forward to only one thing – his or her own death? I am not in favour of the death penalty, as I could never accept one innocent man or women being killed in error by a miscarriage of justice, but you could argue that leaving a man or woman to rot behind bars for the whole of the rest of their natural life is almost as fierce and ferocious a punishment.

It does not need to be so. Changes to sentencing to fix a maximum term of fifty years would ease that burden. But there would need to be other changes to go hand in hand with that alteration. The prisons in this country that currently contain some of the worst offenders serving whole life terms – particularly the Victorian-built 'Monster Mansion' of Wakefield Prison in Yorkshire – are ill-equipped for the task. There needs to be a rebalancing of the prison estate to take into account the increasing number of violent prisoners serving very long sentences indeed.

I would argue for the construction of one large and well-staffed 'supermax' prison, which would house a large proportion of these most vicious offenders and be staffed and financed to provide the maximum security while offering its inmates the latest therapeutic psychological help. It should be run by prison officers who have been specially trained to deal with offenders serving extended sentences and who may well suffer the signs of ageing as a result of their long period of incarceration.

At present we rely on the experience of dedicated prison officers who are expected to cope with an ageing prison population as though it is nothing new. The reality, of course, is that as the population overall is steadily ageing so the prison population itself follows it, with the result that an ever-increasing proportion of prisoners are now susceptible to 'ageing' diseases like dementia and heart conditions that were certainly less the case twenty years ago.

If you think back to Dick Clement and Ian La Frenais' superb BBC television comedy *Porridge*, there was hardly a character over fifty, and that includes Ronnie Barker's Norman Stanley Fletcher. Written almost forty years ago, that programme painted an entirely different picture of the prison system than the one that exists now in the twenty-first century. Now we need a prison system and its officers equipped to deal with an ever-ageing population and inmates who are serving longer and longer sentences, including whole life terms. That requires very different regimes, and even the ever-stern and vigilant Mr MacKay would accept that. The possibility that Fletcher might need incontinence pads after a stroke or special nursing for dementia would transform the regime at Slade Prison beyond all recognition. That may sound far-fetched, but it is the reality that the prison system will increasingly have to deal with over the coming decades.

Contrast the almost homely feel of Fletcher's cell in Slade with the grim reality of a whole life prisoner's regime, which – in the worst cases – can mean twenty-three hours in solitary confinement every day of the week, sometimes completely segregated from any other contact, even with other prisoners. If there is an element of education in the system, the prisoner will be in one cell with the teacher in an adjoining cell protected by bars between them. There is no privacy, little human contact, little exercise, and less humanity.

When asked whether there was any possibility of rehabilitation, one whole lifer replied bitterly, 'Rehabilitation is just a word politicians use and psychologists dream about.' But he went on to explain with equal force, 'People rehabilitate themselves when they're ready to change, when conditions are conducive to it. They can't be bribed, blackmailed or forced to rehabilitate themselves.'

Surely the prison system should at least be able to offer the worst offenders that opportunity, but that is not the case, and there is little sign of any political will to change the existing flawed system. But I must also acknowledge that amendments to the prison system and sentencing for the worst of the worst offenders will never satisfy the families of the victims of the men and women subjected to whole life terms.

As one whole lifer once put it, 'If someone killed a member of my family in a similar fashion to what I did, I wouldn't want them released either. It's only natural.'

That is the dilemma that lies at the heart of the question of whole life sentences – are they for punishment alone? Do they in any way imply an opportunity for rehabilitation and redemption? It is my view that by sentencing a whole life term, society is implicitly saying that they are for punishment alone – a trade-off against the loss of the death penalty for the worst offenders – and that is something that makes me feel deeply uncomfortable.

If whole life terms are, in fact, a 'delayed death penalty', then that should be made clearer, and the circuitous argument that they still represent some remote possibility of release should be ditched once and for all. If we are intent on 'throwing away the key', let us not make any bones about it.

The present ambiguous and confused compromise which can see offenders convicted of exactly the same crime, be it the murder of Fusilier Lee Rigby by Michael Adebolajo and Michael Adebowale, or the rapes and murders by the 'Railway Killers' John Duffy and David Mulcahy, in which one offender in a partnership of murder is given a whole life term while the other is not, serves only to undermine the sentencing process and confuse society.

If life must mean life then let us say so unequivocally – and reserve that sentence for the very worst offenders – rather than diluting it by implicitly encouraging the judiciary to hand out more and more whole life sentences while the public fail to understand what they mean. One group who do clearly understand, however, are the prisoners themselves. Perhaps it is fitting to leave the last words to one whole lifer who wrote, 'If I ever walk out them gates, great, so be it, I won't look back. If I never walk out them gates, that's just how it is. I expect nothing.'

Afterword

This is my third book about murder and the men and woman who commit this most foul of all crimes, and I am as certain as I can be that it will be my last. There is only so much brutality and ugliness that any imagination can take, and I have had more than my fair share. To relive the tragedies contained in these pages in detail was sometimes almost too much to bear. Murder affects not only the victim but also a far wider circle, including, of course, their families and friends. It stains the world forever, and no amount of scrubbing will ever rub out its memory.

The only reason that I embarked on the stories of the group of individuals who earned the greatest penalty the law in England and Wales can provide – a whole life period of imprisonment – was that the subject seemed to me to have been all but ignored in the discussion of the crimes themselves. I wanted to draw attention to the fact that the steady increase in the number of these sentences has happened almost without anyone noticing, or considering its implications for a civilized society.

My old friend legal commentator Joshua Rozenberg was kind enough to agree with my argument and to point me in the right direction, and I must also pay tribute to a number of members of the British judiciary who offered me their opinions freely, on the simple grounds that I never identify them. I thank them all, just as I must thank Richard Whittam QC, the First Senior Treasury Counsel, who was consistently helpful in ensuring that I was working from the right documents in cases that came before the Court of Appeal.

My editor, Dan Bunyard, was as enthusiastic about raising the issue as I was, and has given me extraordinary support throughout the process, for which I am profoundly grateful. His assistant Fiona Crosby has been equally generous, not least in assembling the plates of pictures, as have their colleagues Martin Higgins in the sales department and Ellie Hughes in publicity. The manuscript was meticulously copy-edited by Fiona Brown.

I also owe special thanks to my excellent young researcher Sahyma Shaid, who trawled through mountains of material to unearth the precise details of some of the darkest crimes ever committed in this country, and did so with consummate skill, no matter how testing the task may have been. I am every bit as grateful to my own assistant and great supporter, Diana Fletcher, who bore, with great strength and dignity, the burden of ensuring that I did not submerge completely beneath the tidal wave of tragedy that sometimes threatened to engulf me.

None of these admirable people are responsible for my conclusions, however. Those are mine alone.

Picture Credits

p1 (Bamber): Alamy EMNNWM © Trinity Mirror / Mirrorpix / Alamy Stock Photo

p2–5 (Bamber letter): Jeremy Bamber

p6 (Dennehy): Alamy DTA0Y5. Geoffrey Robinson / Alamy

p7 top (McLoughlin): Rex 2659241a. REX Shutterstock

p7 bottom (Newell): Rex 3032766a. REX Shutterstock

p8 top (Cooke): Rex 288507b. REX Shutterstock

p8 bottom (Restivo): Rex 1153704a. IPA/REX Shutterstock

p9 top (Bronson): Rex 553601a. Cherri Gilham/REX Shutterstock

p9 bottom (Regan): Rex 532433a. Rex Shutterstock

p10 top (Huntley): Getty 51792974. AFP/Getty Images

p10 bottom (Bridger): Rex 2312166a. Rex Shutterstock

p11 top (Whiting): PA 1503939. PA / PA Archive/Press Association Images

p11 bottom (Tobin): Rex 1204538a. Rex Shutterstock

p12 top (Roberts): Rex 4218038a. Rex Shutterstock

p12 bottom left (Cregan): Rex 1860615b. Gavin Rodgers/ REX Shutterstock

p12 bottom right (Bieber): Getty 51814689. West Yorkshire Police / Getty Images

p13 (Wests): Rex 227355c. Rex Shutterstock

Index